THE
LYLE
OFFICIAL
ARTS
REVIEW 1984

Converted at the rate of exchange on the day of sale.

SBN 0 - 86248 - 042 - 6

Copyright © Lyle Publications MCMLXXXIII
Glenmayne, Galashiels, Scotland.

Printed and bound by R. J. Acford, Chichester, Sussex, England.

Copyright © 1983 by Voor Hoede Publicaties B. V.

Distributed in the United States by Coward, McCann & Geoghegan, Inc., 200 Madison Avenue, New York, N. Y. 10016

THE
LYLE
OFFICIAL
ARTS
REVIEW 1984

COMPILED BY JENNIFER KNOX
EDITED BY TONY CURTIS

L

Auction Acknowledgements

Anderson & Garland, *Anderson House, Market Street, Newcastle on Tyne*
Australian Art Auctions, *31 George Street, Sydney, Australia*
G. H. Bayley & Sons, *Vittoria House, Vittoria Walk, Cheltenham*
Biddle & Webb, *Ladywood, Middlewade, Birmingham*
Bonhams, *Montpelier Galleries, Montpelier St., London*
Bracketts, *Royal Sussex Assembly Rooms, The Pantiles, Tunbridge Wells*
Butler & Hatch Waterman, *86 High Street, Hythe, Kent*
Butterfield's, *1244 Sutter Street, San Francisco, U.S.A.*
Calart, *4bis, Rue Provost-Martin, 1205, Geneve, Switzerland*
Capes, Dunn & Co., *38 Charles Street, Manchester*
H. C. Chapman & Son, *The Auction Mart, North Street, Scarborough*
Christie, Manson & Woods Int. Inc., *502 Park Avenue, New York*
Christie's, *8 King Street, St. James, London*
Christie's & Edmiston's, *164-166 Bath Street, Glasgow*
Christie's South Kensington, *85 Old Brompton Road, London*
Chrystals Auctions, *Exchange House, Athol Street, Douglas, I.O.M.*
Dacre, Son & Hartley, *1-5 The Grove, Ilkley*
Dee & Atkinson, *Exchange Salerooms, Driffield*
Dickinson, Davy & Markham, *10 Wrawby Street, Brigg, South Humberside*
Wm. Doyle Galleries Inc., *175 East 75th Street, New York 10028*
Dreweatt, Watson & Barton, *Donnington Priory Salerooms, Newbury*
Hy. Duke & Son, *40 South Street, Dorchester*
Du Mouchelles, *409 E. Jefferson Ave., Detroit, Michigan, U.S.A.*
Edwards, Bigwood & Bewlay, *The Old School Tiddington, Stratford-on-Avon*
Elliot & Green, *40 High Street, Lymington, Hants*
R. H. Ellis & Sons, *44-46 High Street, Worthing*
Entwistle Green, *The Galleries, Kingsway Ansdell, Lytham St. Annes*
Escritt & Barrell, *Elmer House, Grantham, Lincs.*
Galerie Moderne, *Rue du Parnasse 3, 1040 Bruxelles, Belgium*
Ronald J. Garwood, *55 Mill Street, Ludlow, Shrops*
Geering & Colyer, *Highgate, Hawkhurst, Kent*
Germann Auktionshaus, *CH 8032, Zeltweg 67, Zurich, Switzerland*
Andrew Grant, *59/60 Foregate Street, Worcester*
Graves, Son & Pilcher, *38 Holland Park, Hove, Sussex*
Geoff. K. Gray Pty. Inc., *34 Morley Ave., Rosebery, N.S.W., Australia*
Hall, Wateridge & Owen, *Welshbridge, Shrewsbury*
Heathcote Ball & Co., *96 Scraptoft Lane, Leicester*

Hilhams, *53 Springfield Road, Gorleston on Sea*
John Hogbin & Son, *53 High Street, Tenterden, Kent*
Norman Hope & Partners, *2 South Road, Hartlepool*
Edgar Horn, *47 Cornfield Road, Eastbourne*
Jackson-Stops & Staff, *14 Curzon Street, London*
W. H. Lane & Son, *The Central Auction Rooms, Wadebridge*
Thomas Love & Sons Ltd., *12 St. John's Place, Perth*
Lawrence of Crewkerne, *South Street, Crewkerne*
McCartney Morris & Barker, *25 Corve Street, Ludlow, Shrops.*
Messenger May & Baverstock, *93 High Street, Godalming, Surrey*
Morphets of Harrogate, *4-6 Albert Street, Harrogate*
Mortons Auction Exchange Inc., *643 Magazine Street, New Orleans, U.S.A.*
Neales of Nottingham, *192 Mansfield Road, Nottingham*
Olivers, *23/24 Market Hill, Sudbury, Suffolk*
Osmond, Tricks & Son, *Regent Street Auctions, Clifton, Bristol*
Outhwaite & Litherland, *Kingsway Galleries, Fontenoy Street, Liverpool*
Pearsons, *Walcote Chambers, High Street, Winchester*
Phillips, *The Old House, Station Road, Knowle*
Phillips, Son & Neale, *Blenstock House, 7 Blenheim Street, London*
John H. Raby & Son, *21 St. Mary's Road, Bradford*
Reeds Rains, *Trinity House, 114 Northenden Road, Sale, Cheshire*
Renton & Renton, *16 Albert Street, Harrogate*
Riddetts of Bournemouth, *Richmond Hill, The Square, Bournemouth*
M. Christian Rosset, *29 Rue du Rhone, 1204 Geneve, Switzerland*
Lacy Scott, *3 Hatter Street, Bury St. Edmunds*
Robt. W. Skinner Inc., *Bolton Gallery, Route 117, Bolton, Mass.*
Sotheby's, *34/35 New Bond Street, London*
Sotheby's, *980 Madison Avenue, New York, U.S.A.*
Sotheby's Belgravia, *19 Motcomb Street, London*
Sotheby Beresford Adams, *Booth Mansion, Watergate Street, Chester*
Sotheby, King & Chasemore, *Station Road, Pulborough*
Sotheby Mak Van Waay, *Rokin 102, Amsterdam, Holland*
H. Spencer & Sons Ltd., *20 The Square, Retford, Notts.*
Stalker & Boos, *280 North Woodward Avenue, Birmingham, Michigan, U.S.A.*
Laurence & Martin Taylor, *High Street, Honiton, Devon*
Woolley & Wallis, *The Castle Auction Mart, Salisbury, Wilts.*
Worsfolds, *40 Station Road West, Canterbury*

ACKNOWLEDGEMENTS

The publishers wish to thank the following for their assistance
in the production of this volume.

Janice Moncrieff, Nichola Fairburn, Karen Kilgour, Margot Rutherford,
Tanya Fairbairn.

Introduction

This is the tenth edition of the Lyle Official Arts Review. The 1984 edition contains details of many thousands of oil paintings, watercolours and drawings, covering a wide spectrum of what is available on the market today. There are over 2,000 illustrations of selected pictures computed from auction results gathered over the past year.

Every entry is listed alphabetically under the Artist's name for easy reference and includes a description of the picture, its size, medium, auctioneer and the price fetched.

As regards authenticity of the works listed, this is often a delicate matter and throughout this book the conventional system has been observed:

The full Christian name(s) and surname of the artist denote that, in the opinion of the auctioneer listed, the work is by that artist.

The initials of the Christian name(s) and the surname denote that, in the opinion of the auctioneer listed, the work is of the period of the artist and may be wholly or partly his work.

The surname only of the artist denotes that, in the opinion of the auctioneer listed, the work is of the school or by one of the followers of the artist or painted in his style.

The word 'after' associated with the surname of the artist denotes that, in the opinion of the auctioneer listed, the picture is a copy of the work of the artist. The word 'signed' associated with the name of the artist denotes that, in the opinion of the auctioneer listed, the work bears a signature which is the signature of the artist .

The words 'bears signature' or 'traces of signature' denotes that, in the opinion of the auctioneer listed, the work bears a signature or traces of a signature that may be that of the artist.

The word 'dated' denotes that the work is dated and, in the opinion of the auctioneer listed, was executed at that date.

HANS VAN AACHEN, Circle of – The Judgement Of Paris – on copper – 9¼ x 12¾in.
(Sotheby's) **$3,009 £1,980**

JOHN ABSOLON – A Young Lady Leaning On A Rocky Bank Holding A Rose – signed and dated 1857 – pencil and watercolour heightened with white – 15¾ x 10½in.
(Christie's) **$615 £410**

JOHN ABSOLON – Harvesters' Refreshment – signed – watercolour heightened with white – 8¾ x 13¾in.
(Christie's) **$456 £302**

JOHN ABSOLON – Women Collecting Rushes – watercolour over pencil – 8 x 17¼in.
(Sotheby's) **$508 £330**

ANDREAS ACHENBACH – A Fishing Boat On Rough Seas – signed and dated – on panel – 7 x 10½in.
(Sotheby's) **$2,675 £1,760**

ANDREAS ACHENBACH – Bringing The Boat Ashore – signed and dated – on panel – 18 x 27cm.
(Phillips) **$4,114 £2,200**

ALICE ACHESON – Birds In A Landscape – signed – oil on board – 13 x 14in.
(Stalker & Boos) **$50 £29**

ACHTSCHELLINCK – A Landscape With A Church – 16½ x 21¾in.
(Sotheby's) **$1,332 £770**

EDMOND ADAM – A Fire At Sea –
signed and dated 1906 – 22½ x 35in.
*(Sotheby Beresford
Adams)* **$628** **£374**

J. D. ADAM – Still Life With Fruit &
Fowl – signed – oil on canvas – 24½
x 30in.
*(Stalker &
Boos)* **$300** **£195**

PATRICK WILLIAM ADAM – Autumn
Study – on panel – 11 x 7in.
*(Christie's &
Edmiston's)* **$480** **£300**

CHARLES ADAMS – A Shepherd With
His Flock Meeting A Farmer With Horse
And Cart On A Country Bridge With
Trees And Cottages In The Background –
signed – watercolour – 19½ x 29½in.
*(Outhwaite &
Litherland)* **$1,114** **£700**

HARRY WILLIAM ADAMS – A Wintry
Landscape – signed and dated 1903 –
24 x 20in.
(Sotheby's) **$500** **£330**

JOHN CLAYTON ADAMS – Sheep On
A Hillside, A Pond In Woodland Beyond
– signed – watercolour heightened with
white – 14¼ x 13¼in.
(Christie's) **$362** **£216**

JOHN CLAYTON ADAMS – A Wooded
River Landscape With Harvesters –
signed and dated 1874 – 13½ x 20½in.
(Christie's) **$2,371** **£1,296**

A. E. ADAMSON – Still Life With Fruit
– signed and dated 1847 – 18 x 20in.
*(Sotheby Beresford
Adams)* **$203** **£121**

C. W. ADDERTON – The 'Johanna' Drying Sails At Ockbrook Near Derby –
signed – watercolour – 12 x 18in.
*(Hy. Duke &
Son)* **$259** **£150**

ADER

W. ADER – Partridge Shooting – indistinctly inscribed on reverse – oil on canvas – 27 x 35½in.
(Sotheby, King & Chasemore)   **$2,722   £1,815**

WILLIAM AFFLECK – Young Maid Before A Cottage – signed – watercolour on board – 16 x 11in.
(Butterfield's)   **$375   £220**

WILLIAM AFFLECK – Gathering Flowers, A Small Girl Wearing A Blue Gown And Pink Bonnet Seated In A Field With Wild Flowers In Her Lap, Trees Beyond – signed – watercolour – 42.5 x 22.5cm.
(Henry Spencer & Sons)   **$1,933   £1,080**

PIETER AERTSEN, Circle of – Kitchen Interiors – 49½ x 77in.
(Sotheby's)   **$12,375   £8,250 Pair**

JOHN ERNEST AITKEN – 'The Market Square, Bruges' – signed – watercolour – 13 x 19½in.
(Sotheby, King & Chasemore)   **$638   £396**

JOHN ERNEST AITKEN – A Fruit Market – signed –heightened with bodycolour – 10 x 14in.
(Sotheby's) **$203** **£132**

JOHN ERNEST AITKEN – 'Amsterdam' – signed – watercolour – 13¾ x 19½in.
(Sotheby, King &
Chasemore) **$313** **£176**

IVAN KONSTANTINOVICH AIVAZOVSKY– Figures On A Beach Awaiting A Rowing Boat, With Capri In The Distance – signed, signed, inscribed and dated 1892 on the reverse – oil on canvas – 17¾ x 29¼in.
(Sotheby's) **$14,212** **£9,350**

IVAN CONSTANTINOVICH AIVAZOVSKY – The Coast Of The Dardanelles – signed with initial and dated 1860 – 11½ x 15¾in.
(Christie's) **$3,260** **£2,160**

IVAN KONSTANTINOVICH AIVAZOVSKY – A Shipwreck – signed and dated 1887 – oil on canvas – 25¼ x 38¼in.
(Sotheby's) **$12,540** **£8,250**

IVAN KONSTANTINOVICH AIVAZOVSKY– A Coastal View – signed and dated 1861 – brush and brown ink – 7½ x 10½in.
(Sotheby's) **$2,508** **£1,650**

JOHANNES EVERT AKKERINGA – Fisherwomen Mending The Nets – signed – 21¾ x 27¼in.
(Sotheby's) **$3,010** **£1,980**

ERNEST ALBERT – The Day's End – signed and dated 1928 – oil on canvas – 24 x 25in.
(William Doyle
Galleries) **$6,000** **£3,550**

ALBRIGHT

ADAM EMORY ALBRIGHT – Two Boys Fishing – signed – oil on canvas – 24 x 18in.
(Butterfield's) **$1,600 £958**

CECIL ALDIN – The South Dorset Hunt: Hounds Running To Warren Hill Covert, With Milborne Wood Beyond, Between Blandford and Dorchester – signed – pastel, on paper on canvas – 41¼ x 74½in.
(Christie's) **$5,080 £3,024**

FREDERICK JAMES ALDRIDGE – Venice: Fishing Boats By A Bridge, The Molo Beyond – signed and inscribed – watercolour – 10¼ x 14¾in.
(Christie's) **$816 £486**

FREDERICK JAMES ALDRIDGE – 'Shipping In Venice' – signed – watercolour – 8 x 23½in.
(W. H. Lane & Son) **$174 £100 Pair**

GEORGE AMES ALDRICH – A Normandy Landscape – signed – oil on canvas – 32¼ x 40½in.
(William Doyle Galleries) **$2,900 £1,715**

CLIFFORD GREAR ALEXANDER – 'Early Spring' – signed – oil on canvas – 16 x 24in.
(Robert W. Skinner Inc.) **$450 £280**

EDWIN ALEXANDER – The Dead Peacock – signed with initials – watercolour and bodycolour – 37 x 76in.
(Christie's & Edmiston's) **$3,840 £2,400**

EDWIN ALEXANDER – Two Collared Doves In A Walnut Tree – signed and dated 1902 – watercolour and gouache – 20 x 18¼in.
(Christie's) **$4,747 £3,024**

JOHN WHITE ALEXANDER – Portrait Of Little Girl – signed and dated '01 – oil on canvas – 48¼ x 35½in.
(Christie's) **$2,200 £1,466**
ALKEN – Taking A Fence – 20 x 24½in.
(Sotheby Beresford Adams) **$370 £220**

ALKEN – A Huntsman And Hounds –
25 x 29in.
(Sotheby Beresford
Adams)   **$480**   **£286**

HENRY ALKEN, JNR. – The Ambulance,
Taking The Pack Back To Kennels At The
End Of A Hard Day – signed – 11¼ x
15½in.
(Sotheby's)   **$2,459**   **£1,430**

HENRY ALKEN, SNR. – The Forest
Stakes, Henley-In-Arden, Warwickshire,
February 23rd 1847 – signed and
inscribed – on canvas on panel – 10 x
14in.
(Sotheby's)   **$26,576**   **£17,600 Four**

HENRY ALKEN, SNR. – The Grand
Leicestershire Steeplechase, March 12,
1829 – each 10½ x 14½in.
(Sotheby's)   **$105,952**   **£61,600 Eight**

ALKEN

HENRY ALKEN – 'Very Wet'; 'Very Dry'
– signed – watercolour – 10½ x 14¾in.
(Sotheby, King &
Chasemore) **$1,540** **£880 Pair**

SAMUEL ALKEN, JNR. – Coursing
– signed and dated 1812 – 26 x 34¼in.
(Christie's) **$1,998** **£1,080**

ROBERT WEIR ALLAN – Venice
From San Giorgio Maggiore – signed –
on panel – 14½ x 20½in.
(Christie's) **$870** **£486**

JOSEPH WILLIAM ALLEN – A Storm
At Even – signed and dated 1850 – 13½
x 17½in.
(Christie's) **$483** **£270**

HELEN ALLINGHAM – Summer
Hedgerows – signed with initials –
watercolour heightened with white –
5¼ x 3½in.
(Christie's) **$579** **£345**

HELEN ALLINGHAM – A Wiltshire Cottage – signed – heightened with scratching out – 9 x 7in.
(Sotheby's) **$7,623 £4,950**

HELEN ALLINGHAM – The Church Of
Santa Maria Della Salute, Venice –
signed and dated 1901 – watercolour –
18¼ x 14¼in.
(Sotheby's) **$3,388** **£2,200**

HELEN ALLINGHAM – By The Cottage
Gate – signed – heightened with body-
colour – 9¾ x 7in.
(Sotheby's) **$3,050** **£1,980**

HELEN ALLINGHAM – A Surrey Cottage – signed – 7 x 10in. *(Sotheby's)*
$3,727 £2,420

JOAQUIN PALLARES Y ALLUSTAUTE – Place De La Concorde, Paris – signed
and dated 1900 – on panel – 10¼ x 12in. *(Christie's)*   **$3,694 £2,052**

ALMA-TADEMA

SIR LAWRENCE ALMA-TADEMA –
Expectation Or Impatient – signed and
inscribed – watercolour – 7¾ x 5¾in.
(Sotheby's)   **$8,662   £4,950**

SIR LAWRENCE ALMA-TADEMA –
The Kiss – signed and inscribed – on
panel – 18 x 25in.
(Sotheby's)   **$82,500   £55,000**

RAPHAEL VON AMBROS – An Arab
Selling Artefacts – signed and dated 1883
– oil on cradled panel – 13½ x 18½in.
(Sotheby, King &
Chasemore)   **$6,886   £4,050**

AMERICAN SCHOOL, 19th century –
Winter On The Farm – oil on canvas –
21½ x 30¼in.
(Christie's)   **$4,400   £2,933**

CUNO AMIET – Mohnblumen – monogrammed and dated '33 – oil on canvas –
72 x 57.5cm.
(Germann
Auktionshaus) **$17,680   £11,050**

JACOPO AMIGONI – Anzia And Abro-
come At The Feast Of Diana – 54¾ x
71in.
(Sotheby's)   **$47,575   £27,500**

more controversial aspects of cleaning.

"In some instances problems have been reported to the Press" the report goes on, "instead of the head teachers following the correct procedure.

GP, John Scott, accident consultant, Howard Sherriff, at Cambridge's Addenbrooke's Hospital and Robin Glover, his counterpart at Peterborough, to raise life-saving standards and become fully-fledged members of the Association.

A. AMOROSI – A Smiling Girl Holding
A Basket Of Fruit – 27 x 23in.
(Sotheby's)   **$2,270**   **£1,320**

FERNANDO AMORSOLO – Washing
By The River – signed and dated 1951
– oil on canvas – 22 x 18in.
(Butterfield's)   **$3,500**   **£2,070**

CAPTAIN J. W. ANDERSON – A Calm,
The Solent From The Esplanade Ryde –
signed – oil – 10½ x 14in.
*(Woolley &
Wallis)*   **$1,047**   **£680**

W. ANDERSON – A Man Of War And A
Peterboat Near Harwich – on panel –
14 x 18in.
(Sotheby's)   **$1,797**   **£1,045**

WILLIAM ANDERSON – Shipping At
The Mouth Of A River – on panel –
9¾ x 14½in.
(Sotheby's)   **$1,170**   **£770**

WILLIAM ANDERSON – Barges And
Men Of War In A Calm – on panel –
12¼ x 16½in.
(Sotheby's)   **$2,006**   **£1,320**

WILLIAM ANDERSON – British Men
Of War In Open Seas – signed – 17½ x
23¼in.
(Sotheby's)   **$5,675**   **£3,300**

WILLIAM ANDERSON – A Man Of War
With Barges In A Calm – signed – on
panel – 7¼ x 8½in.
(Sotheby's)   **$1,513**   **£880**

WILLIAM ANDERSON – Shipping On A
River With A Dockyard Nearby And A
Rowing Boat In The Foreground – on
panel – 8¼ x 12¾in.
(Christie's)   **$1,598**   **£864**

ANDREENKO

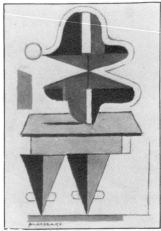

MICHEL ANDREENKO – Composition –
signed – pencil on paper – 11¾ x 8¾in.
(Christie's)   **$372**   **£237**

ALEX DE ANDREIS – The Laughing
Cavalier – signed – 31½ x 25¼in.
(Sotheby's)   **$869**   **£572**

ALEX DE ANDREIS – The Connoisseurs
– signed and dated 1922 – 25½ x 31¼in.
(Sotheby's)   **$1,772**   **£990**

FREDERIGO ANDREOTTI – 'An Inter-
esting Document' – watercolour, heightened with white – 8¾ x 6¾in.
(Sotheby, King &
Chasemore)   **$363**   **£242**

EDITH ALICE ANDREWS – Autumn
Flowers In A Jug – signed – 13½ x 18in.
(Lawrence)   **$87**   **£55**

HENRY ANDREWS – The Hawking
Party With A Grey Horse By A Forge –
oil on canvas – 19½ x 15½in.
(Dreweatt Watson &
Barton)   **$1,875**   **£1,250**

HENRY ANDREWS − A Hawking Party
Taking Refreshments Outside An Inn −
signed and dated 1850 − 42½ x 56½in.
(Christie's)   **$3,260**   **£2,160**

PIETER ANGILLIS − The Kitchen Of An
Inn − 25 x 30in.
(Sotheby's)   **$5,328**   **£3,080**

**THE HON. AND REV. CHARLES
FRANCIS ANNESLEY** − The Pass Of
Finstermuntz On The Inn, Switzerland
− signed or inscribed on the reverse −
pen and brown ink and watercolour −
20 x 14¼in.
(Christie's)   **$171**   **£102**

RICHARD ANSDELL − Children With
Pets − dated 1877 − oil − 67 x 48cm.
(Reeds Rains)   **$1,487**   **£850**

R. ANSDELL − The Noon Day's Rest
− 19 x 30in.
*(Christie's &
    Edmiston's)*   **$608**   **£380**

ANSDELL

RICHARD ANSDELL – Quarrying In The Highlands, Loch Laggan – signed and dated 1875 – 54 x 97in.
(Sotheby's)   **$21,450   £14,300**

HORST ANTES – Frau Und Taube – signed – gouache – 19 x 12cm.
(Germann Auktionshaus)   **$1,325   £828**

JAMES ARCHER – A Girl Holding A Posy Of Wild Flowers, In A Landscape – signed with monogram and dated '74 – 12 x 9in.
(Christie's)   **$676   £378**

JAMES ARCHER – How The Little Lady Stood To Van Dyck – signed with monogram and dated 1868 – 24 x 18in.
(Sotheby's)   **$13,200   £8,800**

EDWARD ARDEN – A Coast Scene With Cottages And Figures – signed – 9½ x 15in.
(Lawrence)   **$52   £33**

E. ARMFIELD – The Otter Hunt At Fault – signed – 30 x 50in.
(Chrystals)   **$1,040   £650**

GEORGE ARMFIELD – Terriers Putting Up A Duck – signed – oil on canvas – 17 x 22½in.
(Sotheby, King &
Chasemore) **$990** **£660**

GEORGE ARMFIELD – 'Out of Reach'; 'Expectation' – signed – oil on canvas – 12¼ x 10¼in.
(Sotheby, King &
Chasemore) **$979** **£550 Pair**

GEORGE ARMFIELD – Rabbits In A Wooded Glade – indistinctly signed – 11½ x 9½in.
(Christie's) **$1,088** **£702**
GEORGE ARMFIELD – Four Gun Dogs On The Stone Floor Of A Sparsely Furnished Room – signed – 15¾ x 23¾in.
(Anderson &
Garland) **$1,185** **£710**
GEORGE ARMFIELD – A Fox Stalking A Rabbit Warren – 20 x 24in.
(Sotheby's) **$752** **£495**

ELIZABETH ARMSTRONG – Little Sisters – signed with monogram – oil on panel – 12 x 9in.
(Christie's) **$1,223** **£810**

FRANCIS ARMSTRONG – An English Village Scene With A Stone Bridge Crossing A River, Villagers On The River Bank And Before The Inn, And With A Church In The Background – initialled and dated '97 – oil on canvas – 54 x 36cm.
(Osmond,
Tricks) **$516** **£300**

GEORGE ARNALD – A View Of Linlithgow Palace – signed, and signed, inscribed and dated 1819 on a label on the reverse – on panel – 7½ x 10in.
(Christie's) **$400** **£216**
ALWIN ARNEGGER – A Winter's Afternoon In The Alps – signed – 30 x 40in.
(Chrystals) **$716** **£400**

DAVID ADOLF CONSTANT ARTZ –
The Little Shepherdess – signed – 36½
x 54in.
(Sotheby's)   **$3,938**   **£2,200**

J. M. ARUNDALE – A Mother And
Child Watching Men Loading A Cart
With Hay – signed – oil on board –
11½ x 23½in.
(Anderson &
Garland)   **$112**   **£70**

WILLIAM F. ASHBURNER – Picking
Delphiniums In A Summer Garden –
signed – pencil and watercolour – 10¼
x 14¼in.
(Christie's)   **$470**   **£280**

SIR JOHN WILLIAM ASHTON – 'Twilight Pastoral' – oil on canvas board –
26 x 38cm.
(Geoff K. Gray)   **$450**   **£268**

SIR JOHN WILLIAM (WILL) ASHTON –
'Morning Light, Paris' – signed – oil on
canvas/board – 36 x 44cm.
(Geoff K. Gray)   **$1,544**   **£882**

JULIAN ROSSI ASHTON – 'Wiseman's
Ferry' – signed and inscribed – water-
colour – 17.5 x 32cm.
(Geoff K. Gray)   **$1,130**   **£672**

JULIAN ROSSI ASHTON – 'Young
Girls Picking Apples' – signed and dated
1914 – oil on canvas – 110 x 96cm.
(Geoff K. Gray)   **$9,610**   **£2,150**

F. K. ASKEW – A Portrait Of A Racehorse With A Jockey Up – indistinctly
signed – oil – 17¾ x 24in.
(Anderson &
Garland)   **$112**   **£70**

BALTHASAR VAN DER AST – Still
Life With An Overturned Basket of Fruit,
Flowers In A Vase And Sea Shells –
signed – on panel – 14½ x 27½in.
(Sotheby's)   **$61,050**   **£40,700**

SAMUEL ATKINS – A British Man-O'-
War In A Storm – signed – watercolour
– 6¼ x 8¾in.
(Christie's)   **$272**   **£162**

ATKINSON – Seaside Rides – height-
ened with bodycolour – 3¼ x 5½in.
(Sotheby Beresford
Adams)   **$147**   **£88**

GEORGE ATKINSON – The Umbrella
Maker – signed – watercolour over pencil
– 13 x 19in.
(Sotheby's)   **$1,440**   **£935**

JOHN ATKINSON – A View Along The Quay At North Shields, Figures And Horse-Drawn Carts Milling At The Dockside, Funnels And Masts Rising In The Middle Distance – signed and dated '08 – watercolour – 9 x 12in.
(Anderson & Garland) **$608** **£380**

JOHN ATKINSON – Figures Seated in Deck Chairs On A Pleasure Beach, A Steam Ship On The Horizon – signed – 7¼ x 11¼in.
(Anderson & Garland) **$368** **£230**

ALBERT AUBLET – Portrait Of Mrs Tarn, In Feathered Collared White Dress – signed and dated 1889 – oil on canvas – 32½ x 20½in.
(Dreweatt Watson & Barton) **$1,200** **£800**

ETIENNE AUBRY – 'La Becquee' – 11 x 14½in.
(Sotheby's) **$2,855** **£1,650**

JOSEPH AUFRAY – 'Finishing The Dregs' – signed – oil on panel – 10¾ x 8¼in.
(Sotheby, King & Chasemore) **$940** **£528**

W. AULTON – 'Fishing Village'; 'Cloisters'; and 'A Castle' – signed – coloured etchings – 9½ x 13½in.
(W. H. Lane & Son) **$17** **£10 Three**

LUG. AUMOND – French Soldiers, One Mounted, Scanning A Battlefield – oil on canvas – 15 x 21in.
(Hy. Duke & Son) **$432** **£250**

RANIERO AURELI – Oriental Dancers – signed – watercolour – 14 x 21in.
(Morphets) **$442** **£150**

MICHAEL AYRTON – Figures In A Street – signed and dated '52 – charcoal on brown paper – 15¾ x 10¼in.
(Christie's) **$178** **£118**

MICHAEL AYRTON – Whistler In The Field – signed and dated '53 – oil on canvas – 15 x 18in.
(Christie's) **$1,060** **£702**

CARL BAAGOE – Sailing Vessels And Steamers In An Estuary – signed and dated 1890 – 26½ x 40in.
(Sotheby's) **$2,954** **£1,650**

VICTOR BACHEREAU-REVERCHON – The Letter – signed and dated 1873 – on panel – 7½ x 6in.
(Sotheby's) **$2,067** **£1,155**

S. BACKUS – 'Tropical Landscape' – signed and dated 1950 – watercolour – 14½ x 21½in.
(Stalker & Boos) **$90** **£53**

STANLEY ROY BADMIN – 'A Nativity – No Room At The Inn' – signed and inscribed – watercolour and pen – 10 x 8¼in.
(Sotheby, King & Chasemore) **$587** **£330**

JOSEPH BAIL – The Evening Meal – signed – 45¼ x 34½in.
(Sotheby's) **$12,512** **£7,150**

DAVID BAILLY, Attributed to – A Vanitas Still Life – on panel – 10 x 12in.
(Sotheby's) **$6,054** **£3,520**

FREDERICK WILLIAM BAKER, JNR. –
At The Cottage Gate – signed – 35 x 21in.
(Sotheby Beresford
Adams) **$2,310 £1,375**

THOMAS BAKER OF LEAMINGTON –
Cattle In A Wooded Landscape – signed
and dated 1860, also signed and dated
on the reverse – on board – 12 x 10in.
(Christie's) **$803 £518**

W. BAKER – An Angler In An Open Boat
On A Loch By A Castle – signed and
dated 1901 – watercolour – 13½ x 17¼in.
(Anderson &
Garland) **$48 £30**

BAKHUYSEN, Follower of – British Man-
O'-War Off The Coast – oil on canvas –
27½ x 35in.
(Sotheby, King &
Chasemore) **$755 £484**

JULIUS JACOBUS VAN DE SANDE
BAKHUYZEN – An Extensive Park Land-
scape – signed – 23½ x 33½in.
(Christie's) **$1,847 £1,026**

LUDOLF BAKHUYZEN – 'French
Ships Sailing On Heavy Seas' – oil on
canvas – 25 x 36½in.
(Robert W. Skinner
Inc.) **$550 £343**

BALDWYN

CHARLES H. C. BALDWYN – Study Of Young Magpies – signed and dated 1890, inscribed on the reverse – 11 x 14in.
(Sotheby, King &
Chasemore)   **$422**   **£264**

J. BALLANTYNE – The Frugal Meal – bears monogram and dated 1875 – 28 x 36¼in.
(Christie's)   **$2,706**   **£1,512**

ALEX BALLINGALL – On The Dutch Coast, Unloading The Catch – signed and dated – watercolour – 18.5 x 29in.
(Woolley &
Wallis)   **$334**   **£200**

ELIAS MOLLINEAUX BANCROFT – A Blanket Weaver, Shetland – signed, inscribed and dated 1881 – watercolour heightened with white – 14 x 21in.
(Sotheby, King &
Chasemore)   **$360**   **£231**

MAX BAND – L'Eglise Saint-Germain-Des-Pres – signed – oil on canvas – 18 x 15in.
(Butterfield's)   **$150**   **£88**

BANKS – A Traveller Walking In A Forest Landscape – bears another signature and date – 17 x 23in.
(Sotheby Beresford
Adams)   **$517**   **£308**

A. BANKS – Country Village – signed and dated 1917 – 13 x 19in.
(Sotheby Beresford
Adams)   **$19**   **£11**

HAMLET BANNERMAN – His First Day At Work – signed and dated 1890 – 39 x 63in.
(Sotheby Beresford
Adams)   **$3,696**   **£2,200**

FILIPPO BARATTI – La Sultane – signed and dated 1901, and signed, inscribed and dated on the reverse – 46½ x 35¼in.
(Christie's)   **$17,820**   **£11,880**

EMILE BARBARINI – A Market Scene, Vienna With The Karlskirche Beyond – signed – on panel – 8¼ x 12¼in.
(Christie's) **$2,511 £1,620**

GIOVANNI BARBARO – Desert Scenes – signed – 13½ x 21in., the other 9½ x 23in.
(Sotheby Beresford Adams) **$37 £22 Two**

CHARLES BURTON BARBER – A Rival Attraction – signed, inscribed and dated 1887 – 14 x 9½in.
(Sotheby's) **$28,050 £18,700**

CHARLES BURTON BARBER – In Disgrace – signed and dated 1893 – 36½ x 25in.
(Sotheby's) **$33,000 £22,000**

BARBER

C. B. BARBER – 'A Day Sport In The Highlands', Ghillie With Pony And Dead Deer And Other Figures – signed – oil on panel – 8½ x 11in.
(R. J. Garwood)   **$463**   **£260**

EDGAR BARCLAY – Wrestling With The Wind – signed and dated 1909 – 56½ x 41in
(Lawrence)   **$1,644**   **£1,034**

RALPH W. BARDILL – The Watermill At Springtime With A Cow Drinking From The River, Overlooked By A Young Maiden On The Bridge – signed – watercolour – 26½ x 35½in.
(Outhwaite & Litherland)   **$954**   **£600**

JOHN JOSEPH BARKER of Bath – A Mountainous Landscape In Merioneth, North Wales – signed and inscribed on the reverse – 30 x 25in.
(Sotheby's)   **$400**   **£264**

JOHN NOBLE BARLOW – 'Moonlight On A Wooded Estuary' – oil on canvas – 16½ x 22in.
(W. H. Lane & Son)   **$140**   **£80**

JOSEPH H. BARNES – A Country Wedding – signed – watercolour, heightened with bodycolour – 23 x 28½in.
(Sotheby's) **$644** **£418**

JOSEPH H. BARNES – Falstaff At Table – signed and dated 1858 – heightened with bodycolour – 11½ x 16½in.
(Sotheby Beresford Adams) **$56** **£33**

HENRI-ALPHONSE BARNOIN – Concarneau – signed, signed, inscribed and dated 1925 – pastel – 20¾ x 28¼in.
(Sotheby's) **$984** **£550**

BARRATT – Continental Street Scenes – indistinctly signed – watercolour – 3 x 9½in. and 6 x 9½in.
(Laurence & Martin Taylor) **$27** **£16** Two

BARRAUD – Portrait Of A Gentleman On His Horse – signed with initials – oil on canvas – 20 x 24in.
(Sotheby, King & Chasemore) **$2,150** **£1,265**

WILLIAM BARRAUD – Portrait Of A Gentleman On A Bay Hunter – signed – 30¾ x 40in.
(Sotheby's) **$6,310** **£4,180**

GEORGE BARRET – Anglers By A Woodland Waterfall – 35 x 56¼in.
(Sotheby's) **$14,285** **£9,460**

BARRET

GEORGE BARRET, JNR. — At Liberty Hall Near Sheffield, West Riding, Yorkshire — watercolour ⚊ 20½ x 32¾in. *(Christie's)*   **$1,814**   **£1,080**

WILLIAM H. BARTLETT — A Venetian Landscape With Children On A Path — signed and indistinctly dated — on board — 9 x 15in. *(Christie's)*   **$1,159**   **£641**

GEORGE BARRETT — View Of Hawarden Castle — 16½ x 24½in. *(Christie's)*   **$4,395**   **£2,376**

BARRY — Hercules — 29¼ x 24¼in. *(Christie's)*   **$380**   **£205**

ROSE MAYNARD BARTON — Child And Pigeons — signed and inscribed on the reverse — watercolour — 5¼ x 6¾in. *(Christie's)*   **$1,814**   **£1,080**

CHARLES WILLILAM BARTLETT — The Cloth Seller — signed — watercolour over pencil — 16 x 19in. *(Sotheby's)*   **$1,036**   **£715**

ROSE MAYNARD BARTON – Azaleas In Bloom, Rotten Row – signed and dated '92, and inscribed on the reverse – watercolour heightened with white – 7 x 10¼in.
(Christie's)   **$4,717**   **£2,808**

EVARISTO BASCHENIS, Circle of – A Still Life Of Fruit And Flowers On A Table – 32¾ x 42in.
(Sotheby's)   **$10,973**   **£6,380**

BATCHELDER – Sailing Barge On A River – watercolour – 9½ x 23¾in.
(Sotheby, King & Chasemore)   **$92**   **£53**

STEPHEN JOHN BATCHELDER – 'Entrance To Ranworth, May 30th 1881' – watercolour – 13¼ x 20½in.
(Hilhams)   **$976**   **£610**

D. BATES – The Road From Cairo To The Pyramids, Water Carriers Who Water The Road – oil on canvas – 21½ x 14½in.
(G. H. Bayley & Sons)   **$1,176**   **£680**

D. BATES – Filling Water Skins By The Roadside Cairo – oil on canvas – 19 x 13in.
(G. H. Bayley & Sons)   **$900**   **£520**

DAVID BATES – A Brook In The New Forest – signed and dated – 18 x 24in.
(Woolley & Wallis)   **$1,169**   **£700**

DAVID BATES – A Rickyard, Baidon's Norton – signed, inscribed on the reverse – 10 x 14in.
(Sotheby's)   **$814**   **£528**

DAVID BATES – At Malvern Wells – signed and dated 1904 – heightened with white – 14 x 20½in.
(Sotheby's)   **$813**   **£528**   .

BATES

DAVID BATES – Caffyn Bridge, Capel Curig – signed and dated 1900 – oil on canvas – 24 x 36in.
(Sotheby, King &
Chasemore) **$1,776 £1,045**

DAVID BATES – At Old Colwall, Hereford – signed, and signed and inscribed on the reverse – watercolour – 14 x 21¼in.
(Christie's) **$1,088 £648**

DAVID BATES – Figures Fishing By A River In North Wales – signed and indistinctly inscribed on the reverse – oil on canvas – 20 x 30in.
(Sotheby, King &
Chasemore) **$1,156 £680**

DAVID BATES – Stepping Stones On The Conway – oil – 50 x 75cm.
(Reeds Rains) **$805 £460**

HARRY BATES – The Old Watermill, Near Dolgelly, North Wales – signed and dated 1871 – 16 x 13in.
(Sotheby Beresford
Adams) **$332 £198**

ARTHUR BATT – Portraits Of Bulls – signed, inscribed and dated 1878 – oil – 15.5 x 19.5in.
(Woolley &
Wallis) **$1,062 £600 Two**

ARTHUR BATT – Donkey And Her Foal – signed and dated 1866 – oil on board – 9½ x 13½in.
(Sotheby, King &
Chasemore) **$294 £165**

BAUMANN – An Arab Hawking Party – signed – on panel – 14 x 10¾in.
(Christie's) **$4,352 £2,808**

BAVICE – Off Needle Point, 1892 – 8 x 12½in.
(Lawrence) **$55 £35**

CHARLES BAXTER – The Egg Seller – signed and dated 1863 – 20½ x 16½in.
(Christie's) **$1,422 £918**

CHARLES BAXTER — A Venetian Beauty — signed and dated — 28½ x 23½in.
(Christie's)   **$2,846**   **£1,836**

CECIL BEATON — Lilies — signed — pen and ink and coloured washes — 24 x 18in.
(Sotheby's)   **$592**   **£385**

A. BEAUMONT — 'Fishing Boats In St. Ives Harbour' — signed — oil on canvas — 14½ x 18½in.
(W. H. Lane & Son)   **$147**   **£85**

SIR G. BEAUMONT — Building By A River In A Classical Landscape — a sketch, on card — 6 x 9½in.
(Sotheby's)   **$329**   **£176**

HARRY BECKER — At The Cottage Door — signed — 20 x 30in.
(Sotheby Beresford Adams)   **$111**   **£66**

WILIFRED CONSTANT BEAUQUESNE — The Midst Of The Battle — signed — oil on canvas — 21½ x 25¾in.
(William Doyle Galleries)   **$2,200**   **£1,301**

FRANCESCO BEDA — The Finishing Touch — signed — 28½ x 22½in.
(Sotheby Beresford Adams)   **$406**   **£242**

CORNELIUS BEELT — The Forge — signed — on panel — 15¼ x 21½in.
(Sotheby's)   **$7,022**   **£4,620**

BEERSTRATEN

A BEERSTRATEN – A Winter Landscape
– 30 x 43½in.
(Sotheby's) **$8,563 £4,950**

A. BEGEYN, Called Bega – Cattle And
Figures At A Farrier's Shop – 25 x 31½in.
(Sotheby's) **$1,807 £1,045**

ROBERT ANNING BELL – 'The Fainting
Dryad' – signed – red chalk drawing –
4¾ x 8in.
(Sotheby, King &
Chasemore) **$348 £205**

ALFRED BENNETT – Collecting Bracken – signed and dated 1867 – 21 x
32in.
(Sotheby Beresford
Adams) **$1,293 £770**

FRANK MOSS BENNETT – Amberley,
Sussex – signed, inscribed and dated
1912 – oil on canvas – 10 x 13½in.
(Sotheby, King &
Chasemore) **$480 £308**

G. BENNETT – Cattle By A Wood In An
Extensive Landscape – signed and dated
'08 – oil on canvas – 35 x 45½in.
(Dreweatt Watson &
Barton) **$510 £340**

W. BENNETT – 'The Fisherman' – signed
– watercolour – 37 x 49.5cm.
(Geoff K. Gray) **$118 £60**

WILLIAM BENNETT – A Punt On A
River, Woods Beyond – signed – watercolour with touches of white heightening
– 14¼ x 20½in.
(Christie's) **$416 £248**

FRANK WESTON BENSON – Interior
With Woman – signed – oil on canvas –
14 x 10in.
(Christie's) **$13,200 £8,800**

C. BENTLEY – 'A Quiet Smoke' –
dated 1853 – watercolour – 11½ x 8¼in.
(Sotheby, King &
Chasemore) **$425 £250**

THOMAS HART BENTON – Forest
Path – signed – watercolour and
pencil on paper – 11 x 7½in.
(Butterfield's) **$1,500 £888**

PIETRO BENVENUTI – Il Giuramento
Dei Sassoni A Napoleone Dopo La
Battaglia Di Jena – signed and dated
1820 – 62 x 88in.
(Christie's) **$29,160 £19,440**

JOSEPH AUSTIN BENWELL – Egypt:
Music Outside A Temple – signed and
dated 1867 – watercolour heightened
with white – 13 x 19½in.
(Christie's) **$2,903 £1,728**

BERAUD

JEAN BERAUD – Paris, On The Boulevard – signed – 25¼ x 31½in.
(Sotheby's) **$214,500 £143,000**

JEAN BERAUD – A Self Portrait In Evening Dress – signed – 39½ x 25½in.
(Sotheby's) **$15,675 £10,450**

NICOLAES BERCHEM – A Southern Landscape With Herdsmen – signed in monogram – 30¼ x 43¼in.
(Sotheby's) **$49,500 £33,000**

NICHOLAS BERCHEM – Cattle, Figures And Dogs Fording A Stream – signed and dated 1655 – sepia drawing – 11 x 15in.
(Laurence & Martin Taylor) **$173 £100**

MORITZ BERENDT – The Marriage Feast At Caana – signed and dated 1835 – 10¾ x 16in.
(Sotheby's) **$1,588 £1,045**

FRANCESCO BERGAMINI – 'The Rosary' – signed and inscribed – oil on canvas – 17 x 25½in.
(Sotheby, King & Chasemore) **$3,795 £2,530**

FRANCESCO BERGAMINI – The Young Harvester – signed and inscribed – 9¼ x 6¼in.
(Christie's) **$1,674 £1,080**

KNUD LARSEN BERGSLEIN – Peasant Woman And Lame Sheep By The Hearth – signed – oil on canvas – 26 x 31in.
(Butterfield's) **$1,700 £1,017**

F. BERLIN – Figures In A Dutch Street – signed and dated '63 – 23¾ x 18¾in.
(Sotheby's) **$1,575 £880**

JOHANN BERTHELSEN – Washington Monument, Mt. Vernon Park – signed – oil on canvas – 20¼ x 42¼in.
(Christie's) **$1,100 £733**

BARTOLOMEO BETTERA, Studio of – Still Life Paintings Of Musical Instruments – 26¼ x 30¼in.
(Sotheby's) **$7,802 £4,510 Pair**

ROBERT BEVAN – Cottage Set In Trees With Two Figures – signed – oil – 14 x 18in.
(Graves, Son & Pilcher) **$7,700 £4,400**

BIANCHINI – 'Parting Words' – signed and dated 1873 – oil on panel – 12¾ x 10¼in.
(Robert W. Skinner Inc.) **$400 £250**

LAURENCE BIDDLE – Pansies, Primroses And Forget-Me-Nots With A China Figure – signed and dated '34 – on panel – 12½ x 21in.
(Sotheby's) **$669 £462**

IRWIN BEVAN – A Napoleonic Encounter – signed and dated 1895 – 13 x 20in.
(Sotheby's) **$508 £330**

WILLIAM REDMORE BIGG, Attributed to – A Tavern Scene With Sailors And Harlots Dancing – 27½ x 35½in.
(Sotheby's) **$1,827 £1,210**

BILIVERTI

GIOVANNI ANTONIO BILIVERTI –
Saint Agnes – signed – 52¾ x 42½in.
(Sotheby's)   **$4,180   £2,750**

SAMUEL JOHN LAMORNA BIRCH –
The Ever Restless Sea, Lamorna Cove –
signed and dated 1905 – 16 x 24in.
(Sotheby's)   **$1,196   £825**

SAMUEL JOHN LAMORNA BIRCH –
Clapper Mill, Lamorna, July – signed and
dated 1952, also signed and inscribed on
the reverse – on panel – 10¾ x 13½in.
(Sotheby's)   **$568   £330**

SAMUEL JOHN LAMORNA BIRCH –
'Cromwell's Castle, Isles Of Scilly' –
signed and dated 1934 – watercolour
– 8 x 5in.
*(W. H. Lane &
Son)*   **$76   £44**

WILLIAM MINSHALL BIRCHALL –
With The Fleet – signed, inscribed
and dated 1913 – heightened with
white – 9½ x 21in.
*(Sotheby Beresford
Adams)*   **$203   £121**

HUGO BIRGER – La Toilette – signed
and dated 1880 – 57½ x 45in.
(Sotheby's)   **$44,550   £29,700**

WILLIAM VERPLANCK BIRNEY – Old
Photos Bring Fond Thoughts – signed,
also signed and inscribed on the reverse
– oil on board – 18 x 24in.
*(William Doyle
Galleries)*   **$5,500   £3,254**

WILLIAM VERPLANCK BIRNEY –
Preparing The Fishing Rod – signed –
watercolour on paper on board – 30½
x 18½in.
(Christie's)   **$935**   **£623**

ABRAHAM BISSCHOP – A Swan, A Cockerel And Other Birds In A Landscape –
signed – 59 x 47¾in.
(Sotheby's)   **$7,612**   **£4,400**

FRANZ BISCHOFF – Mt. Alice – signed
– oil on canvas – 12½ x 16½in.
(Butterfield's)   **$800**   **£473**

A. BISSCHOP – Exotic Duck And Other
Birds In A Park Setting – 35¾ x 30in.
(Sotheby's)   **$3,027**   **£1,760**

EUGEN VON BLAAS – Girl With
Bouquet – signed – oil on cradled panel
– 21¼ x 14in.
(Butterfield's)   **$12,000**   **£7,185**

BLAAS

EUGENE DE BLAAS – An Italian Beauty
– signed – on panel – 14¾ x 10¼in.
(Sotheby's)   **$6,497   £3,630**

EUGENE DE BLAAS – The Fair Washer
Girl – signed and dated 1898 – 57½ x
30in.
(Christie's)   **$5,832   £3,240**

D. BLACKHAM – Still Lives With Fruit
– one signed and dated 1910 – 15½ x
23½in.
*(Sotheby Beresford
       Adams)*   **$58   £33 Pair**

WILLIAM KAY BLACKLOCK – Sunny
Beach, Walberswick – signed, inscribed
on the reverse – on board – 9 x 12in.
*(Sotheby Beresford
       Adams)*   **$2,296   £1,320**

WILLIAM KAY BLACKLOCK – Playing
With The Kitten – signed – watercolour
– 26 x 51cm.
*(Sotheby, King &
       Chasemore)*   **$1,963   £1,155**

WILLIAM KAY BLACKLOCK – 'Children Before A Mill On The Wooded
Banks Of A River With Punt' – oil on
board – 10½ x 13½in.
*(W. H. Lane &
       Son)*   **$574   £330**

E. J. BLADON – Moored Vessel – signed
and dated 1902 – 18½ x 28½in.
*(Sotheby Beresford
       Adams)*   **$189   £110**

EDMUND BLAMPIED – 'Camelias' – signed – oil on board – 27 x 30in. *(Sotheby, King & Chasemore)* **$1,617** **£924**

ANTOINE BLANCHARD – Paris Street Scene – signed – oil on canvas – 18 x 21½in. *(Butterfield's)* **$800** **£473**

ANTOINE BLANCHARD – La Rue Tronchet, Paris – signed, inscribed on the reverse – 13 x 18in. *(Sotheby Beresford Adams)* **$887** **£528**

EMILY BEATRICE BLAND – 'Miscellaneous Bunch' – signed and inscribed on reverse – oil on board – 30 x 24¼in. *(Sotheby, King & Chasemore)* **$346** **£198**

ANTOINE BLANCHARD – Place De L'Opera, Cafe De La Paix, Paris En 1900 – signed, inscribed on the reverse – 13 x 18in. *(Sotheby Beresford Adams)* **$924 £550**

BLARENBERGHE

LOUIS NICOLAS VAN BLARENBERGHE – A Northern Winter Landscape – gouache on vellum – 5 x 7½in. *(Sotheby's)* **$3,406 £1,980**

CARLE J. BLENNER – 'Portrait Of A Woman Holding Buttercups' – signed – oil on canvas – 26 x 20in. *(Robert W. Skinner Inc.)* **$1,100 £688**

JABEZ BLIGH – Still Life Of Fruit – watercolour – 10½ x 12½in. *(Lawrence)* **$112 £71**

THOMAS BLINKS – Full Cry; and A Check – one signed – 13½ x 20½in. *(Sotheby Beresford Adams)* **$227 £132 Pair**

DOUGLAS PERCY BLISS – Summer In The Hebrides – signed and dated 1955 – 30 x 40½in. *(Christie's & Edmiston's)* **$320 £200**

ALBERT BLOCH – Motley – signed – oil on board – 17¾ x 20½in. *(Christie's)* **$3,850 £2,566**

EUGENE DE BLOCK – Waiting For The Boats To Return – signed and dated 1874 – 30¾ x 23¼in.
(Sotheby's) **$1,204** **£792**

VAN BLOEMEN – Italian Landscape With Figure In A Rowing Boat On A Lake – 25 x 30in.
(Sotheby's) **$1,174** **£682**

ARNOLDUS BLOEMERS – Still Life Of Summer Flowers – signed with monogram – oil on canvas – 20 x 17in.
(William Doyle Galleries) **$16,000** **£9,467**

ABRAHAM BLOEMAERT – The Latin Fathers Of The Church – signed and dated 1645 – 82 x 61in.
(Sotheby's) **$32,350** **£18,700**
HENDRICK BLOEMAERT – A Man Eating From An Earthenware Bowl – 36 x 27in.
(Sotheby's) **$2,932** **£1,705**
BLOEMEN – Sheep And A Cow In A Landscape – 14 x 19½in.
(Sotheby Beresford Adams) **$702** **£418**

PEETER DE BOC – Music – signed and dated 1631 – 31 x 36¼in.
(Sotheby's) **$4,758** **£2,750**

BOCK

THEODORE DE BOCK – August .
Zandvoort – signed and inscribed – oil
on canvas – 9½ x 15½in.
(Sotheby, King &
Chasemore) **$782** **£460**

HENRY JOHN BODDINGTON – 'On
The Conway, North Wales' – signed and
inscribed on a label – oil on canvas – 14 x
22in.
(Sotheby, King &
Chasemore) **$1,485** **£990**

E. BODE – 'Sydney Heads From Obelisk
Bay' – signed and inscribed – water-
colour – 32 x 46cm.
(Geoff K. Gray) **$360** **£215**

JOHANNES DE BOECKHURST,
Attributed to – Herse Approached By
Mercury – oil on canvas – 41 x 51in.
(Butterfield's) **$1,100** **£658**

PIERRE LE BOEUFF – French Town
Views – signed – heightened with body-
colour – 14½ x 21½in.
(Sotheby Beresford
Adams) **$267** **£154 Pair**

PIERRE LE BOEUFF – Lisieux, Calvados
– signed – 24½ x 29in.
(Sotheby's) **$689** **£385**

HENRY JOHN BODDINGTON, Follower of – Cottage Scenes, With Children In
The Background – on panel – 11¾ x 10¾in. *(Sotheby, King & Chasemore)*
$4,032 £2,585 Pair

LOUIS-LEOPOLD BOILLY, Attributed
to – A Girl And A Boy Playing In A
Park – bears signature – 20½ x 15¼in.
(Sotheby's)   **$4,347   £2,860**

FERDINAND BOL – Anna Rijkens, In
A Crimson Dress And Gold Brocade
Skirt – 44 x 34in.
(Sotheby's)   **$13,320   £7,700**

GIOVANNI BOLDINI – A Portrait Of
Madame Lacroix – signed and dated 1910
– watercolour, Indian ink and charcoal
heightened with white – 19¼ x 19¼in.
(Sotheby's)   **$28,875   £16,500**

DAVID BOMBERG – Self Portrait –
signed and dated '31 – oil on canvas –
30 x 25¼in.
(Christie's)   **$3,587   £2,376**

ELIAS PIETER VAN BOMMEL –
Figures On The Outskirts Of Amsterdam
– signed, signed, inscribed and dated
1866 on a label – 10½ x 13¾in.
(Sotheby's)   **$1,575   £880**

BOMMEL

ELIAS PIETER VAN BOMMEL – A Dutch Canal At Dusk – signed with initials – on panel – 7¼ x 9in.
(Sotheby's)   **$1,180**   **£660**

CARLO BONAVIA – An Italian Port At Sunset – 30 x 54¼in.
(Sotheby's)   **$15,675**   **£10,450**

WILLIAM JOSEPH J. C. BOND – Dutch Fishing Boats – signed – 6 x 8in.
(Sotheby's)   **$287**   **£187**

SIR MUIRHEAD BONE – On The Grand Canal, Venice – signed and dated 1912 – pencil on beige paper – 9¼ x 8¼in.
(Christie's)   **$422**   **£280**

SIR MUIRHEAD BONE – The Molo, Venice – signed – pencil, pen, ink and wash – 7¼ x 11½in.
(Christie's & Edmiston's)   **$352**   **£220**

PIERRE BONNARD – 'Deux Femmes' – etching – 6½ x 9in.
(Du Mouchelles)   **$800**   **£470**

RICHARD PARKES BONINGTON – View In Venice, With The Church Of St. George – on board – 12 x 16in. *(Sotheby's)*   **$232,540 £154,000**

FLORENCE MARY BONNEAU – Tiger
Skin Rug – signed – 7½ x 15½in.
(Sotheby Beresford
   Adams)   **$172**   **£99**

PIETRO PAULO BONZI, Attributed to –
A Still Life Of Grapes, Apples And Pears
– oil on canvas – 33¼ x 45in.
(Sotheby's)   **$7,682**   **£6,820**

WALTER BOODLE – Rural Cottage With
A Lake In The Foreground – signed – oil
on canvas – 17¼ x 23½in.
(Bracketts)   **$352**   **£220**

BERNARD LOUIS BORIONE – 'A
Musical Cardinal' – signed and inscribed
– oil on canvas – 16 x 13in.
(Sotheby, King &
   Chasemore)   **$1,527**   **£858**

WILLEM JACOBUS BOOGARD – Horses Feeding At A Manger – signed and
dated 1896 – on panel – 8 x 10¾in. *(Sotheby's)*   **$3,010** **£1,980**

BOSER

KARL FRIEDRICH ADOLF BOSER –
After Church – signed and dated 1861 –
27½ x 22in.
(Christie's) **$9,720 £6,480**

A. BOSL – 'After A Summer Storm',
Wreckage In The Sea At Dawn –
indistinctly signed and dated – oil
– 17¾ x 31¾in.
(Anderson &
Garland) **$8 £5**

PIETER VAN DEN BOSSCHE, Attributed
to – An Elderly Woman And A Boy In A
Kitchen Interior – on panel – 11 x 17in.
(Sotheby's) **$3,009 £1,980**

JULIUS BOSSE – Idle Thoughts – signed
and inscribed – 38½ x 59in.
(Sotheby's) **$1,755 £1,155**

BOSTON SCHOOL – 'Profile Portrait
Of A Seated Woman' – oil on canvas – 36
x 28in.
(Robert W. Skinner
Inc.) **$350 £218**

JAN BOTH, Follower of – Herdsmen In A
Landscape – on panel – 8½ x 10½in.
(Sotheby's) **$1,170 £770**

BOUCHER – The Infant Bacchus And
Two Cherubs – canvas on panel – 31
x 23in.
(Christie's &
Edmiston's) **$960 £600**

PIERRE VAN BOUCLE – A Still Life Of
Fish – 17½ x 21¼in.
(Sotheby's) **$1,839 £1,210**

SAMUEL BOUGH – 'Twilight' – water-colour – 4½ x 10¾in.
*(Sotheby, King &
    Chasemore)* **$297**   **£198**

SAMUEL BOUGH – 'Glencaple' –
signed and inscribed on the reverse –
watercolour – 7¼ x 10¾in.
*(Sotheby, King &
    Chasemore)* **$693**   **£462**

SAMUEL BOUGH – Brough By Sands
Church – inscribed – 23 x 18in.
(Sotheby's) **$501**   **£330**

SAMUEL BOUGH – Coastal Scene,
With Sailing Vessels In A Choppy Sea
In The Foreground – watercolour –
13¾ x 19in.
*(Sotheby, King &
    Chasemore)* **$578**   **£385**

SAMUEL BOUGH – 'The Quiraing', Skye'
– signed, inscribed and dated 1867 – oil
on canvas – 25 x 42½in.
*(Sotheby, King &
    Chasemore)* **$5,940** **£3,960**

SAMUEL BOUGH – 'The Reapers' – signed – oil on canvas – 24 x 36in.
(Sotheby, King &
Chasemore) **$3,465 £2,310**

SAMUEL BOUGH – 'Solway' – signed, inscribed and dated 1866 – watercolour heightened with bodycolour – 10½ x 16½in.
(Sotheby, King &
Chasemore) **$1,174 £660**

GEORGE HENRY BOUGHTON – Alone ·
– signed and dated '74 – oil on canvas
– 30½ x 20½in.
(Christie's) **$5,500 £3,666**

HIPPOLYTE BOULENGER – A View In Fontainebleau Forest – on panel – 13¾ x 11in.
(Sotheby's) **$1,004 £660**

LOUIS DE BOULLONGNE, The Younger — Male Nude Seated On A Rock — signed — black and white chalk on blue paper — 50.3 x 37.8cm.
(Sotheby's) **$7,771** **£4,950**

BURTON SHEPARD BOUNDEY — House In Monterey — signed — oil on canvas — 24½ x 30½in.
(Butterfield's) **$1,500** **£998**

J. BOURNE — A Paddle Steamer — signed — on board — 11½ x 17½in.
(Sotheby Beresford Adams) **$102** **£60**

JAMES BOURNE — 'Snowdon', With Figures On Path — watercolour — 7 x 10in.
(John Hogbin & Son) **$80** **£47**

P. BOUT AND A. F. BOUDEWIJNS — A Southern Landscape With Peasants On A Roadway — on panel — 7¾ x 12in.
(Sotheby's) **$5,328** **£3,080**

F. CECIL BOULT — 'Gone To Ground'; and 'The Chase' — one signed — oil on canvas — 24 x 18in.
(Sotheby, King & Chasemore) **$1,496** **£935 Pair**

PIETER BOUT — Winter Landscape With A Hunting Party — on panel — 11½ x 16in.
(Sotheby Beresford Adams) **$12,012** **£7,150**

BOUVARD

ANTOINE BOUVARD – A View Of Venice With The Campanile Di S. Marco In The Distance – signed – 10¾ x 13¾in.
(Christie's) **$875** **£486**

ANTOINE BOUVARD, JNR. – Venetian Canal – signed – 9¾ x 13½in.
(Sotheby Beresford Adams) **$1,914** **£1,100 Pair**

ANTOINE BOUVARD, JNR. – Twilight, Venice – signed – 19 x 25in.
(Sotheby Beresford Adams) **$1,848** **£1,100**

ANTOINE BOUVARD, SNR. – Sunset Over A Venetian Canal – signed – 19 x 25in.
(Sotheby's) **$1,772** **£990**

ANTOINE BOUVARD, SNR. – Sunset Over A Venetian Canal – signed – 19 x 24¾in.
(Sotheby's) **$1,672** **£1,100**

ANTOINE BOUVARD, SNR. – A Gondola On A Venetian Side Canal – signed – 10 x 13in.
(Sotheby's) **$826** **£462**

AUGUSTE JULES BOUVIER – Helen At Her Toilet With Attendants – signed and dated '73 – watercolour heightened with white – 14¼ x 22in.
(Christie's) **$580** **£345**

JULES BOUVIER – A Stitch For Freedom – signed – watercolour – 11½ x 9½in.
(Sotheby, King & Chasemore) **$343** **£220**

OWEN BOWEN – 'River Landscape With Cows' – oil – 18 x 24in.
(Dacre, Son & Hartley) **$326** **£190**

WILLIAM THOMAS NICHOLAS BOYCE – A Trawler In A Stiff Breeze – signed and dated 1911 – 15 x 29in.
(Sotheby Beresford Adams) **$133** **£77**

ALICE BOYD – The Incantation Of Hervor – signed with monogram – 23½ x 19¼in.
(Christie's & Edmiston's) **$320** **£200**

DAVID BOYD – 'The Secluded Pool' – signed – oil on canvas – 51 x 61cm.
(Geoff K. Gray) **$904** **£538**

DAVID BOYD – 'Preparing For The Picnic' – signed – oil on board – 41 x 46cm.
(Geoff K. Gray) **$1,130** **£672**

EMILE BOYER – Paris Street Scene – signed – oil on canvas – 13 x 18in.
(Butterfield's) **$225** **£133**

HERCULES BRABAZON BRABAZON – San Juan Daroca, Spain – signed with initials – pencil and watercolour heightened with white – 9¼ x 13½in.
(Christie's) **$619** **£410**

HERCULES BRABAZON BRABAZON – Monaco From Cap St. Martin – signed, inscribed and dated 1875 on the reverse – heightened with white – 8½ x 12½in.
(Sotheby Beresford Adams) **$364** **£209**

HERCULES BRABAZON BRABAZON – Vesuvius From Naples – pencil and watercolour heightened with white – 9¼ x 13¼in.
(Christie's) **$260** **£172**

NEWTON BRABY – The Little Dutch Girl – signed and dated 1905 – oil on canvas – 11½ x 8½in.
(Sotheby, King & Chasemore) **$290** **£187**

BRACKEN

WILLIAM BRADFORD – The Ice Blockade On The Labrador Coast – signed and inscribed – oil on canvas – 18 x 30in. *(William Doyle Galleries)* **$24,000 £14,200**

JOHN BRACKEN – Portrait Of Elizabeth, Lady Chaworth – 36 x 29¾in. *(Sotheby's)* **$830 £550**

RICHARD BRACKENBERG – An Interior With Figures Merrymaking – inscribed – 26½ x 35¾in. *(Sotheby's)* **$10,032 £6,600**

PAUL BRADDON – Abbeville; St. Nicholas, Ghent; Rouen; and Bruges – signed – 30 x 21in. *(Sotheby Beresford Adams)* **$351 £209 Four**

HELEN BRADLEY – The Wakes Come To Lees – signed, signed, inscribed and dated on the reverse – oil on canvas board – 30 x 40in. *(Christie's)* **$4,077 £2,700**

WILLIAM BRADFORD – 'Fishing Boats In The Arctic' – signed – oil on canvas – 12 x 20in. *(Robert W. Skinner Inc.)* **$14,000 £8,750**

WILLIAM BRADLEY – Eton College – signed – pencil and watercolour heightened with white – 17½ x 26in.
(Christie's)   **$1,782**   **£1,188**

BRAEKELEER – A Boy And His Monkey – on panel – 20 x 16in.
(Sotheby Beresford
      Adams)   **$406**   **£242**

FERDINAND DE BRAEKELEER – The Game Of Cards – signed and dated 1863, and signed and dated on the reverse – 15¾ x 19¼in.
(Sotheby's)   **$11,704**   **£7,700**

RICHARD BRAKENBURGH – A Fiddle Player In A Tavern – 16 x 12in.
(Sotheby's)   **$1,797**   **£1,045**

BRANDEIS

ANTONIETTA BRANDEIS – The Church Of Santa Maria Della Salute – signed – oil on board – 6¼ x 8¾in.
(Sotheby, King & Chasemore)   **$1,403   £825**

ANTONIETTA BRANDEIS – Venice, The Bridge Of Sighs – signed – 17¾ x 10¼in.
(Sotheby's)   **$2,165   £1,210**

BRANDI – Italianate Rocky Landscape – 11½ x 8½in.
(Sotheby's)   **$1,324   £770 Pair**

FRANK BRANGWYN – 'Mediterranean Landscape' – etching – 12 x 15½in.
(Dacre, Son & Hartley)   **$86   £50 Pair**

SIR FRANK BRANGWYN – The Moroccan Boy – oil on panel – 9½ x 11½in.
(Christie's)   **$489   £324**

SIR FRANK BRANGWYN – The Orange Sellers – signed and dated – oil on canvas – 20 x 24in.
(Christie's)   **$8,154   £5,400**

CHARLES BRANWHITE – 'Goring Church On The Thames', Cattle Before The Church And A Figure In A Punt On The River – inscribed – oil on panel – 44 x 28cm.
(Osmond, Tricks)   **$498   £290**

CHARLES BROOK BRANWHITE – Kilsgarren Castle, South Wales With A Fisherman On The Banks Of The River Before The Castle At Sunset – signed and dated '74 – watercolour – 45 x 30cm.
(Osmond, Tricks)   **$413   £240**

LOUIS BRAQUAVAL – The Quay At Martigues, Bouches Du Rhone – signed – on board – 15 x 18in.
(Sotheby's)   **$481   £660**

A. BRATINGHAM-SIMPSON – 'Cows In A Meadow' – watercolour – 7 x 10in.
(W. H. Lane & Son)   **$48   £28**

KARL OTTO BRAUN – At The Doorway
– signed and inscribed – 24 x 16½in.
(Christie's) **$5,219 £3,456**
MAURICE BRAUN – Mountain Lake –
signed – pastel on paper – 8½ x 6½in.
(Butterfield's) **$175 £103**

LODOVICO BREA, Circle of – A Trip-
tych: The Virgin And Child Enthroned
With Angels; Saint James The Greater;
A Bishop Saint – on panel – centre 45¼
x 23½in; wings, each 45¼ x 15¾in.
(Sotheby's) **$18,078 £10,450**

WILLIAM A. BREAKSPEARE – The
Tiff – signed – 27¼ x 20¼in.
(Christie's) **$2,176 £1,404**

CLAUDIO BRAVO – A Lady And Girl
Before A Surreal Courtyard – signed
and dated – conte crayon and graphite
on paper – 42 x 30½in.
(Butterfield's) **$7,000 £4,190**

ALFRED DE BREANSKI – Mountainous
Landscape With Cattle Watering – oil –
19 x 29in.
*(Capes, Dunn
& Co.)* **$800 £500**

ALFRED DE BREANSKI, SNR. — A Spring Morning, The Callander Falls — signed, inscribed on the reverse — 21 x 14in.
(Sotheby's) **$1,003** **£660**

ALFRED DE BREANSKI, JNR. — Evening Gwn-Y-Llan, Wales — signed and inscribed on reverse — 24 x 36in.
(Sotheby, King & Chasemore) **$950** **£500**

ALFRED FONTVILLE DE BREANSKI — Early Morning, The Slopes Of Ben Aan; and Evening In Glan Falloch — signed, inscribed on the reverse — 23 x 15in.
(Sotheby Beresford Adams) **$1,293** **£770 Pair**

ALFRED FONTVILLE DE BREANSKI — Windsor From The River — signed — watercolour — 10½ x 14½in.
(Sotheby's) **$373** **£242**

ALFRED DE BREANSKI, SNR. — 'A July Evening, Loch Katrine' — signed and inscribed on the reverse — oil on canvas — 20 x 30in. *(Sotheby, King & Chasemore)* **$2,524 £1,485**

GUSTAVE DE BREANSKI – Sailing Boat
Entering Harbour – signed – oil on canvas
– 18 x 30in.
(Sotheby, King &
Chasemore) $548   £308

MICHAEL GEORGE BRENNAN –
Portrait Of A Young Woman Looking At
An Artist's Folio – signed and dated –
oil – 56 x 43.5in.
(Woolley &
Wallis) $635   £380

JULES ADOLPHE BRETON – The
Reapers – signed and dated 1860 – 29½ x
44in.
(Sotheby's) $36,575   £20,900

HARRIS BRETT – Morning And Evening Near Cairo – signed – gouache –
6¼ x 9¼in.
(Sotheby Beresford
Adams) $56   £33 Two

HENRY CHARLES BREWER – 'Oxford'
– signed – watercolour heightened with
white – 19¼ x 12½in.
(Sotheby, King &
Chasemore) $528   £330

BREYDEL

KAREL BREYDEL – A Cavalry Battle
– 21 x 24½in.
(Sotheby's)   **$3,678   £2,420**

ALFRED THOMPSON BRICHER –
Grand Manan Channel, Maine – signed
– oil on canvas – 15¼ x 33¼in.
*(William Doyle
Galleries)*   **$13,000   £7,692**

ALFRED THOMPSON BRICHER –
Mountain Landscape – signed – oil on
canvas – 9 x 18¼in.
(Christie's)   **$4,400   £2,933**

ALFRED THOMPSON BRICHER – 'Reading By The Shore, Narragansett Bay' –
signed – watercolour and gouache on
paper on board – 11¾ x 20in.
*(Robert W. Skinner
Inc.)*   **$24,000   £15,000**

HARRY BRIGHT – The Carol Singer
– signed and dated 1891 – watercolour
heightened with white – 15 x 10½in.
(Christie's)   **$362   £216**

HENRY BRIGHT – Old Mill, Killarney,
An Old Watermill by Stunted Trees With
A Girl In A Red Dress Crossing A Stream
On Stepping Stones, Rugged Hills Beyond
– signed – oil on canvas – 51 x 75.5cm.
*(Henry Spencer &
Sons)*   **$895   £500**

HENRY BRIGHT – Coastal Scenes – 16
x 30cm.
(Reeds Rains)   **$2,625   £1,500 Pair**

P. BRIL – Saint Isidore Seated In A
Garden Contemplating – on metal – 7 x
9in.
(Sotheby's)   **$2,838   £1,650**

CARL BRINNIR – Sussex, After A Shower
Of Rain – signed, inscribed and dated 1879
on the reverse – 15 x 25½in.
*(Sotheby Beresford
Adams)*   **$178   £104**

HENRI BRISPOT – Cardinals At Table In An Interior – signed – 22½ x 28¾in.
(Christie's)   **$3,850 £2,484**

EDMUND BRISTOW – Still Life With A Hare, Pheasant, Partridge And Other Birds
– signed and dated – oil – 36.2 x 48.2in. *(Woolley & Wallis)*   **$2,505 £1,500**

BROCHART

GERALD LESLIE BROCKHURST –
Girl, Standing – signed – soft pencil –
15¼ x 8¼in.
(Christie's)   **$815**   **£540**

GERALD LESLIE BROCKHURST –
Woman In A Hat – signed and dated
1930 – pencil – 9 x 7in.
(Christie's)   **$1,140**   **£756**

GERALD LESLIE BROCKHURST – A
Portrait Of Miss Von Damm – signed –
oil – 27 x 24in.
*(Woolley &
   Wallis)*   **$2,655**   **£1,500**

GERALD LESLIE BROCKHURST –
Standing Girl With Her Left Arm Raised
– signed – pencil – 14¾ x 9in.
(Christie's)   **$1,140**   **£756**

WILLIAM BROMLEY – Feeding The Bird
– signed – 14 x 12in.
(Christie's)   **$4,018**   **£2,592**

C. J. BROCHART – Classical Studies Of
Ladies – bears signature – oil on panel –
18 x 12in.
*(Sotheby, King &
   Chasemore)*   **$560**   **£330 Pair**

JAN GERRITSZ. BRONKHORST, Manner
of – Philosophy, History And Geometry –
45½ x 49½in.
(Sotheby's)   **$1,304**   **£858**

ALEXANDER BROOK – Red Vase –
signed and dated 1927 – oil on canvas
– 36 x 30¼in.
(Christie's)   **$2,860   £1,906**

ADRIAEN BROUWER, Follower of – A
Man Pulling Off A Bandage – on panel –
6 x 5in.
(Sotheby's)   **$869   £572**

SAMUEL JOHN MILTON BROWN – A
Three-Masted Sailing Ship – signed –
pencil – 5 x 7½in.
*(Sotheby Beresford
      Adams)*   **$23   £13**

SAMUEL JOHN MILTON BROWN –
Sail And Steam – signed – 16 x 21in.
(Sotheby's)   **$643   £418**

VINCENT BROWN – 'Sunset' – signed
– oil on canvas board – 29 x 36cm.
(Geoff K. Gray)   **$360   £215**

WILLIAM BROWN – Horses Grazing At
Sunset – signed and dated '97 – 27½ x
36in.
*(Sotheby Beresford
      Adams)*   **$19   £11**

WILLIAM MARSHALL BROWN –
'Mussel Gatherers' – signed – oil – 10
x 14in.
*(Woolley &
      Wallis)*   **$690   £390**

HABLOT KNIGHT 'PHIZ' BROWNE –
The Peat-Cutter's Family; and A Quiet
Ride – one signed – black chalk, pen
and brown ink and watercolour – 13½
x 19¾in.
(Christie's)   **$1,549   £1,026 Pair**

LAZARE BRUANDET – Cattle, Sheep
And A Figure Beside A Gateway – on
panel – 13 x 18½in.
(Sotheby's)   **$950   £550**

BRUEGHEL

PIETER BRUEGHEL, The Younger – Peasants Feasting Out-Of-Doors – signed
– on panel – 17 x 24½in. *(Sotheby's)*   **$173,250 £115,000**

PIETER BRUEGHEL, The Younger – A Peasant Wedding Procession – signed and
dated 1630 – on panel – 29 x 49in. *(Sotheby's)*   **$266,420 £154,000**

BRUEGHEL – River Landscape With Boats And Figures – oil on copper panel – 6 x 8in.
(Woolley & Wallis) **$5,698 £3,700 Pair**

BRUEGHEL AND RUBENS – Saint Hubert – 37¾ x 50in.
(Sotheby's) **$6,811 $3,960**

LEON BRUNIN – A Proud Cavalier – signed and inscribed – 19½ x 13½in.
(Sotheby's) **$1,505 £990**

P. T. VAN BRUSSEL – Still Life, A Vase Of Flowers With Bird's Nest On Marble Ledge – signed with initials and dated – oil on panel – 27 x 18in.
(Woolley & Wallis) **$4,956 £2,800**

H. C. BRYANT – At The Vegetable Market – signed and dated 1874, and signed and inscribed on the reverse – 17½ x 22¼in.
(Christie's) **$4,185 £2,700**

ADAM BUCK, After – Mother And Child – watercolour – 7¼ x 10in.
(Olivers) **$74 £44**

C. F. BUCKLEY – Coniston Water – watercolour – 10 x 14¾in.
(Christie's) **$435 £259**

BERNARD BUFFET – Vase Avec Tulipes – signed and dated '65 – gouache on paper – 25 x 20in.
(William Doyle Galleries) **$6,700 £3,964**

BUFFET

BERNARD BUFFET – 'Still Life' –
signed and dated '63 – oil on canvas – 53
x 63cm.
(Geoff K. Gray) **$3,191 £1,823**

EDGAR BUNDY – The Envoy – signed
– watercolour over traces of pencil,
heightened with bodycolour – 20 x 27in.
(Sotheby's) **$813 £528**

HENRY WILLIAM BUNBURY – The
Dancing Bear – 16½ x 21in.
(Sotheby's) **$798 £528**

EDGAR BUNDY – Angry Moments –
signed and inscribed on the reverse –
watercolour over pencil heightened with
bodycolour – 10¾ x 12¼in.
(Sotheby's) **$678 £440**

EDGAR BUNDY – The Raid – signed –
heightened with bodycolour – 10¼ x 12in.
*(Sotheby Beresford
    Adams)* **$628 £374**

EDGAR BUNDY – Reminiscences –
signed – 20 x 30in.
(Sotheby's) **$836 £550**

EDGAR BUNDY – Flirtation – signed –
14 x 20in.
(Sotheby Beresford
Adams) **$1,244** **£715**

RUPERT CHARLES WULSTEN BUNNY
– 'Figure On A Path, Vineyard And Villa'
– signed with monogram – oil on canvas
– 53 x 64cm.
(Geoff K. Gray) **$9,935** **£5,914**
ELBRIDGE AYER BURBANK –
Fishing Wharf – signed – pencil on
paper – 9½ x 16in.
(Butterfield's) **$90** **£53**
FERDINAND BURGDORFF – Holy
Grail – signed and dated 1966 – oil on
board – 15½ x 12in.
(Butterfield's) **$125** **£74**
JOHN BAGNOLD BURGESS – Far Away
Thoughts – on board – 10¾ x 7in.
(Christie's) **$803** **£518**

JOHN BAGNOLD BURGESS – A
Spanish Beauty – signed and dated 1872
– 30½ x 21½in.
(Christie's) **$1,088** **£702**

CLEMENT BURLISON – A Portrait Of
Mary Johnson Of Aykley Heads Seated
In A Chair Wearing A Low Cut Red Dress
– 19 x 16in.
(Anderson &
Garland) **$434** **£260**

J. BURLUDGE – The Interior Of Sher-
borne Abbey With Figures – signed –
watercolour – 28 x 18½in.
(Lawrence) **$770** **£484**

BURNE-JONES

SIR EDWARD COLEY BURNE-JONES –
The Wedding Of Sire Degravaunt – signed
with initials – watercolour – 9½ x 11½in.
(Sotheby's) **$5,775** **£3,300**

SIR EDWARD COLEY BURNE-JONES –
Ixion – gouache on prepared paper – diam.
8¾in.
(Sotheby's) **$1,251** **£715**

SIR EDWARD COLEY BURNE-JONES
– Study Of A Lady's Head – 14½ x
15¾in.
(Christie's) **$9,720** **£6,480**

ALEXANDER HOHENLOHE BURR –
The Interrupted Courtship – signed and
dated '81 – 12 x 9½in.
(Christie's &
Edmiston's) **$1,120** **£700**

EDWARD BURRA – Man Outside A
Bordello – signed – pen and black ink
– 10 x 8½in.
(Christie's) **$896** **£594**

BRYSON BURROUGHS – The Boatman
– signed and dated 1902 – oil on canvas
– 30 x 24in.
(Butterfield's) **$1,000** **£590**

WALTER BURROUGHS-FOWLER – A
Chill November Evening – signed – on
board – 9¾ x 13¾in.
(Christie's &
Edmiston's) **$112** **£70**

CHARLES THOMAS BURT – A Sunny
Country Lane With Figures – signed –
watercolour – 18.5 x 14in.
(Woolley &
Wallis) **$217** **£130**

CHARLES THOMAS BURT – Unloading
The Catch – signed and dated 1894 –
15 x 23in.
(Sotheby Beresford
Adams) **$924** **£550**

HOWARD RUSSELL BUTLER – Pink Phlox – signed – oil on canvas – 16 x 21in.
(Christie's) **$2,420** **£1,613**

HOWARD RUSSELL BUTLER – Girl In A White Dress – oil on canvas – 24½ x 15in.
(Butterfield's) **$1,000** **£598**

JAMES E. BUTTERSWORTH – Two Racing Schooners Setting Their Topsails – signed – oil on canvas – 14¼ x 22in.
(Butterfield's) **$11,000** **£6,586**

JAMES E. BUTTERSWORTH – The Hibernia, A Cable Laying Steamship – signed – 17¼ x 23¼in.
(Sotheby's) **$4,162** **£2,420**

THOMAS BUTTERSWORTH – Sailing Vessels Offshore, A Harbour In The Background – signed – oil on canvas – 17 x 21in.
(Hy. Duke & Son) **$4,152** **£2,400**

J. H. BUTTERWORTH – Peel Castle And Harbour – signed – 15 x 27in.
(Chrystals) **$537** **£300**

ABRAM LOUIS BUVELOT – 'Cattle By The Creek' – signed – watercolour – 18 x 26cm.
(Geoff K. Gray) **$4,220** **£2,410**

W. BYGRAND – Extensive Townscapes, Mediterranean Ports With Figures To Foreground – signed on verso and dated 1853 – oil on canvas – 51.5 x 34cm.
(Osmond, Tricks) **$584** **£340 Pair**

ALEXANDRE CABANEL – An Eastern Beauty – signed – oil on canvas – 16¼ x 13in.
*(William Doyle
     Galleries)*   **$3,500   £2,071**

HECTOR CAFFIERI – 'The Lobster Pots' – signed – watercolour with scratching out – 13½ x 22¾in.
*(Sotheby, King &
     Chasemore)*   **$2,745   £1,760**

HECTOR CAFFIERI – Girls Seated In A Garden With A Basket – signed – watercolour heightened with white – 10 x 14¼in.
(Christie's)   **$2,903   £1,728**

HECTOR CAFFIERI – 'Two Children On A Seashore' – signed – watercolour – 20½ x 13¾in.
*(Sotheby, King &
     Chasemore)*   **$844   £528**

GUSTAVE CAILLEBOTTE – Yellow Roses In A Vase – signed and dated 1882 – oil on canvas – 21½ x 18½in.
*(William Doyle
     Galleries)*   **$32,500   £19,230**

ALEXANDRE CALAME – Children In An Alpine Landscape – signed indistinctly and dated 1847 – oil on canvas – 31 x 47in.
(William Doyle Galleries)   **$5,000**   **£2,958**

RANDOLPH CALDECOTT, Attributed to – A Portrait Of Mrs George Henry Boughton – signed with a monogram – 16 x 14½in.
(Sotheby's)   **$4,620**   **£2,640**

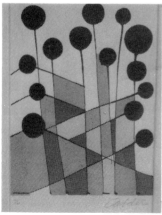

ALEXANDER CALDER – 'Color Field' – signed – pencil lithograph – 9½ x 12in.
(Du Mouchelles)   **$375**   **£215**

PHILIP HERMOGENES CALDERON – The Virgin's Bower – signed and dated 1870, and signed and inscribed on the reverse – 73¼ x 47in.
(Christie's)   **$2,754**   **£1,836**

EDMUND CALDWELL – Wildebeest Grazing – signed and dated – watercolour – 10 x 14in.
(Woolley & Wallis)   **$212**   **£120**

SIR AUGUSTUS WALL CALLCOTT – York Minster – signed – 10 x 13in.
(Sotheby Beresford Adams)   **$406**   **£242**

SIR AUGUSTUS WALL CALLCOTT – A View Of Eton College – signed, and signed and inscribed on a label on the reverse – 29 x 43¾in.
(Christie's)   **$7,592**   **£4,104**

CALLOW

CALLOW – Choppy Seas Off The Coast
– 29 x 43in.
(Sotheby Beresford
Adams) **$332** **£198**

BENJAMIN CALLOW – Haddon Hall –
signed and dated 1858, inscribed on the
reverse – on board – 14½ x 20in.
(Sotheby Beresford
Adams) **$170** **£99**

GEORGE D. CALLOW – On The
Cheshire Coast; and On The Sands –
signed and dated 1866 – 11½ x 21½in.
(Sotheby Beresford
Adams) **$1,664** **£990 Pair**

W. CALLOW – A Ship Off The Coast, A
Fleet In The Distance – watercolour –
6.7 x 9.2in.
(Wooley &
Wallis) **$208** **£125**

WILLIAM CALLOW – The Riva Degli
Schiavoni; and The Island Of S. Giorgio
Maggiore, Venice – signed and dated 1894
– watercolour – 14¾ x 21¾in. and 13¾ x
20in.
(Geering &
Colyer) **$8,532** **£5,400 Pair**

WILLIAM CALLOW – Caesar's Tower,
Warwick – signed, inscribed and dated
'52 – pencil and watercolour – 13 x
9¼in.
(Christie's) **$997** **£594**

WILLIAM CALLOW – Fishing Boats At
Marseilles – signed – pencil and water-
colour – 11¾ x 9in.
(Christie's) **$1,360** **£810**

WILLIAM CALLOW – Lynmouth Coastal Scene With Buildings – signed and inscribed and dated '47 – watercolour – 10 x 14½in. *(W. H. Lane & Son)* **$425 £250**

SIR DAVID YOUNG CAMERON – Afterglow, Arran – signed, signed, dated 1912 and inscribed on the reverse – on panel – 12½ x 15½in. *(Christie's & Edmiston's)* **$400 £250**

HUGH CAMERON – 'A Hazy Summer Day' – signed and dated 1893, inscribed – 16 x 36in. *(Sotheby, King & Chasemore)* **$2,722 £1,815**

JOHN HENRY CAMPBELL – The Island Of Lambay From Malahide – signed and inscribed and dated 1805 – watercolour – 4¼ x 6in. *(Sotheby, King & Chasemore)* **$348 £205**

CAMPI

FEDERICO DEL CAMPO — Journeying Through The Island — signed and dated 1885 — 14½ x 9¼in.
(Sotheby's) **$5,350 £3,520**

CANADIAN SCHOOL, Mid 19th century — An Encampment Near The Coast — brown washes — 7 x 10¼in.
(Sotheby's) **$172 £110**

ANTONIO CANALE, Called Canaletto — Venice, A View From The Fondamenta Nuove Looking Towards Murano — 55¾ x 59¼in.
(Sotheby's) **$323,510 £187,000**

BERNARDINO CAMPI — The Crucifixion — on panel — 81 x 28in.
(Sotheby's) **$26,642 £15,400**

CANALETTO – View Of The Church Of S. Giovanni And Paolo; and View Of The Doge's Palace And The Piazzetta – 21¼ x 31in.
(Sotheby's) **$6,470** **£3,740 Pair**

CANALETTO, Follower of – A View In The Piazzetta Towards The Clock Tower – 12¼ x 17¾in.
(Sotheby's) **$3,784** **£2,200**

CANALETTO, Follower of – A View Of The Grand Canal, Venice – 19 x 29¾in.
(Sotheby's) **$3,176** **£2,090**

HANS CANON – Frauenbildnis – signed and dated 1880 – oil on canvas – 71 x 58cm.
(Germann Auktionshaus) **$2,650** **£1,657**

JOHAN OSCAR CANTZLER – The Violinist – signed – 28½ x 39in.
(Sotheby's) **$2,508** **£1,650**

JOHAN OSCAR CANTZLER – The Poultry Maid – signed and dated 1884 – 31 x 39¼in.
(Sotheby's) **$2,508** **£1,650**

CAPPELLE

VAN DE CAPPELLE – A Dutch Yacht
And Other Vessels In A Calm – on panel
– 20½ x 26¾in.
(Sotheby's)   **$9,515   £5,500**

CAPRIOLI – The Mocking Of Christ –
31¾ x 28¼in.
(Sotheby's)   **$1,797   £1,045**

JACQUES CARABAIN – A Rhine Landscape With Figures By A Tower – signed
and dated 1865 – 30 x 24in.
(Christie's)   **$14,677   £9,720**

JACQUES FRANCOIS CARABAIN –
'Street Scene Belgium' – signed – oil on
canvas – 12 x 10in.
*(Robert W. Skinner
Inc.)* **$750** **£468**

JACQUES FRANCOIS CARABAIN –
'At The Quay' – signed – oil on canvas
– 12 x 10in.
*(Robert W. Skinner
Inc.)* **$850** **£530**

CLAUDE CARDON – Cows Grazing In
A Meadow – oil – 29 x 38cm.
(Reeds Rains) **$1,260** **£720 Pair**

CONSALVE CARELLI – The Bay Of
Naples – signed and inscribed – on panel
– 10 x 17in.
(Christie's) **$2,527** **£1,404**

JOHN CARLAW – 'Sunday Morning Gal-
lop' – signed – watercolour – 12¼ x
19¼in.
*(Sotheby, King &
Chasemore)* **$132** **£82**

L. CARLEVARIJS – A View In The
Piazzetta – 17 x 22½in.
(Sotheby's) **$7,946** **£4,620**

DINES CARLSEN – The White Jug –
signed with initials – oil on canvas –
24¼ x 20¼in.
(Christie's) **$3,850** **£2,566**

CARMICHAEL

JAMES WILSON CARMICHAEL – A View Of Como From The South – signed and inscribed – 23½ x 35½in. *(Sotheby's)* **$2,989 £1,980**

HENRI CARNIER – A Cairo Street Scene – signed – 14½ x 22¾in. *(Sotheby's)* **$886 £495**

JEAN CAROLUS – A Musical Trio – signed with initials – on panel – 25¼ x 30¼in. *(Christie's)* **$837 £540**

JEAN CAROLUS – Le Peintre De Fleurs – signed, signed and indistinctly dated on the reverse – 30¼ x 37¼in. *(Sotheby's)* **$4,922 £2,750**

GIROLAMO DA CARPI – The Assumption Of The Virgin – on panel – 22¼ x 16¾in. *(Sotheby's)* **$7,920 £5,280**

SAMUEL S. CARR – Fetching Water At The Spring – signed and dated 1873 – oil on canvas – 12 x 10in. *(William Doyle Galleries)* **$3,000 £1,775**

GEORGIA CARROLL – 'Mother And Child' – signed – pastel – 22 x 18in. *(Stalker & Boos)* **$450 £269**

GEORGIA CARROLL – Male And Female Ballet Dancers – signed – pastel drawing – 15 x 10¼in. *(Stalker & Boos)* **$70 £42**

E. CARTER – A Study Of A Vase Of Flowers Before A Window – signed – oil – 19 x 28¾in.
(Anderson & Garland) **$96** **£60**

FRANK T. CARTER – An Extensive Lakeland Landscape – signed – 9 x 17¾in.
(Anderson & Garland) **$50** **£30**

FRANK T. CARTER – A Crag In Borrowdale – signed – oil on board – 11½ x 15½in.
(Anderson & Garland) **$67** **£40**

FRANCIS THOMAS CARTER – The High Force, Teesdale – signed, inscribed and dated 1891 on the reverse – 36 x 24in.
(Sotheby Beresford Adams) **$227** **£132**

H. B. CARTER – 'Off Scarborough', A Coastal Scene With Rough Sea, A Shipwreck, Rowing Boats And Figures – watercolour – 28 x 19in.
(G. H. Bayley & Sons) **$1,003** **£580**

HENRY BARLOW CARTER – Peel Castle, Isle Of Man; and Scarborough Castle, Yorkshire – one signed and dated 1857 – 10½ x 16in.
(Sotheby Beresford Adams) **$350** **£209 Pair**

HENRY BARLOW CARTER – Iona – watercolour – 8½ x 12¼in.
(Christie's) **$235** **£140**

WILLIAM CASLEY – The Steeple Rock; and Mullion Cove, Cornwall – signed – watercolour over pencil – 15¾ x 11¾in.
(Sotheby's) **$339** **£220 Pair**

W. CASMELL – A Naval Battle – signed – 27 x 42½in.
(Sotheby Beresford Adams) **$887** **£528**

L. G. CASO – Feeding The Turkey – signed – oil on canvas – 19½ x 27in.
(Butterfield's) **$1,400** **£828**

JAMES CASSIE – King's College, Old Aberdeen – signed and dated 1848 – oil on board – 12 x 18in.
(Sotheby, King & Chasemore) **$1,403** **£935**

SIR HUGH CASSON – Farmyard, Alcudia – signed with initials – pen and wash – 2.5 x 4.5in.
(Woolley & Wallis) **$222** **£125**

GIUSEPPE CASTIGLIONE – Distant Thoughts – signed – 11¼ x 15¼in.
(Sotheby's) **$1,181** **£660**

S. CATATANO – A Knife Grinder Watched By Children Outside A House – oil on board – 9½ x 12in.
(Hy. Duke & Son) **$311** **£180**

CHARLES CATTERMOLE – Cavaliers – signed and one dated '73 – watercolour with bodycolour – 14 x 8½in.
(Sotheby's) **$373** **£242 Two**

CHARLES CATTERMOLE – The Abbot's Blessing – signed – watercolour heightened with white – 16¾ x 30in.
(Christie's) **$1,180** **£702**

GEORGE CATTERMOLE – A Procession
– signed and dated – 13 x 18¾in.
(Sotheby, King &
    Chasemore)   **$372**   **£209**

EUGENE-HENRI CAUCHOIS – A
Pumpkin, Grapes And Peaches In A
Basket On A Stone Slab – signed – 27
x 41¼in.
(Christie's)   **$2,176**   **£1,404**

EUGENE-HENRI CAUCHOIS – Vase
Fenetre – Bordeaux – signed, signed on
the reverse – 23½ x 19¼in.
(Sotheby's)   **$836**   **£550**

DE CAULLERY – A View Of St. Mark's
Square And The Doge's Palace – on panel
– 18 x 57in.
(Sotheby's)   **$2,855**   **£1,650**

CAULLERY

LOUIS DE CAULLERY – A Banquet On A Terrace In A Park – on panel – 19½ x 16½in.
(Sotheby's) $4,567   £2,640

BERNARDO CAVALLINO – Saint Cecilia – 38 x 29½in.
(Sotheby's)   **$18,150   £12,100**

PETER LA CAVE – Returning From The Market – watercolour over pencil – 6½ x 9in.
(Sotheby's)   **$243**   **£130**

PETER LA CAVE – A Woman On A Donkey Fording A River, Anglers On The Bank; and A Man And His Dog By A River With Cattle Watering – pen and grey ink and watercolour – 7¼ x 9¼in.
(Christie's)   **$507**   **£302 Pair**

NEVILLE HENRY PENISTON CAYLEY – 'Kookaburra' – signed – watercolour – 29 x 25cm.
(Geoff K. Gray)   **$100**   **£60**

EDMOND CERIA – Le Pont Des Arts – signed – oil on canvas – 23 x 35½in.
(Sotheby's)   **$1,420**   **£935**

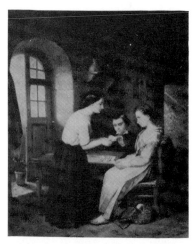

THEODORE CERIEZ – The Game Of Cards – signed – 21¾ x 18¼in.
(Sotheby's)   **$826**   **£462**

P. CERNERI – Fishing Boats Moored On The Outskirts Of Dortmund – signed – 28¼ x 38½in.
(Sotheby's)   **$984**   **£550**

ANTONIO DEL CERRAIUOLO, Follower of — The Mystic Marriage Of Saint Catherine Of Siena — on panel — 6¼ x 8¼in.
(Sotheby's)   **$3,678**   **£2,420**

GIUSEPPE CESARI, Attributed to, Called Cavaliere D'Arpino — God The Father Seated On A Cloud — 24¾ x 19¼in.
(Sotheby's)   **$836**   **£550**

CORNELIS JANSSENS VAN CEULEN — Portrait Of A Lady Of The De Waert Family — inscribed — 32 x 26in.
(Sotheby's)   **$4,125**   **£2,750**

CHAFFEE

OLIVER NEWBERRY CHAFFEE –
Magnolia And Oranges – signed on the
reverse – oil on canvas – 36¼ x 30¼in.
(Christie's)   **$660**   **£440**

HECTOR CHALMERS – A Shepherd And
His Flock Leaving The Farmstead – signed
– oil on canvas – 10 x 14in.
*(Sotheby, King &
   Chasemore)*   **$660**   **£440**

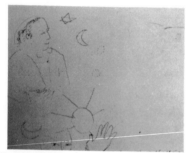

MARC CHAGALL – Chagall Et Son
Ami L'Astronome – signed and dated
1952 – pen and ink – 7½ x 7¼in.
(Sotheby's)   **$1,970**   **£1,100**

HENRY BERNARD CHALON – A Bay
Hunter With Two Dogs In Parkland, A
Country House Beyond – signed and
dated 1828 – 22¼ x 29¼in.
(Sotheby's)   **$5,676**   **£3,300**

JOHN JAMES CHALON – A Ferry – signed – 29½ x 59¼in. *(Sotheby's)*
$7,972 £5,280

MASON CHAMBERLIN, JNR. – A
Country Pasture – signed and dated 1835
– 27¼ x 34¼in.
(Sotheby's) **$1,420** **£935**

GEORGE CHAMBERS – A Sailing Barge
On A Rough Estuary – signed and indis-
tinctly dated – 14½ x 17½in.
(Sotheby, King &
Chasemore) **$969** **£570**

J. WILLIS CHAMPNEY – Young Girl
Before An Open Fire – inscribed and
dated '74 – oil on canvas – 22 x 17¾in.
(Dreweatt Watson &
Barton) **$1,230** **£820**

CHARLES CHAPLIN – A Good Book
– signed – 10¾ x 8½in.
(Christie's) **$434** **£280**

HAMILTON CHAPMAN – 'River Scene
With Church And Bridge In The Background' – signed and dated 1903 –
watercolour – 9¼ x 14¼in.
(Bracketts) **$48** **£30**

REUBEN CHAPPELL, Follower of – A
Study Of The Brig 'Sailor Of Shields'
Entering The Port Of Palermo – water-
colour – 19 x 26in.
(Sotheby, King &
Chasemore) **$1,023** **£682**

RUEBEN CHAPPELL – Sappho Of
Padstow – signed and inscribed – 14½
x 22in.
(Sotheby Beresford
Adams) **$170** **£99**

JAMES CHARLES – Boy On A White
Horse – signed with initials – 9¾ x 13¾in.
(Sotheby's) **$530** **£308**

ERNEST CHATEIGNON – A Young
Lady In A Park – signed – 39½ x 28½in.
(Christie's) **$1,255** **£810**

PIERRE PUVIS DE CHAVANNES –
Abraham And Isaac – signed – 11½ x
15¼in.
(Sotheby's) **$11,357 £6,490**

E. S. CHEESWRIGHT – Rocky Coastal
Scene – signed – watercolour – 9 x 14in
*(Laurence & Martin
Taylor)* **$55 £32**

GEORGE CHESTER – 'A Shepherd And
His Flock In A Wooded Landscape' –
signed and dated 1855 – oil on canvas –
44 x 35½in.
*(Sotheby, King &
Chasemore)* **$563 £352**

L. CHIALIVA – 'The Fishing Lesson'
– signed – oil on canvas – 9½ x 15½in.
*(Stalker &
Boos)* **$3,600 £2,155**

N. H. CHRISTIANSEN – Winter Scene
'The Road To Hamlet's Grave' – signed –
oil on canvas – 19½ x 15¾in.
(Bracketts) **$768 £480**

SIR WINSTON CHURCHILL – A Farm
At The Head Of Lake Como – oil on
canvas – 19¾ x 23¾in.
(Christie's) **$10,600 £7,020**

THOMAS CHURCHYARD – A Landscape With A Windmill – oil on board
on panel – 7½ x 9½in.
(Sotheby's) **$334 £220**

THOMAS CHURCHYARD – A Weir On
A River – on panel – 5½ x 7in.
(Christie's) **$259 £140**

T. E. CHURNSIDE – A Shepherd And
His Flock On A Track Near Arundel
Castle – signed – watercolour – 10¼
x 15in.
*(Anderson &
Garland)* **$64 £40 Pair**

BEPPE CIARDI – Cattle In A Field –
signed – 54¾ x 85in.
(Sotheby's) **$11,370 £7,480**

EMMA CIARDI – View Of Murano –
signed – on panel – 14½ x 19½in.
(Christie's) **$5,443 £3,024**

PIERRE-LUC-CHARLES CICERI – A
Capriccio Landscape – signed and dated
1829 – watercolour – 7¾ x 10¼in.
(Sotheby's) **$297 £154**

CHURCH, Sir Arthur Herbert KCVO FRS FSA fl.1854-1870
London painter of landscapes and still-life. Exhib. at RA and BI several landscapes of Cornwall. Was Professor of Chemistry to the Royal Academy 1879-1911.
Bibl: Hutchison.

CHURCHER, G.P. fl.1886
Exhib. one watercolour of Christchurch, Oxford at SS, 1886. Oxford address.

CHURCHILL, H. fl.1872
Exhib. one watercolour 'An Arab of Algiers' at SS, 1872. London address.

CHURCHYARD, Thomas 1798-1865
Suffolk landscape painter. Lived in Woodbridge, where he practised as a lawyer. Occasionally visited London, but mostly painted in his native Suffolk, in a style similar to that of Constable, who he may have known. Exhib. in London 1830-3, and in Norwich in 1829 and 1852. He had several children, many of whom were also painters.
Bibl: D. Thomas, *Thomas Churchyard of Woodbridge*, 1966.

CLABBURN, Arthur E. fl.1875-1879
Portrait painter. Exhib. three pictures at RA, 1875-9. Lived in London and Norwich.

CLACK, Richard Augustus fl.1827-1875
London portrait painter. Exhib. at RA, BI and SS. RA exhibits all portraits, and a few landscapes.

CLACK, Thomas 1830-1907
Painter of figure subjects and landscape. Lived in Coventry but then moved to London. Exhib. at RA, and elsewhere. RA subjects mostly domestic genre, also some landscape and portraits. Was Master at the

CLARK, B. fl.1875
Exhib. one picture of a grey mare at SS, 1875. London address.

CLARK, Christopher RI 1875-1942
Painter and illustrator of military and historical subjects. Elected RI, 1905. Published and illustrated several military history books.

CLARK, C.W. fl.1839-1843
London painter of portraits. Exhib. at RA only, 1839-43.

CLARK, Dixon fl.1890-1902
Animal painter from Blaydon-on-Tyne. Exhib. at RA from 1890-1902, but worked mostly in the north-east. Subjects usually cattle or sheep in pastoral landscapes, in the style already popularised by T.S. Cooper. Pictures by him are in the Sunderland AG.
Bibl: Hall.

CLARK, Falconer fl.1888-1889
Exhib. two watercolours of domestic subjects at NWS, 1888-9. Address Dorking, Surrey.

CLARK, Francis fl.1853-1865
London painter of figure subjects. Exhib. at RA, BI and SS. RA subjects also include a portrait and still-life.

CLARK, James RI ROI 1858-1943
Painter and watercolourist of religious and other figure subjects, portraits, landscape and flowers. Also book illustrator and designer of stained glass. Studied at first in Hartlepool, Co. Durham, later in Paris, and settled in London. Exhib. at RA, SS, NWS, and at the NEAC, of which he was a member.
Bibl: Hall

*CLARK, Joseph ROI 1834-1926

at the RA from 1857-1904. Received a medal and award at Philadelphia in 1876 sending there his 'Sick Child' and 'The Bird's Nest'. Among his more important works are 'The Wanderer Restored' 1861, and 'Early Promise'. Graves, R. Acad, lists him as 'Joseph Clarke'.

Bibl: AJ 1863 pp.49 ff. (reprd. 'The Return of the Runaway', 'The Wanderer Restored' and 'Hagar and Ishmael'); AJ 1859 p.165; 1860 p.78; 1869 p.296; Clement and Hutton; Ruskin, Academy Notes, 1875; Who's Who 1912; Wood.

CLARK, Joseph Benwell   fl.1876-1894

London painter of rustic subjects. Exhib. at RA, SS, GG and elsewhere. At the RA he exhibited also a portrait of H.S. Tuke (q.v.), a picture copied from Joseph Clark (q.v.), and two military subjects set in Afghanistan painted in collaboration with V.M. Hamilton (q.v.).

CLARK, J. Wait   fl.1880-1900

Painter of seascapes and coastal scenes; lived at South Shields, Co. Durham. Exhib. one picture 'Whitley Sands' at RA, 1900.

CLARK, Miss Mary   fl.1844-1848

London painter of figure subjects. Exhib. at RA and SS. Titles: 'Rose Bradwardine', etc. London address.

CLARK, Miss Mary Brodie   fl.1889-1902

Painter of fruit and flowers. Exhib. once at RA and SS. Address Brentford, Middlesex.

CLARK, S.J.

Very little-known painter of horses, animals and farmyard scenes, whose works have appeared frequently at auction sales in London and the provinces. His style is similar to that of J.F. Herring, Junior, but he did not exhibit in London.

Bibl: Annual Art Sales Index 1969-1975.

CLACY, Miss Ellen   fl.1870-1900

Historical and genre painter. Exhib. 1870-1900 at SS and RA, 1872-1900 at RA. Titles at RA: 'The List of Conspirators', 'A Hunted Jewess, France 1610', 'The Letter', etc. 'Will Myers, Ratcatcher and Poacher', RA 1885, is in the Walker AG, Liverpool.

CLAPHAM, James T.   fl.1862

Painter of fruit. Exhib. two pictures at SS, 1862. Address Crayford, Kent.

CLAPHAM, Miss Mary   fl.1885

Exhib. one picture of moonlight in 1885. London address.

CLARE, George   fl.c.1860-1900

Birmingham fruit and flower painter. Exhib. 1864, 1866 and 1867 at RA, also BI and SS. Imitator of W.H. Hunt's small, detailed pictures of fruit, flowers, blossom and birds' nests. Probably the father of Oliver and Vincent C (qq.v.).

CLARE, Miss   fl.1858

Exhib. one picture of flowers at RA, 1858. London address.

*CLARE, Oliver   c.1853-1927

Painter of fruit and flowers; son of George C (q.v.). Exhib. one picture at RA in 1883, two at SS. Like his brother, probably worked mainly in Birmingham. Oliver Clare's pictures are very similar to those of George Clare's, but not of such good quality.

CLARE, Vincent   c.1855-1930

Still-life painter; brother of Oliver Clare (q.v.). His work is similar to that of the other two Clares, but coarser in quality. He worked in Birmingham, but did not exhibit in London.

CLARIS, F.G.   fl.1884

Exhib. one picture 'A Sombre Day' at SS, 1884. London address.

CARLO CIGNANI and Studio — Joseph And Potiphar's Wife — 87½ x 73¼in.
(Sotheby's)   **$14,025**   **£9,350**

A. CLAESSINS — The Crucifixion — on panel — 40½ x 32¾in.
(Sotheby's)   **$756**   **£440**

GEORGE CLARE — A Still Life Study Of Apple-Blossom And Primroses — signed — on canvas — 10 x 14in.
(Sotheby, King &
Chasemore)   **$924**   **£616**

GEORGE CLARE — A Still Life Study Of Primrose And Cherry-Blossom — signed — oil on canvas — 6 x 8in.
(Sotheby, King &
Chasemore)   **$990**   **£660 Pair**

GEORGE CLARE — Still Life, Fruit On A Bank — signed and dated — oil — 20 x 24in.
(Woolley &
Wallis)   **$668**   **£400**

OLIVER CLARE — Plums And Raspberries In Cabbage Leaf — signed and dated '90 — oil on board — 9 x 12in.
(Butterfield's)   **$950**   **£568**

OLIVER CLARE — Still Life Study Of A Bird's Nest And Primroses — oil on canvas — 6 x 8in.
(Sotheby, King &
Chasemore)   **$950**   **£594 Pair**

CLARE

OLIVER CLARE – Still Lives, Fruit On Mossy Banks – signed, one dated – oil – 12 x 10in.
(Woolley & Wallis)   **$1,018**   **£610 Pair**

OLIVER CLARE – Still Life Study Of Flowers – signed – oil on canvas – 6 x 8¾in.
(Sotheby, King & Chasemore)   **$340**   **£200**

VINCENT CLARE – Still Life With Blossom And Nest – signed – 9½ x 7in.
(Sotheby's)   **$669**   **£440**

ALBERT CLARK – 'Beauty And Harry' – signed and dated 1896 – oil on canvas – 20 x 30in.
(Sotheby, King & Chasemore)   **$1,000**   **£572**

DIXON CLARK – Two Shire Horses Watering At A Mill Stream – signed and dated 1886 – oil on canvas – 13 x 19in.
(Sotheby, King & Chasemore)   **$650**   **£407**

JAMES CLARK – A Chestnut Stallion – signed and dated 1878 – 20 x 24in.
(Sotheby's)   **$568**   **£374**

OCTAVIUS T. CLARK – In The Surrey Hills – signed – 20 x 30in.
(Sotheby Beresford Adams)   **$628**   **£374**

WILLIAM CLARK – The British Frigate 'David' And Other Shipping In A Light Breeze – signed and dated 1830 – 15¼ x 22¼in.
(Christie's)   **$2,597**   **£1,404**

HARRY HARVEY CLARKE – Working In The Barn – signed – 30 x 25in.
(Sotheby's)   **$446**   **£308**

JAMES CLARKE – A Chestnut Stallion
– signed – 20 x 24in.
*(Sotheby Beresford
Adams)* **$277   £165**

WARREN CLARKE – 'Rural Scene, Near
Lyndhurst' – watercolour – 8¾ x 15½in.
(Bracketts) **$96   £60**

EUGENE CLARY – Paysage A La
Riviere – signed – 9¾ x 15¼in.
(Sotheby's) **$1,476   £825**

JEAN MAXIME CLAUDE – La Pesee A
Longchamps – signed and dated 1867 –
22½ x 19½in.
(Christie's) **$40,770 £27,000**

SIR GEORGE CLAUSEN – Trees At
Sunset – watercolour – 10 x 8½in.
(Christie's) **$244   £162**

SIR GEORGE CLAUSEN – Girl By The
Zuyder Zee – signed and dated 1876 –
oil on canvas – 18¼ x 15in.
(Christie's) **$6,523   £4,320**

SIR GEORGE CLAUSEN – The Vale Of
Clwyd, Rainy Evening – signed – water-
colour – 9¼ x 11½in.
(Christie's) **$310   £205**

SIR GEORGE CLAUSEN – Rural Landscape With Corn Stooks And Cottages –
signed and dated – watercolour – 6.5 x
12in.
*(Woolley &
Wallis)* **$602   £340**

CLAUSEN

SIR GEORGE CLAUSEN – Autumn Leaves – signed and dated 1889, also signed, inscribed and dated 1890 on the backboard – pastel on grey paper – 9¼ x 6¼in.
(Christie's)   **$1,794   £1,188**

SIR GEORGE CLAUSEN – 'Cottages' – signed – watercolour – 9.5 x 12in.
(Woolley &
Wallis)   **$584   £350**

SIR GEORGE CLAUSEN – Head Of A Girl – signed with initials – black and red chalk – 9¼ x 6¼in.
(Christie's)   **$1,060   £702**

PAUL JEAN CLAYS – Fishing Boats In An Estuary – 10¾ x 17½in.
(Sotheby's)   **$886   £495**

J. HUGHES CLAYTON – Thatched Cottages In Midsummer With Trees And Fields In The Distance – signed – watercolour – 13½ x 20½in.
(Outhwaite &
Litherland)   **$628   £398 Pair**

JAMES HUGHES CLAYTON – Landing Fish On The Shore At Penzance – signed – watercolour – 23 x 31in.
(Chrystals)   **$537   £300**

JOSEPH HUGHES CLAYTON – Fishing Boats At Cemaes; and Anglesey Cottages – signed – heightened with white – 10 x 14in.
(Sotheby Beresford
Adams)   **$277   £165 Pair**

HENDRICK DE CLERCK, Follower of – Christ And Saint Veronica On The Road To Calvary – 54½ x 42½in.
(Sotheby's)   **$1,797   £935**

JOHN CLEVELEY, SNR. – A British Frigate In Three Positions – signed – 42¼ x 62in.
(Sotheby's)   **$24,915 £16,500**

THOMAS CLOUGH – Newlyn Bay, Cornwall, Fisher Folk With Their Boats And Smacks At Low Tide, Below The Village – watercolour – 75 x 125cm.
(Henry Spencer & Sons) $716   £400

EDWARD JOHN COBBETT – Littlehampton – signed – heightened with bodycolour – 12 x 18in.
(Sotheby Beresford Adams) $203   £121

EDWARD JOHN COBBETT – Little Red Riding Hood – signed – oil on canvas – 24 x 20in.
(Dreweatt Watson & Barton) $930   £620

JOHN AMORY CODMAN – Bathers On The Beach – oil on canvas – 15 x 20in.
(Butterfield's) $850   £508

WILLIAM HASKELL COFFIN – Karma – signed and dated 1897 – oil on canvas – 72 x 36in.
(Butterfield's) $1,100   £650

EDWARD JOHN COBBETT – Pleasant Thoughts – signed and dated 1864 – 23 x 19in.
(Sotheby Beresford Adams) $1,016   £605

LEON COGNIET – Soldiers With Their Wounded By A Ruined Castle – signed – on panel – 7¾ x 9in.
(Sotheby's) $492   £275

HAROLD COHN – 'Grapes And Peach' – signed – oil on board – 11½ x 19½in.
(Stalker & Boos) $100   £59

COLE

GEORGE COLE – Shepherd And Sheep
In A Moorland Landscape At Sunset –
signed and dated – oil – 34 x 48in.
(Woolley &
Wallis) **$4,602 £2,600**

GEORGE VICAT COLE – Autumn Tints
– watercolour heightened with bodycolour – 9½ x 12in.
(Sotheby's) **$2,371 £1,540**

GEORGE VICAT COLE – A Grey Day
On The Thames – signed and dated 1866
– on board – 7 x 10in.
(Christie's) **$635 £410**

JOSEPH FOXCROFT COLE – 'Brittany Sea
Coast' – signed – oil on canvas – 19 x 26in.
(Robert W.
Skinner Inc.) **$2,100 £1,100**

REX VICAT COLE – The Old Barn –
signed and dated 1932, inscribed on the
reverse – 34 x 44½in.
(Sotheby's) **$877 £605**

THOMAS WILLIAM COLE – View Of
Bosham; and View Of A Country Cottage
– signed and dated 1928 – watercolour
– 15¼ x 29in.
(Sotheby, King &
Chasemore) **$618 £396 Pair**

HENRY COLEMAN – Horses And Cart
In A Stormy Landscape, Roma 1877, and
Maccarese, February '78, Roma – signed,
dated and inscribed – watercolour –
12.7 x 22.2in.
(Woolley &
Wallis) **$584 £350 Pair**

MARION COLEMAN – Indian Child
With Beads – signed – oil on canvas –
10 x 8in.
(Butterfield's) **$150 £90**

WILLIAM STEPHEN COLEMAN –
'Happy As The Day Is Long' – signed –
oil on canvas – 22¼ x 13in.
(Sotheby, King &
Chasemore) **$2,112 £1,320**

SAMUEL JAMES COLKETT, Attributed to – A Stormy Landscape, With Rustics In The Foreground – bears signature and dated 1853 – oil on panel – 9½ x 13½in. *(Sotheby, King & Chasemore)* **$1,458** **£935**

SAMUEL DAVID COLKETT – Crossing A River – signed – on panel – 9½ x 12½in. *(Sotheby's)* **$1,003** **£660**

WILLIAM STEPHEN COLEMAN – Feeding The Kitten – signed and dated 1888 – oil on canvas – 25½ x 16¾in. *(Sotheby, King & Chasemore)* **$4,290** **£2,860**

SAMUEL DAVID COLKETT, Follower of – Rustics On A Country Path – oil on canvas – 12¼ x 17in. *(Sotheby, King & Chasemore)* **$308** **£198**

COLLET

JOHN COLLET – The Rescue Or The
Tars Triumphant – signed – 27¼ x
35¼in.
(Sotheby's) **$6,644 £4,400**

JOHN COLLET – The Unlucky Attempt
– 13¼ x 11¼in.
(Sotheby's) **$1,994 £1,320**

COLLIER – Trompe L'Oeil – oil on
canvas – 24 x 11½in.
*(Dreweatt Watson &
Barton)* **$1,080 £720**

SAMUEL COLMAN – Woods By The Stream – signed – oil on canvas – 8 x 15in.
(Christie's) **$7,150 £4,766**

EDWARD COLLIER – Still Life With An Inkwell, A Watch, Books And Documents – signed – 24¾ x 29¾in.
(Sotheby's) **$3,986 £2,640**

EVERT COLLIER, Follower of – Still Life With Books, A Folio And Other Objects On A Ledge – 29¼ x 24¼in.
(Sotheby Beresford Adams) **$4,065 £2,420**

R. COLLIER – Moorland View – signed – on board – 7½ x 11½in.
(Sotheby Beresford Adams) **$37 £22**

SAMUEL COLMAN – Rotterdam – signed and dated also signed and inscribed on the reverse – 9¼ x 12¾in.
(Christie's) **$2,640 £1,760**

WILLIAM COLLINS – Woodland Scene With Children Playing On A Five Bar Gate – 17 x 22cm. *(Henry Spencer & Sons)* **$1,030 £670**

COLMAN

SAMUEL COLMAN – Abigail Confronting The Army Of David – on panel – 29¼ x 41½in.
(Sotheby's) **$9,966** **£6,600**

NINA COLMORE – A Portrait Of Mrs R. E. More On Horseback, On A Beach – signed – oil – 30 x 40in.
(Woolley & Wallis) **$619** **£350**

NICOLAS COLOMBEL – Rebecca At The Well – 78¾ x 47in.
(Sotheby's) **$7,612** **£4,400**

ROBERT COLQUHOUN – Actors – signed – oil on canvas – 40 x 28in.
(Christie's) **$4,240** **£2,808**

FRANCIS EDWARD COLTHURST – Studies Of Male And Female Nudes As The Bathers – signed – pencil and red chalk – 13 x 9in. approx.
(Lawrence) **$34** **£22 Four**

E. HARRISON COMPTON – A Breezy Day – signed and dated 1902 – heightened with bodycolour – 10 x 17in.
(Sotheby Beresford Adams) **$277** **£165**

EDWARD THOMAS COMPTON – An Alpine Lake Scene – signed and dated 1886 – watercolour – 7¾ x 12½in.
(Sotheby, King & Chasemore) **$264** **£176**

EDWARD THOMAS COMPTON – Mediterranean Coastal Landscapes – signed and dated 1877 – 16 x 24½in.
(Christie's) **$3,180** **£2,052 Pair**

NICHOLAS MATTHEW CONDY, JNR. – The Constance In Plymouth Harbour, Alongside A Hulk Fitting Out – on panel – 8¾ x 12in.
(Sotheby's) **$1,495** **£990**

DAVID DE CONINCK, Circle of − A Spaniel And Hounds With A Bag Of Game − 36 x 51¼in.
(Sotheby's) **$4,681 £3,080**

GILLIS VAN CONINXLOO, After − Landscape With Judgement Of Paris − on panel − 17¼ x 27½in.
(Sotheby's) **$6,688 £4,400**

JOHN CONSTABLE − A View Of Dedham Vale From East Bergholt − paper on panel − 10½ x 15in.
(Sotheby's) **$53,152 £35,200**

JOHN CONSTABLE, Follower of − Extensive Landscape With A Man And Dog On A Track − 19½ x 23½in.
(Sotheby's) **$2,508 £1,650**

JEAN JOSEPH BENJAMIN CONSTANT − An Odalisque In A Harem − signed − 20 x 38in.
(Christie's) **$8,910 £5,940**

CONTARINI

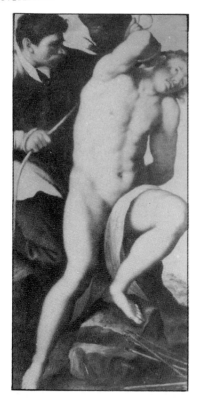

GIOVANNI CONTARINI – The Binding Of Saint Sebastian – signed – 77 x 38½in.
(Sotheby's) **$6,660 £3,850**

CONTINENTAL SCHOOL, Mid 18th century – Hunting Scene – oil on canvas – 29 x 45in.
(McCartney, Morris & Barker) **$2,666 £1,550**

CONTINENTAL SCHOOL, 18th century – Portrait Of An Officer – oil on canvas – 182 x 78cm.
(Sotheby, King & Chasemore) **$884 £520 Pair**

MEIFFREN CONTE – A Still Life With A Chest And A Silver-Gilt Dish – 28¼ x 36¼in.
(Sotheby's) **$11,220 £7,480**

CONTINENTAL SCHOOL, 17th century – Still Life Of Fruit With A Squirrel And A Parrot – oil on canvas – 27¾ x 34½in.
(Dreweatt Watson & Barton) **$4,350 £2,900**

CONTINENTAL SCHOOL, 18th century
– A Portrait Study Of A Lady – oil on
canvas – 182 x 78cm.
(Sotheby, King &
Chasemore) **$884** **£520 Pair**

SAMUEL COOK OF PLYMOUTH – Plymouth – signed, indistinctly inscribed and
dated '59 – pencil and watercolour
heightened with white – 18 x 25in.
(Christie's) **$521** **£280**

WILLIAM COOK OF PLYMOUTH – A
Rocky Coastline – signed with monogram
and dated '78 – watercolour heightened
with white – 11¾ x 20¾in.
(Christie's) **$111** **£60**

EBENEZER WAKE COOKE – Watering
The Horses – signed and dated 1885 –
watercolour – 6¾ x 9½in.
(Sotheby, King &
Chasemore) **$720** **£462**

EBENEZER WAKE COOKE – The
Fountain Of Bacchus – signed and dated
'95 – pencil and watercolour heightened
with white – 35¼ x 12¼in.
(Christie's) **$896** **£594**

COOKE

EDWARD WILLIAM COOKE – Fishermen – inscribed and dated 1875 – pen and ink – 10 x 14in.
(Sotheby's) **$75** **£49**

R. COOKE – 'Bognor Beach', Figures In Victorian Costume On The Seashore – signed and dated on the reverse – oil on card – 2¾ x 8¾in.
(W. H. Lane & Son) **$63** **£36**

MARGARET MURRAY COOKESLEY, After Waterhouse – Consulting The Oracle – 30½ x 50¼in.
(Christie's) **$13,770** **£9,180**

PIERRE OLIVIER JOSEPH COOMANS – The Bath – signed – oil on canvas – 40 x 33in.
(Butterfield's) **$2,250** **£1,347**

HUBERT COOP – Fishermen Disembarking – signed – 18½ x 27½in.
(Sotheby Beresford Adams) **$462** **£275**

HUBERT COOP – 'Sunrise' – signed – watercolour – 17 x 18¾in.
(Sotheby, King & Chasemore) **$299** **£187**

ALFRED HEATON COOPER – The Cottage Door – signed and dated 1896 – 20 x 28½in.
(Sotheby Beresford Adams) **$480** **£286**

ASTLEY DAVID MONTAGUE COOPER – Indian Teepee In A Forest Clearing – signed – oil on canvas – 30 x 50in. *(Butterfield's)* **$2,500 £1,497**

ASTLEY DAVID MONTAGUE COOPER
— Indian Encampment On The Plains —
signed and dated 1915 — oil on canvas —
40 x 56in.
(Butterfield's)   **$4,000   £2,395**

COLIN CAMPBELL COOPER — Wall
Street — signed and dated 1913 — oil on
canvas — 31 x 19¾in.
(Christie's)   **$3,300   £2,200**

T. S. COOPER — Cattle Watering In A
Landscape — signed and dated 1850 —
18¼ x 24in.
(Christie's)   **$585   £378**
T. S. COOPER — Cattle And Sheep —
bears signature and date — on panel — 8
x 11in.
(Sotheby Beresford
Adams)   **$277   £165**

THOMAS SIDNEY COOPER — Sheep
In A Byre — signed and dated 1839 —
on panel — 12½ x 19¼in.
(Sotheby's)   **$502   £330**
THOMAS SIDNEY COOPER — In The
Marshes, Canterbury — signed and dated —
oil on panel — 18 x 24in.
(Woolley &
Wallis)   **$4,312   £2,800**

THOMAS SIDNEY COOPER — Canterbury
Meadows — signed and dated 1884 —
watercolour over pencil — 9 x 12in.
(Sotheby's)   **$813   £528**

THOMAS SIDNEY COOPER — Sheep
Resting On A Mound, With Shepherd
And Dog — signed and dated — oil —
28 x 42in.
(Woolley &
Wallis)   **$9,285   £5,600**
THOMAS SIDNEY COOPER — Sheep In
The Snow — signed and dated 1865 — 8
x 11½in.
(Sotheby's)   **$813   £528**

COOPER

THOMAS SIDNEY COOPER – The Fallen Oak Stops The Way – signed – 49 x 71in.
(Sotheby's)   **$32,725 £18,700**

DIXON COPES – 'Still Life With Roses And Fruit' – signed – 54 x 74cm.
(Geoff K. Gray)   **$450   £268**

DIXON COPES – 'Cremorne Wharf' – signed – oil on board – 58 x 48cm.
(Geoff K. Gray)   **$278   £165**

COQUES – A Lady And A Gentleman On A Terrace – on panel – 17 x 19¾in.
(Sotheby Beresford Adams)   **$1,071   £638**

MATTHEW RIDLEY CORBETT – A Tuscan Hill Town – signed and dated 1897 – 20 x 32in.
(Sotheby's)   **$602   £396**

JEAN BAPTISTE CAMILLE COROT – Prairies Au Bord De L'Eau – signed – 17¾ x 14½in.
(Sotheby's)   **$62,563   £35,750**

JEAN BAPTISTE CAMILLE COROT – La Prairie Aux Deux Gros Arbres – signed – 17¼ x 23½in.
(Sotheby's)   **$108,900   £72,600**

HERMANN DAVID SALOMON CORRODI – Figures On The Steps Of A Lakeside Shrine – signed – on panel – 7¾ x 6¼in.
(Sotheby's)   **$824   £450**

**HERMANN DAVID SALOMON
CORRODI** – Fishing Village – signed
and dated 1872 – watercolour on paper
– 16 x 26in.
(Butterfield's) **$400** **£236**

SALOMON CORRODI – A View Of Venice
With Santa Maria Della Salute – signed and
dated 1826 – watercolour – 12 x 18½in.
(Sotheby, King &
Chasemore) **$1,584** **£1,056**

HENDRIK FRANS DE CORT – View Of
St. Michael's Mount From Marazion,
Cornwall – on panel – 34¼ x 46½in.
(Sotheby's) **$5,315** **£3,520**

EDOUARD CORTES – Paris, A View
Towards Notre-Dame – signed – 10¼ x
13½in.
(Christie's) **$5,016** **£3,300**

EDOUARD CORTES – Le Boulevard,
Paris – signed – 17¾ x 25in.
(Sotheby's) **$5,016** **£3,300**

EDOUARD CORTES – Place De L'Opera
– signed – oil on canvas – 13 x 18in.
(Butterfield's) **$3,000** **£1,796**

GUISEPPE COSENZA – Fisherfolk Resting On A Beach – signed and inscribed –
on panel – 9 x 7in.
(Christie's) **$777** **£432**

EMANUELLE COSTA – Portrait Of The
Virgin And Child – oil on canvas – 33 x
26in.
(Hy. Duke &
Son) **$311** **£180**

COSTA

GIUSEPPE COSTA – A Smiling Beauty – signed – 47¼ x 27¼in.
(Christie's)   **$1,944   £1,080**

RICHARD COSWAY – Portrait Of A Lady, Wearing A White Dress – 35½ x 27½in.
(Christie's)   **$1,098   £594**

COTES – Portrait Of A Girl, Half Length, Wearing A White Dress – oval 22¼ x 19in.
(Christie's)   **$1,098   £594**

JOHN JOSEPH COTMAN – 'The River Bend', With Trees – watercolour – 7 x 10in.
(Hilhams)   **$672   £420**

JOHN SELL COTMAN – Gillingham Hall, Suffolk – signed and dated, inscribed on the reverse – pencil and wash – 6 x 11in.
*(Woolley &
    Wallis)*   **$985   £640**

JOSEPH W. COTTON – 'Sailing On A Lake' – signed – watercolour – 29 x 34cm.
(Geoff K. Gray)   **$154   £90**

HORATIO HENRY COULDERY – The New Arrival – signed – oil on canvas – 20 x 27in.
*(Sotheby, King &
    Chasemore)*   **$7,378   £4,730**

HORATIO HENRY COULDERY – 'Quick Someone Is Coming' – signed – oil on canvas – 14 x 18in.
(Sotheby, King & Chasemore) **$3,622 £2,035**

THOMAS W. COULDERY – The Flower Seller And The Chimney Sweep – signed – 13 x 19in.
(Sotheby's) **$678 £440**

JOSEPH DESIRE COURT – The Bather – signed – 35 x 26¾in.
(Christie's) **$1,846 £1,026**
COURTOIS – A Cavalry Skirmish – 12 x 16in.
(Sotheby Beresford Adams) **$739 £440**

GORDON COUTTS – Cattle Along A Path At Sunset – signed – oil on canvas – 15 x 20in.
(Butterfield's) **$425 £250**

LEON COUTURIER – Soldiers Gathering Fire Wood – signed – 18½ x 22¾in.
(Sotheby's) **$630 £352**

J. VAN COUVER – Figures And Boats On The Coast – bears signature – oil on panel – 3.5 x 6in.
(Woolley & Wallis) **$275 £155**

J. R. COUZENS – 'The Vale Of Chamouny, Savoy' – inscribed – watercolour – 12¾ x 20in.
(Laurence & Martin Taylor) **$276 £170**

A. J. COX – 'Sheep Grazing On A Hillside' – signed and dated 1889 – watercolour – 6¾ x 10in.
(W. H. Lane & Son) **$105 £60**

C. COX – A River Landscape With Foreground Figure Fishing From A Punt – watercolour – 10½ x 7in.
(G. H. Bayley & Sons) **$294 £170**

D. COX – Children And A Dog Playing On A Path By A Cottage – bears signature – watercolour – 6 x 9¾in.
(Anderson & Garland) **$83 £52**

COX

D. COX – A Beach Scene With Foreground Boats And Figures – watercolour – 12 x 8½in.
(G. H. Bayley & Sons)   **$311**   **£180**

D. COX – River Scene With A Hay Barge – watercolour – 8½ x 14in.
(Sotheby, King & Chasemore)   **$411**   **£231**

DAVID COX – Yarmouth Pier – signed and dated – watercolour – 5½ x 7½in.
(Woolley & Wallis)   **$2,926**   **£1,900**

DAVID COX – A Cascade – pencil and watercolour – 20½ x 16in.
(Christie's)   **$130**   **£86**

DAVID COX, JNR. – Ludlow Castle – indistinctly signed – 12½ x 19½in.
(Sotheby's)   **$270**   **£176**

DAVID COX, JNR. – Grenoble – signed and dated 1854 – pencil and watercolour heightened with white – 18½ x 26¼in.
(Christie's)   **$585**   **£388**

DAVID COX, JNR. – 'Mip Mills', A Figure On A Path By A Cottage – watercolour – 6.7 x 10.2in.
(Woolley & Wallis)   **$217**   **£130**

DAVID COX, SNR. – 'Crossing The Sands' – signed and dated – oil on panel – 11.2 x 15.7in.
(Woolley & Wallis)   **$8,016**   **£4,800**

CRADOCK – Ducks And Their Chicks On A Pond – oil on canvas – 16 x 39in.
(Sotheby, King & Chasemore)   **$585**   **£285**

MARMADUKE CRADOCK, Follower of – A Study Of Wildfowl – oil on canvas – 24½ x 29in.
(Sotheby, King & Chasemore)   **$4,620**   **£3,080**

THOMAS BIGELOW CRAIG — 'Land-scape With Cows At A Stream' — signed — watercolour — 13½ x 21½in.
(Robert W. Skinner Inc.) **$350 £218**

PERCY ROBERT CRAFT — A Bit Of St. Just — indistinctly signed — 30 x 16½in.
(Sotheby's) **$501 £330**

LUCAS CRANACH, The Elder — Melencolia — signed and dated 1532 — on panel — 30 x 22in.
(Sotheby's) **$152,240 £88,000**

LUCAS CRANACH, The Elder — Diana And Actaeon — on panel — 22¾ x 30¼in.
(Sotheby's) **$107,250 £71,500**

WALTER CRANE — The Laidley Worm
Of Spindleton Heugh — signed with mono-
gram and dated 1881 — 29¾ x 66¾in.
(Sotheby's) **$105,875 £60,500**

WALTER CRANE — A Midsummer
Night's Dream — signed with monogram
and inscribed — watercolour and bodycolour — 11 x 15in.
(Christie's) **$1,995 £1,296**

EDMUND THORNTON CRAWFORD —
Market Boats, Scene On The Meuse Near
Dort — signed and dated 1854, and signed
and inscribed on the reverse — 36 x 51in.
(Christie's) **$7,828 £5,184**

ROBERT C. CRAWFORD — A Young Girl
Resting By A Haystook — signed and dated
1878 — oil on canvas — 20 x 24in.
*(Sotheby, King
& Chasemore)* **$800 £420**

JOHN CREALOCK — The Open Window —
signed — oil on canvas — 39½ x 32in.
*(Sotheby, King &
Chasemore)* **$380 £253**

PIERRE CREIXÁMS — Jeune Acrobate
Assis — signed — oil on canvas — 81 x
65cm.
*(Germann
Auktionshaus)* **$5,745 £3,590**

THOMAS CRESWICK, Follower of —
An Angler — on board — 8½ x 10¼in.
(Sotheby's) **$368 £242**

THOMAS CRESWICK – Returning With Flock – signed and dated 1878 – oil on canvas – 20 x 24in.
(Butterfield's) **$300** **£177**

GEORGES CROEGAERT – Pheasant For Dinner – signed and inscribed – on panel – 19¼ x 23½in.
(Christie's) **$21,060** **£14,040**

JAMES SHAW CROMPTON – A Statute Fair – signed – watercolour – 13½ x 20in.
(Sotheby's) **$880** **£572**

W. CROMPTON – 'On The Ludwig'; and 'Borrowdale' – watercolour and gouache – 15½ x 23½in.
(Dacre, Son & Hartley) **$146** **£85 Pair**

J. H. CRONSHAW – Herring Fleet – signed – watercolour – 9.2 x 13in.
(Woolley & Wallis) **$167** **£100**

RAY AUSTIN CROOKE – 'The Guitarist' – signed – oil on board – 23 x 24cm.
(Geoff K. Gray) **$464** **£276**

ANTHONY JANSZ. VAN CROOS – A Landscape With Tree-Fellers And A Distant View Of Haarlem – 42½ x 33½in.
(Sotheby's) **$9,075** **£6,050**

JASPER FRANCIS CROPSEY – Autumn By The Brook – signed and dated 1855 – oil on canvas – 10 x 15¼in.
(Christie's) **$4,180** **£2,786**

ENOCH CROSLAND – River Landscape With A Woman And Child On The Path – signed – oil – 17.5 x 24in.
(Woolley & Wallis) **$320** **£190**

ALISTAIR CROWLEY – 'The Green Man' – signed – oil on panel – 24 x 18cm.
(Sotheby, King & Chasemore) **$374** **£220**

ALISTAIR CROWLEY – 'Three Witches'
– signed – oil on panel – 41 x 32cm.
(Sotheby, King &
Chasemore) **$408** **£240**

WILLIAM CRUICKSHANK – A Bird's
Nest And Flowers – heightened with
bodycolour – oval 8¾ x 10in.
(Sotheby's) **$880** **£572**

HENRY HADFIELD CUBLEY – The
Old Harbour, Barmouth; and Welsh Hills
– signed, one inscribed on the reverse –
on board – 15¾ x 22in.
(Sotheby Beresford
Adams) **$38** **£22 Two**

EDWARD CUCUEL – Under The Parasol
– signed – oil on canvas – 25¼ x 18¼in.
(William Doyle
Galleries) **$5,000** **£2,958**

CUITT – The Castle Moat – 36 x 48in.
(Sotheby Beresford
Adams) **$406** **£242**

GEORGE CUITT – A View Of Scruton
Hall, Yorkshire – 20¾ x 28in.
(Sotheby's) **$3,986** **£2,640**

CHARLES CUNDALL – Anticoli Corrado,
Italy – signed and dated 1921 – on panel
– 12¾ x 15¾in.
(Sotheby's) **$405** **£220**

JAMES JACKSON CURNOCK – Y-Garn-
Idwal, North Wales – signed and dated
1899 – heightened with scratching out –
27 x 36in.
(Sotheby's) **$847** **£550**

JAMES JACKSON CURNOCK – 'In
The Fir Wood', Two Stags, Hinds And
Calves In A Woodland Clearing – signed
and dated 1891 – watercolour – 59 x
46cm.
(Osmond,
Tricks) **$430** **£250**

JEAN CZENCZ – Nude With A Fan –
signed and dated '924 – 30¼ x 35¾in.
(Sotheby's) **$945** **£528**

RICHARD DADD – Contradiction,
Oberon And Titania – signed and dated
1854/1858, inscribed on the reverse –
24 x 29¾in.
(Sotheby's) **$825,000 £550,000**

CHARLES VAN DEN DAELE – The
Suitor – signed and dated 1856 – on
panel – 24¾ x 19¼in.
(Sotheby's) **$1,254** **£825**

DAVID DALBY OF YORK – A Bay
Hunter With Two Hounds – signed and
dated 1823 – 24½ x 29½in.
*(Sotheby Beresford
Adams)* **$5,544** **£3,300**

SALVADOR DALI – 'Valaquez Painting
The Infanta Margrita' – poster – 75 x
46cm.
(Geoff K. Gray) **$54** **£32**

SALVADOR DALI – 'Knight On Horse'
– poster – 55 x 40cm.
(Geoff K. Gray) **$27** **£16**

SALVADOR DALI – Cyclone With Don
Quixote And Sancho Panza – signed –
ink on paper – 16½ x 11in.
(Butterfield's) **$2,000** **£1,183**

JAMES B. DALZIEL – Figures And A
Pony And Trap In An Avenue, With A
Village Beyond – signed – 28 x 36in.
(Christie's) **$2,344** **£1,512**

CESARE DANDINI, Attributed to – The
Thalian Muse – 26¾ x 22in.
(Sotheby's) **$2,173** **£1,430**

DANIELL

THOMAS DANIELL, Attributed to – The Falls Of Poulaphouca, County Wicklow –
37½ x 51¾in. *(Sotheby's)* **$1,328 £880**

WILLIAM DANIELL – The Battle Of Trafalgar, Vice-Admiral Lord Collingwood's
Flagship The Royal Sovereign Dismasted – signed – 32½ x 47¼in. *(Sotheby's)*
$3,156 £2,090

HENRI-PIERRE DANLOUX – Portrait Of A Young Girl With A Pink Hat – oval 8 x 9½in.
(Sotheby's)   **$13,321   £7,700**

HUGO DARNAUT – Woodcutters In A Forest – signed and dated 1890 – 54¼ x 78in.
(Christie's)   **$6,523   £4,320**

ALLAN D. DAVIDSON – An Old Salt – signed – oil on board – 20½ x 17in.
(Butterfield's)   **$200   £118**
C. T. DAVIDSON – Figures On A Bridge, Near Calstock – 6 x 8½in.
(Lawrence)   **$60   £38**
ALAN DAVIE – Serpent's Breath – oil on canvas – 122 x 152.5cm.
*(Germann
     Auktionshaus)* **$5,745   £3,590**
R. B. DAVIES – In Full Cry – 24¼ x 31in.
(Christie's)   **$799   £432**
F. DAVIS – Cottages Near Kenmare – 8¼ x 12¼in.
*(Sotheby Beresford
     Adams)*   **$84   £49**
H. B. DAVIS – An Angler Fishing From A River, With A Woman Feeding Poultry In The Garden Of A Cottage On The Further Bank – signed and dated 1903 – 19¾ x 29½in.
*(Anderson &
     Garland)*   **$100   £60**

HENRY WILLIAM BANKS DAVIS – 'A Summer Forenoon' – signed and dated – 15 x 30in. *(Woolley & Wallis)*   **$2,087 £1,250**

DAVIS

HENRY WILLIAM BANKS DAVIS –
Gorse In Spring – signed with initials –
on board – 13½ x 22½in.
(Sotheby Beresford
Adams) **$151** **£88**

MONTAGUE DAWSON – The Clipper
Ship, Lightning – signed – oil on canvas
– 23½ x 35½in.
(Butterfield's) **$19,000 £11,378**

MONTAGUE DAWSON – Cruising In The
Solent – signed – pencil and watercolour,
heightened with bodycolour – 16½ x 26½in.
(Sotheby's) **$6,054 £3,520**

J. VALENTINE DAVIS – Crystal Clear
Is The Autumn Air – signed – oil on
canvas – 9¼ x 13½in.
(Sotheby, King &
Chasemore) **$1,544** **£990**

NELSON DAWSON – Yachts Off The
Coast – 5 x 8½in.
(Lawrence) **$35** **£22**

T. DAWSON – A View Of Alnwick
Castle From The West – signed – oil
on board – 11½ x 17¾in.
(Anderson &
Garland) **$61** **£38**

HENRY DAWSON, Attributed to – View
On A Bridge – on board – 18 x 23in.
(Sotheby's) **$535** **£352**

MONTAGUE DAWSON – Yachts
Rounding The Buoy – signed – water-
colour and gouache – 16 x 26½in.
(Sotheby, King &
Chasemore) **$5,148** **£3,300**

EDWIN DEAKIN – Below Pont Neuf
– signed and dated 1882 – oil on canvas
– 30 x 20in.
(Butterfield's) **$2,500** **£1,497**

FRANZ VON DEFREGGER – Portrait
Of A Tyrolean Girl – signed – oil on
panel – 9 x 7in.
(Butterfield's) **$5,500 £3,293**

ADELCHI DEGROSSI – In The Tavern
– signed and inscribed – on panel – 12
x 9in.
*(Sotheby Beresford
Adams)* **$739 £440**

LEON DELACHAUX – Touching A
Thistle – signed and dated 1884 – oil
on canvas – 31¾ x 21¼in.
*(William Doyle
Galleries)* **$5,500 £3,254**

ALBERT DELERIVE – Village Scenes
– signed – on panel – 10¼ x 7½in.
(Sotheby's) **$8,240 £5,500 Pair**

EUGENE DELACROIX – Hamlet And
Horatio In The Graveyard – signed and
dated 1835 – 39 x 31¾in.
(Sotheby's) **$23,100 £13,200**

CORNELIS JACOBSZ. DELFF – A
Kitchen Still Life With A Man Holding A
Glass – 39 x 58½in.
(Sotheby's) **$13,041 £8,580**

DELPRAT

PAUL DELPRAT – 'An Evening With Bach' – signed and dated '69 – hand-coloured etching – 43 x 58cm.
(Geoff K. Gray) **$54** **£32**

VIRGINIE DEMONT-BRETON – 'A Mother And Her Children' – signed and dated 1881 – oil on canvas – 80 x 49in.
(Sotheby, King & Chasemore) **$6,715** **£3,950**

GABRIEL DESCHAMPS – 'St. Tropez Harbour' – signed – oil on canvas – 21¼ x 25½in.
(Sotheby, King & Chasemore) **$1,045** **$615**

LOUIS DESCHAMPS – L'Impatient – signed – 28 x 20in.
(Christie's & Edmiston's) **$1,120** **£700**

RAYMOND DESVARREUX – French Cuirassier Capturing The Colors Of A British Infantry Regiment – signed – oil on canvas – 64 x 52in.
(Butterfield's) **$1,500** **£898**

EMILY DESVIGNES – The Cowgirl – signed and dated 1877 – 29 x 39.5cm.
(Sotheby Beresford Adams) **$358** **£200**

EDOUARD DETAILLE – At Rezonville – 56¾ x 67¾in.
(Sotheby's) **$5,907** **£3,300**

EDWARD JULIUS DETMOLD – 'The Ass And The Goat' – signed with monogram and dated 1909 – 19½ x 14¼in.
(Sotheby, King & Chasemore) **$380** **£200**

CESARE AUGUSTE DETTI – The Chess Players – signed – oil on canvas – 29 x 24½in.
(Butterfield's) **$8,000** **£4,790**

LUDWIG DEUTSCH – A Moorish Woman – signed – 14 x 11½in. *(Christie's)* **$2,008** **£1,296**

ANTHONY DEVAS – Nude Reclining On A Chaise Longue – signed – oil on canvas – 19 x 24in. *(Christie's)* **$734** **£486**

THOMAS COLMAN DIBDIN – Banstead Church, Surrey – signed and dated 1861 – pencil and watercolour heightened with white – 14¼ x 20¼in. *(Christie's)* **$489** **£324**

ROBERT DICKERSON – 'Head Of A Girl' – signed – pastel – 38 x 28cm. *(Geoff K. Gray)* **$270** **£160**

SIR FRANCIS BERNARD DICKSEE – In The Shadow Of The Church – inscribed on the reverse – watercolour over pencil, heightened with bodycolour – 8 x 5½in. *(Sotheby's)* **$508** **£330**

JOHN ROBERT DICKSEE – A Portrait Of An Oriental Woman Reclining In A Palanquin – signed with monogram – 18¼in. diam. *(Anderson & Garland)* **$635** **£380**

JOHN ROBERT DICKSEE – 'Fortune Telling' – signed with monogram, and signed, inscribed and dated 1876 on the reverse – 24¼ x 20in. *(Christie's)* **$3,014** **£1,944**

JULES DIDIER – Cattle By A Pond In A Wooded Landscape – signed – 21¾ x 18in. *(Sotheby's)* **$669** **£440**

VAN DIEST – An Extensive Wooded Landscape With Peasants, Cattle And Sheep – 11½ x 47in. *(Christie's)* **$1,398** **£756**

DIETRICH

ADELHEID DIETRICH – Flowers, Berries, And Insects By A Stream – signed and dated 1880 – oil on canvas – 31½ x 27in. *(William Doyle Galleries)* $52,500 £31,065

ANDREAS DIRKS – Boats Moored In An Estuary At Twilight – signed – 25 x 20½in. *(Sotheby's)* **$1,420** **£935**

CHARLES DIXON – Clipper Race – signed and dated 1926 – watercolour heightened with bodycolour – 10¼ x 29½in. *(Sotheby, King & Chasemore)* **$430** **£242**

CHARLES DIXON – 'Drifting' – signed and inscribed – watercolour – 8¼ x 22in. *(Sotheby, King & Chasemore)* **$712** **£407**

ADOLF DIETRICH – Seelandschaft Am Untersee – signed and dated 1929 – oil on canvas – 41 x 59cm. *(Germann Auktionshaus)* **$24,310 £15,193**

CHARLES EDWARD DIXON – 'The Pool' – signed and dated 1901 – watercolour – 10¾ x 30in. *(Sotheby, King & Chasemore)*   **$1,238 £825**

CHARLES EDWARD DIXON – 'On The Hamble' – signed and dated 1921 – watercolour – 6 x 16in. *(Sotheby, King & Chasemore)*   **$858 £572**

CHARLES EDWARD DIXON – 'Greenwich Reach' – signed and dated 1899 – watercolour – 10½ x 29½in. *(Sotheby, King & Chasemore)*   **$1,733 £1,155**

H. J. DOBSON – Elderly Clockmaker At Work – oil on canvas – 21½ x 29½in. *(Thos. Love & Sons Ltd.)*   **$1,654   £940**

GEORGE HAYDOCK DODGSON – The Fountain – inscribed on a label – 8 x 13¼in. *(Sotheby Beresford Adams)*   **$57   £33**

SIR WILLIAM DOBELL – 'A Friend In London (Fred Coventry 1937)' – signed – oil on board – 60 x 50cm. *(Geoff K. Gray)* **$11,325   £6,470**

PIETER CHRISTIAN DOMMERSEN – The Zandhoek, Amsterdam – signed and dated 1885 – on panel – 16 x 23¾in. *(Sotheby's)*   **$7,285   £4,070**

WILLIAM DOMMERSEN – Lagocomo, Italy – signed, one inscribed on the reverse – oil on canvas – 15¾ x 24in.
(Sotheby, King & Chasemore)   **$1,020**   **£638 Pair**

WILLIAM DOMMERSEN – Jouberg On The Maas, Holland – signed and signed on the reverse – 9 x 12in.
(Sotheby's)   **$535**   **£352**

WILLIAM DOMMERSEN – Fisherfolk By Their Boats On An Estuary – indistinctly signed on the reverse – 15¾ x 23½in.
(Sotheby's)   **$3,344**   **£2,200**

WILLIAM DOMMERSEN – Cappice, Italy, A Coastal Scene – signed and indistinctly inscribed on the reverse – oil on canvas – 9 x 12in.
(Sotheby, King & Chasemore)   **$1,175**   **£660**

WILLIAM DOMMERSEN – Continental Harbour Scenes – signed – on canvas – 16 x 24in.
(Sotheby, King & Chasemore)   **$945**   **£605 Pair**

WILLIAM RAYMOND DOMMERSEN –
A Lakeside Town – signed – 29½ x
49½in.
(Christie's)   **$3,013   £1,944**

WILLIAM RAYMOND DOMMERSEN –
An Estuary Scene With Fishermen And
Boats By A Village – signed – 30 x 50in.
(Christie's)   **$1,555   £864**

WILLIAM RAYMOND DOMMERSEN –
Oudoorp On The Maas, Holland; and
Shiedam On The Scheldt, Holland –
signed and signed and inscribed on the
reverse – 12¼ x 24in.
(Christie's)   **$2,916   £1,620 Pair**

STEFANO DONADONI – The Colisseum
– signed – 19¼ x 31¾in.
(Christie's)   **$2,176   £1,404**

JOHN MILNE DONALD – Borthwick
Castle – on board – 11¾ x 18½in.
(Christie's &
Edmiston's)   **$208   £130**

M. DONNE – Beer, Devon – oil on paper
– 10 x 12½in.
(Lawrence)   **$60   £38**

**EDWARD ALGERNON STUART
DOUGLAS** – Hot On The Scent; and The
Kill – signed and dated 1892 – pencil
and watercolour – 5 x 7½in.
(Christie's)   **$777   £518 Pair**

EDWIN DOUGLAS – 'The Baron's Hall'
– signed with monogram and dated
1890 – 12¼ x 14¼in.
(Christie's)   **$600   £388**

P. DOUX – 'A River With A View Of A
Town With Hills Beyond' – dated 1922
– oil on board – 10 x 13½in.
(W. H. Lane &
Son)   **$96   £55**

H. E. DOWNING – Fishermen And Boats
On A Beach – signed and dated 1834 –
pencil and watercolour heightened with
white – 6¼ x 9¼in.
(Christie's)   **$470   £280**

W. DRAKE – A Rural Scene With Cattle
And A Drover In The Foreground –
signed on canvas – 24 x 42in.
(Sotheby, King &
Chasemore)   **$578   £385**

ALFRED DE DREUX – Tamerlan, The Mount Of Abd-El-Kader – signed – 38½ x 31in.
(Sotheby's)   **$40,425 £23,100**

ALFRED DE DREUX – A Lady On A Dark Bay Horse In A Landscape – on panel – 12¾ x 9½in.
(Christie's)   **$2,008   £1,296**

ALFRED DE DREUX – Huntsmen In An Extensive Landscape – signed – 16¼ x 24in.
(Sotheby's)   **$21,175 £12,100**

WILLEM VAN DRIELENBURGH – An Evening River Landscape – signed – 17 x 21in.
(Sotheby's)   **$3,344   £2,200**

ANTOINE DRUET – A Midi Chez Bignon – signed and dated 1884 – 50¾ x 76¼in.
(Sotheby's)   **$63,525 £36,300**

DRUMMOND – Old Salts – 13½ x 10½in.
(Sotheby Beresford Adams)   **$52   £30 Two**

SIR GEORGE RUSSELL DRYSDALE – 'Female Nude' – signed – ink drawing – 38 x 24cm.
(Geoff K. Gray)   **$540   £322**

SIR GEORGE RUSSELL DRYSDALE – 'Pearl Fisherman And Abo At Broome' – signed and dated 1958 – oil on canvas – 76 x 127cm.
(Australian Art Auctions)   **$56,309 £32,738**

WILLIAM DUFFIELD, Attributed to —
Still Life Study Of Fruit — inscribed —
oil on canvas — 10 x 13in.
(Sotheby, King &
Chasemore) **$308** **£198**

RAOUL DUFY — Cote d'Azur — signed
— gouache — 72 x 54cm.
(Germann
Auktionshaus) **$21,215** **£13,260**

JEAN DUFY — Hydrangea — signed and
dated 1920 — gouache and watercolour
on paper — 21¾ x 16in.
(William Doyle
Galleries) **$2,100** **£1,242**

RAOUL DUFY — Rue a Marseille Avec
Des Soldats Senegalais Et Des Prostituees
— signed — pen and black ink on paper —
9¼ x 7¼in.
(Christie's) **$2,712** **£1,728**

DUGHET

GASPARD DUGHET, Attributed to –
A Southern Landscape – 25½ x 29½in.
(Sotheby's) $836   £550

J. VAN DUITT – A Dutch River – signed
– 9 x 13in.
*(Sotheby Beresford
    Adams)* $170   £99

ALFRED DUKE – 'The Village Gossip'
– signed – oil on canvas – 24 x 36in.
*(Sotheby, King &
    Chasemore)* $1,020   £638

EDMUND DULAC – Tamerlane –
signed and dated – pen and ink – 3¾ x
6in.
(Christie's) $292   £194

E. DUNCAN – 'Running For Home', A
Coastal Storm And Shipping Scene With
Figures – watercolour – 36 x 17½in.
*(G. H. Bayley
    & Sons)* $4,325   £2,500

JOHN DUNCAN – Iona, A Summer's Day
– on panel – 15 x 17½in.
*(Christie's &
    Edmiston's)* $112   £70

WALTER DUNCAN – The Serenade –
signed and dated 1879 – watercolour over
pencil, heightened with bodycolour – 11½
x 21in.
(Sotheby's) $677   £440

P. DUMONT – A French Harbour Scene – signed – oil on canvas – 38 x 56in.
(Sotheby, King & Chasemore)
                    $1,320 £880

WALTER DUNCAN – A Gossip In The Woods – signed and dated 1913 – heightened with bodycolour – 10½ x 7½in.
(Sotheby's)   **$542**   **£352**

WALTER DUNCAN – Windsor Castle – signed – watercolour heightened with white – 7¼ x 10¾in.
(Christie's)   **$689**   **£410**

RONALD OSSORY DUNLOP – Jean By Candlelight – signed – 19¾ x 15in.
(Sotheby's)   **$473**   **£275**

F. DUNNINGTON – 'The Old Aquaduct, Barton On Irwell' – signed and inscribed on reverse – oil on canvas – 15½ x 24in.
(Hall, Wateridge & Owen)   **$391**   **£230**

JULIEN DUPRE – Farm Girls Gathering Hay – signed and dated 1881 – 24¾ x 31in.
(Sotheby's)   **$19,800 £13,200**

GEORGE HENRY DURRIE – Woodsman In Winter – oil on canvas – oil on canvas – 18¼ x 24in.
(Christie's)   **$33,000 £22,000**

GEORGE HENRY DURRIE – Summer Landscape – signed and dated 1862 – oil on canvas – 22 x 30¼in.
(Christie's)   **$46,200 £30,800**

DUSART

CORNELIUS DUSART, Manner of —
Travellers Outside An Inn — 26¼ x 34½in.
(Sotheby's) **$2,173 £1,430**

DUTCH SCHOOL, 17th century — A
River Landscape — signed with initials —
on panel — 14¾ x 19¼in.
(Sotheby's) **$2,648 £1,540**

DUTCH SCHOOL, 18th century — A
Gypsy Eating Mussels — signed or
inscribed — on panel — 11½ x 9in.
(Sotheby's) **$802 £528**

DUTCH SCHOOL — River Landscape
With Figures Fishing, Sheep And A Shepherd — oil on panel — 14.5 x 19in.
*(Woolley &
Wallis)* **$2,088 £1,250**

DUTCH SCHOOL, 19th century –
'Sailing Ships In The Moonlight' – signed
– oil on canvas – 33½ x 23½in.
(Stalker &
Boos) **$1,200** **£718**

DUTCH SCHOOL, 17th century – Christ
And The Woman Taken In Adultery – 47
x 66½in.
(Sotheby's) **$3,344** **£2,200**

DUTCH SCHOOL, 18th century – Still
Life Study Of Grapes, Cherries And A
Bird – oil on canvas – 28 x 25in.
(Sotheby, King &
Chasemore) **$1,567** **£1,045**

DUTCH SCHOOL, 19th century – River
Landscape – oil on canvas – 43 x 63in.
(Sotheby, King &
Chasemore) **$1,345** **£790**

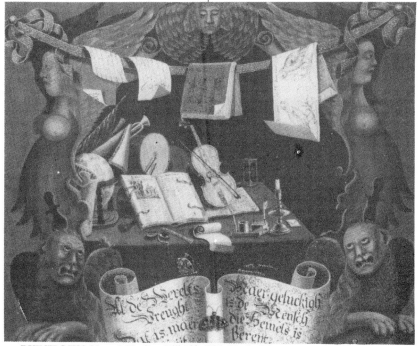

DUTCH SCHOOL – A Vanitas Still Life With Musical Instruments And Books
– inscribed, signed and dated 1680 – 23 x 26½in. *(Sotheby's)* **$2,508 £1,650**

DUTCH SCHOOL

DUTCH SCHOOL, Early 19th century —
'Figures And Boats On A Canal' — oil on
copper — 6¾ x 8¼in.
(Sotheby, King &
Chasemore) **$633** **£396**
MARCEL DYF — Amandiers En Fleurs —
signed — 23 x 28in.
(Lawrence) **$1,574** **£990**

MARCEL DYF — 'Danseuse' — signed —
29 x 24in.
(Lawrence) **$2,624** **£1,650**

MARCEL DYF — Scene Marocaine —
signed — oil on canvas — 17½ x 21in.
(Sotheby's) **$2,006** **£1,320**

ALEX DZIGURSKI — Monterey Surf
— signed — oil on canvas — 32 x 52in.
(Butterfield's) **$700** **£414**

CHARLES EARLE – Landscape Near Dorking – signed – watercolour heightened with white – 9¼ x 23½in.
(Sotheby's)   **$406**   **£264**

CHARLES EARLE – 'Durham' – signed – watercolour – 20 x 30in.
(Sotheby, King & Chasemore)   **$1,287**   **£858**

HENRY EARP, SNR. – Sheffield Park; and Haywards Heath – signed – heightened with bodycolour – 10 x 7½in.
(Sotheby Beresford Adams)   **$535**   **£308 Pair**

HENRY EARP, SNR. – Going Home – signed – heightened with white – 9 x 6½in.
(Sotheby Beresford Adams)   **$184**   **£110**

WILLIAM HENRY EARP – Loch Long – signed – 10 x 22½in.
(Lawrence)   **$130**   **£82**

WILLIAM HENRY EARP – Coastal Views – signed – 9 x 16in., the other 10 x 22in.
(Sotheby Beresford Adams)   **$41**   **£24 Two**

SIR ALFRED EAST – Drying Umbrellas After A Storm, Chryenji – signed, indistinctly inscribed and also inscribed on the reverse – watercolour over pencil – 9½ x 14in.
(Sotheby's)   **$745**   **£484**

SIR ALFRED EAST – Lelant, Moonlight – signed and dated – 27½ x 35½in.
(Sotheby's)   **$378**   **£220**

SIR ALFRED EAST – Harbour Scene With Figures And Boats – signed – watercolour – 13½ x 20in.
(Lawrence)   **$525**   **£330**

FRITZ CARL WERNER EBEL – Figures On A Woodland Path – signed and dated 1860 – 16 x 20¾in.
(Sotheby's)   **$3,678**   **£2,420**

FRITZ CARL WERNER EBEL – A Castle In An Extensive Wooded Landscape – signed and dated 1861 – 20¼ x 28¼in.
(Sotheby's)   **$3,010**   **£1,980**

EBERLE

LIONEL EDWARDS – Racehorses With Their Grooms Walking By Their Sides, In A Country Landscape – watercolour drawing – 19½ x 14in.
(Thos. Love & Sons Ltd.) **$2,464** **£1,400**

JANE SOPHIA EGERTON – On The Terrace – signed and dated 1857 – heightened with white – 19½ x 25½in.
(Sotheby's) **$281** **£150**

ADOLF EBERLE – The Zither Player – signed and inscribed – on panel – 13¾ x 10½in.
(Sotheby's) **$8,466** **£4,730**

LIONEL EDWARDS – 'Caught' And 'Even Me', Two Race Horses Heading For The Post – signed, inscribed and dated – watercolour and gouache – 14.7 x 13.7in. *(Woolley & Wallis)* **$3,451 £1,950**

EILEV RASMUSSEN EILERSEN – A Winter Landscape At Funen – signed with monogram and dated 1854 – 16½ x 22½in.
(Sotheby's) $502   £330

NICK EGGENHOFER – Cattle Rustler – signed – watercolour on paper – 10½ x 8in.
(Butterfield's) $1,200   £718

WYCLIFFE EGGINTON – March Weather, Near Torquay – signed – watercolour – 15 x 22in.
(Sotheby's) $370   £220

EILSJEMIUS – 'Seaside Landscape, In The Foreground A Roadway On Which Walks A Young Girl Going To The Sea' – signed – oil on canvas – 14 x 20in.
(Stalker & Boos) $1,000   £598

GEORGE SAMUEL ELGOOD – The Terrace Garden – signed and dated 1909 – watercolour over pencil – 14 x 20½in.
(Sotheby's) $1,439   £939

MARIA EGNER – Spatherbstmorgen In Der Steiermark – signed – oil on canvas – 68 x 50cm.
(Germann Auktionshaus) $4,198   £2,624

FREDERICK ELLIOTT – 'Ships In Sydney Harbour' – signed – watercolour – 50 x 76cm.
(Geoff K. Gray) $540   £322

ELLIOT

RICHARD ELLIOT — Taking Home The Eggs — signed — 19½ x 29½in.
(Sotheby Beresford Adams) **$665** **£396**

EDWIN JOHN ELLIS — Figures Beside A Pool — signed and indistinctly dated — watercolour and bodycolour — 5¼ x 8in.
(Sotheby's) **$592** **£385**

FREMONT F. ELLIS — Acequeia Maqure, New Mexico — signed — oil on board — 10 x 13¾in.
(Butterfield's) **$1,300** **£778**

ALFRED W. ELMORE — A Scene From The Merchant Of Venice — signed — 27¾ x 35¾in.
(Christie's) **$463** **£259**

ARTHUR JOHN ELSLEY — Springtime — signed and dated 1911 — 37 x 47in.
(Sotheby's) **$22,275** **£14,850**

E. J. ELWELL — A Still Life Of Summer Flowers In A Vase — signed with monogram, also signed with monogram and dated 1896 on the reverse — 28 x 22in.
(Sotheby's) **$468** **£308**

HENRY HETHERINGTON EMMERSON — A Family Portrait Of A Gentleman Holding The Reins Of A Bay Horse, His Wife Mounted Side Saddle Upon A Grey With Two Women Nearby And Three Dogs At Their Feet — signed — 39½ x 49¼in.
(Anderson & Garland) **$1,670** **£1,000**

JOHN EMMS — 'A Refractory Customer' — signed and dated '87 — oil — 17 x 14in.
(Laurence & Martin Taylor) **$1,032** **£600**

JOHN EMMS — Drawing In The Hounds — signed and dated '83 — 24 x 35in.
(Sotheby Beresford Adams) **$10,534** **£6,270**

JOHN EMMS — A Cow With Her Calf In A Barn — signed — 19 x 23in.
(Christie's) **$2,008** **£1,296**

ENGLISH SCHOOL — 'Country Cottage' — inscribed — pencil — 8 x 13cm.
(Geoff K. Gray) **$27** **£16**

ENGLISH SCHOOL, 19th century, After Landseer — 'Stags And Does In A Landscape' — oil on canvas — 11½ x 13½in.
(Bracketts) **$320** **£200**

ENGLISH SCHOOL, Early 19th century — The Schoolmaster's Return — 13½ x 16¼in.
(Sotheby's) **$535** **£352**

ENGLISH PROVINCIAL SCHOOL, Late 17th century — Portrait Of A Young Boy Of The Graves Family — 47¼ x 37½in.
(Sotheby's) **$1,992** **£1,320**

ENGLISH SCHOOL, Mid 18th century — Landscape With Rustics Near A Country Village — bears a signature — 13¼ x 24¾in.
(Sotheby's) **$434** **£286**

ENGLISH SCHOOL, circa 1810 — Landscape With Figures Walking Near A Lake — indistinctly inscribed — 35½ x 49½in.
(Sotheby's) **$4,318** **£2,860**

ENGLISH SCHOOL

ENGLISH SCHOOL, 19th century –
A Still Life Study Of Flowers – oil on
canvas – 19¼ x 24¼in.
(Sotheby, King &
Chasemore) **$823** **£528**

ENGLISH SCHOOL, 19th century –
'Portrait Of A Woman' – oil on canvas –
28½ x 23½in.
(Stalker &
Boos) **$175** **£113**

ENGLISH SCHOOL, 19th century – The
Ambleside To Coniston Coach – water-
colour – 16 x 26in.
(Sotheby, King &
Chasemore) **$495** **£330**

DELPHIN ENJOLRAS – A Young Nude
Woman Reclining On A Chaise Longue –
signed – pastel – 28 x 20½in.
(Graves, Son &
Pilcher) **$2,535** **£1,450**

JOHN JOSEPH ENNEKING – 'Country
Interior' – signed and dated '83 – oil
on canvas – 22 x 34in.
(Robert W. Skinner
Inc.) **$600** **£375**

JOHN JOSEPH ENNEKING – Pulling
Out The Splinter – signed and dated
'94 – oil on canvas – 33 x 45in.
(Butterfield's) **$25,000** **£14,970**

JOHN JOSEPH ENNEKING – 'Autumn Along The Neponset' – oil on canvas – 10 x 14in.
(Robert W. Skinner Inc.) **$1,900** **£1,187**

SIR JACOB EPSTEIN – Gladioli – signed – gouache – 23½ x 17in.
(Christie's) **$1,060** **£702**

SIR JACOB EPSTEIN – Sunita And A Young Girl Reclining – signed – soft pencil – 18 x 21¼in.
(Christie's) **$490** **£324**

SIR JACOB EPSTEIN – Portrait Of Jackie – signed – black chalk – 22 x 17¼in.
(Sotheby's) **$938** **£572**

R. S. ERRINGTON – River Landscape With A Castle On A Mountainside; and Sunset Over A River Landscape, A Castle In The Distance – one signed – oil – 10in. diam.
(Woolley & Wallis) **$192** **£115 Pair**

JEAN-BERNARD ESCHEMANN – Enticement – signed and dated 1900 – 80 x 62in.
(Sotheby's) **$2,508** **£1,650**

RUDOLF ERNST – 'Pipe Dreams' – signed – watercolour – 12¼ x 18¼in.
(Robert W. Skinner Inc.) **$3,800 £2,375**

ESPOUT

V. D. ESPOUT – 'Harbour Scene With Ships – Malta' – watercolour – 8¾ x 13in.
(W. H. Lane & Son) **$19** **£11**

A. ESPOY – Landscape – signed – oil on canvas – 24 x 30in.
(Butterfield's) **$400** **£236**

JACOB ESSELENS – Sportsmen On A Country Road – signed – on panel – 14½ x 19½in.
(Sotheby's) **$5,709** **£3,300**

ESTRADA – 'Madonna And Child' – bears signature – oil on canvas – 27 x 28in.
(W. H. Lane & Son) **$330** **£190**

WILLIAM ETTY – Cupid Reclining On A Scallop Shell – on panel – 10½ x 13¼in.
(Christie's) **$837** **£540**

WILLIAM ETTY – A Female Nude Reclining, recto; Nude Figure Sketches, verso – on board – 16½ x 19½in.
(Sotheby's) **$1,514** **£880**

EUROPEAN SCHOOL, 19th century – 'Portrait Of A Friar' – oil on canvas – 15½ x 11½in.
(Stalker & Boos) **$90** **£58**

BERNARD EVANS – Extensive Landscape With Figures And A Town In The Distance – watercolour – 15 x 29in.
(W. H. Lane & Son) **$544** **£320**

BERNARD EVANS – 'Goldsborough Hall Yorkshire' – signed, inscribed and dated 1889 – watercolour – 15½ x 29½in.
(Sotheby, King & Chasemore) **$665** **£374**

BERNARD WALTER EVANS – Grasse, South Of France – signed – watercolour over pencil – 16 x 29¼in.
(Sotheby's)   **$1,524**   **£990**

RICHARD EVANS, After Coreggio – The Magdalene – on board – 12 x 15in.
(Sotheby Beresford Adams)   **$220**   **£132**

SIDNEY EVANS – Eton College – signed and dated '98 – pencil and water-colour – 9 x 12¾in.
(Christie's)   **$507**   **£302**

WILLIAM EVANS – A Cottage In A Welsh Mountain Valley – signed and dated 1836 – pencil and watercolour heightened with white – 9½ x 18¼in.
(Christie's)   **$544**   **£324**

ADRIANUS EVERSEN – Figures In A Street – signed – on panel – 9 x 6¾in.
(Christie's)   **$2,916**   **£1,620**

H. EVERET – Clipper At Sea – signed – oil on canvas – 30 x 40in.
(Sotheby, King & Chasemore)   **$577**   **£330**

EVERSEN – A Dutch Street In Summer – bears initials – on board – 10½ x 9in.
(Sotheby Beresford Adams)   **$283**   **£165**

A. EVERSEN – A Hay Wagon On A Dutch Street – bears signature – on panel – 7½ x 5¾in.
(Sotheby's)   **$590**   **£330**

ADRIANUS EVERSEN – A Dutch Street Scene – signed with monogram – on panel – 7¾ x 6in.
(Sotheby's)   **$2,173**   **£1,430**

EWORTH – The Head Of Christ – inscribed – 17½ x 15in.
(Christie's)   **$638**   **£345**

GLADSTONE EYRE – 'Upper Reaches Of Sydney Harbour' – signed – water-colour – 86 x 92cm.
(Geoff K. Gray)   **$1,235**   **£706**

FABIO FABBI – Selling A Slave – signed
– watercolour on paper – 25 x 18in.
(Butterfield's)   **$700**   **£415**

GENTILE DA FABRIANO, Follower of
– Susannah And The Elders – on panel
– 13 x 22in.
(Sotheby's)   **$6,520**   **£4,290**

THOMAS FAED – A Fisherwoman On
The Seashore – signed – 10½ x 8in.
(Christie's)   **$1,340**   **£864**

C. FACHINETTI – Mother Playing With
Her Child – signed – oil on canvas –
29½ x 22in.
(Butterfield's)   **$1,500**   **£888**

THOMAS FAED, Follower of – 'Study
Of A Bull Terrier With A Dead Rabbit' –
oil on canvas – 17 x 13½in.
*(Sotheby, King &
   Chasemore)*   **$475**   **£297**

E. FALANGA – 'Idle Hours' – signed –
oil on canvas – 20 x 28in.
(Stalker &
Boos)   **$175**   **£113**

LUIS RICCARDO FALERO – Mystic
Blessing – signed and dated 1883 –
oil on canvas – 29 x 16in.
(Butterfield's)   **$7,000**   **£4,190**

SARAH FALLON – Knitting On The
Shore – signed – canvas on board –
18½ x 24½in.
(Sotheby's)   **$1,435**   **£990**

L. FANZONI – A Good Bottle; and
Testing The Wine – signed – on panel
– 14¾ x 10¾in.
(Christie's)   **$1,841**   **£1,188 Pair**

WALTER FARNDON – A New England
Fishing Port – signed – oil on canvas –
30 x 36in.
(William Doyle
Galleries)   **$950**   **£562**

DAVID FARQUHARSON – Loch Achray,
Well Wooded Track Beside The Loch With
A Man Walking Under The Shade Of The
Trees, A Mare And Foal Grazing By A Wire
Fence – signed and dated (18)90 – oil on
canvas – 39 x 60cm.
(Henry Spencer &
Sons)   **$930**   **£520**

JOSEPH FARQUHARSON – Summer
Days, Sheep In A Highland Landscape
– oil on canvas – 59 x 36in.
(Thos. Love & Sons
Ltd.)   **$4,224**   **£2,400**

ROBERT B. FARREN – Cymbeline –
signed and dated 1887 – 40 x 28in.
(Sotheby's)   **$535**   **£352**

OTTO FEDDER – Winterlandschaft
– signed and dated 1900 – oil on canvas
– 35 x 50cm.
*(Germann
    Auktionshaus)*   **$4,199**   **£2,624**

FRANK FELLER – Cossacks In The
Snow – signed – heightened with body-
colour – 13 x 21in.
*(Sotheby Beresford
    Adams)*   **$739**   **£440**

CHARLES FRANCOISE FELU – An
Early Eighteenth Century Classical Group
– signed and indistinctly dated 1861 –
oil on panel – 9½ x 11in.
*(Sotheby, King &
    Chasemore)*   **$314**   **£209**

FRANS DE PAULA FERG – A River Landscape With A Ferry – indistinctly signed –
on metal – 9¾ x 13½in.
(Sotheby's)   **$4,758**   **£2,750**

FRANS DE PAULA FERG – A Mountainous Landscape With Travellers – inscribed
– 26 x 34in.
(Sotheby's)   **$7,356**   **£4,840**

ALESSANDRO FERGOLA – 'Pestum' – signed – oil on canvas – 11½ x 15½in. *(Sotheby, King & Chasemore)* **$448** **£264**

W. FERGUSON – 'Alpine Scene With A Stream' – signed – watercolour – 13½ x 20in. *(Bracketts)* **$56** **£35**

JOHN DUNCAN FERGUSSON – A Village Street – charcoal and watercolour – 9 x 12in. *(Christie's & Edmiston's)* **$512** **£320**

JOHN FERNELEY, JNR. – A Group Of Hunters – signed – 27¼ x 35⅓in. *(Sotheby's)* **$2,658** **£1,760**

JOHN FERNELEY, JNR. – A Bay And A Chestnut Hunter In A Landscape – signed and indistinctly dated – 25 x 30in. *(Christie's)* **$1,098** **£594**

JOHN FERNELEY, SNR. – Charlemagne, A Grey Arabian Stallion Standing In A Desert – signed – 28 x 36in. *(Sotheby's)* **$59,794 £39,600**

FERNELEY

SARAH FERNELEY, Attributed to —
The Game Of Bowls — 27 x 44½in.
(Sotheby's) **$802** **£528**

JAMES FERRIER — Fishing Boats Disembarking — signed — heightened with
bodycolour — 7 x 12½in.
(Sotheby Beresford
Adams) **$51** **£30 Two**

ANSELM FEUERBACH — Portrait Of A
Lady, Bust Length, In A Black Dress —
signed and dated 1864 — 19¼ x 15¾in.
(Christie's) **$1,458** **£810**

HARRY FIDLER — Ploughing Scene With
Two Grey Shire Horses Drawing A Plough
— signed — oil — 50 x 67cm.
(Henry Spencer &
Sons) **$2,618** **£1,700**

**JOHANN CHRISTIAN FIEDLER, Studio
of** — Portrait Of Ludwig VIII Landgraf
Von Hessendarmstadt — inscribed on the
reverse — 33 x 26½in.
(Sotheby's) **$1,003** **£660**

R. W. FIELDER — A Surrey Windmill —
signed — 10½ x 19in.
(Lawrence) **$113** **£71**

**ANTHONY VANDYKE COPLEY
FIELDING** — River Landscape With
Mountain — signed — watercolour —
8.5 x 12in.
(Woolley &
Wallis) **$534** **£320**

BENJAMIN EUGENE FICHEL — The
Studio — signed — on panel — 7 x 4in.
(Christie's) **$1,088** **£702**

COPLEY FIELDING – Penrhyn Castle – watercolour – 6¾ x 9in.
(Hall, Wateridge & Owen)   **$332**   **£190**

COPLEY FIELDING – A Landscape With Lake Scene And Mountains With Flock Of Sheep In The Foreground – signed and dated 1836 – oil on canvas – 18 x 22½in.
(Hall, Wateridge & Owen)   **$1,400**   **£800**

HERBERT JOHN FINN – Portraits Of Deal Fishermen, Polishing A Lamp And Drinking Ale – signed and dated '92 – oil on panel – 8.2 x 10in.
(Woolley & Wallis)   **$267**   **£160 Pair**

FRANCESCO FIERAVINO, Called Il Maltese – Still Life With A Celestial Globe And A Vase Of Flowers – 67 x 51in.
(Sotheby's)   **$25,575**   **£17,050**

PIER FRANCESCO FIORENTINO – The Virgin And Child With The Infant Saint John – on panel – 22 x 16in.
(Sotheby's)   **$11,730**   **£6,820**

SIR SAMUEL LUKE FILDES – Simpletons – signed – 15¾ x 26¼in. *(Christie's)*
    $4,536 £3,024

MARK FISHER – Cattle Grazing In An Orchard – signed – oil on canvas – 15½ x 29½in.
(Dreweatt Watson & Barton) **$975** **£650**

PAUL FISCHER – Copenhagen, Figures On The Oster Farimagsgade, The Kobenhavns Kommunehospital In The Background – signed and dated 1896 – 39 x 24½in.
(Sotheby's) **$13,475** **£7,700**

ROWLAND FISHER – 'Fusam & Arabritt', At Yarmouth 1958 – watercolour – 9½ x 13in.
(Hilhams) **$256** **£160**

JANET FISHER – 'On The Breezy Hillside' – signed and inscribed on the reverse – oil on canvas – 20 x 35½in. *(Sotheby, King & Chasemore)* **$550 £352**

ROWLAND FISHER – 'Gorleston Harbour', With Brush Bend, Lighthouse And Tug – watercolour – 12½ x 17in.
(Hilhams) **$144** **£90**

WILLIAM MARK FISHER – Cattle And Geese By A Pond In A Wooded Landscape – indistinctly signed and dated – 20 x 30in.
(Christie's) **$1,255** **£810**

FRED FITCH – Members Of A Hunt At The Edge Of A Field, Ploughmen And Their Team Working Nearby – signed – watercolour – 9½ x 19½in.
(Anderson & Garland) **$58** **£36**

JOHN ANSTER FITZGERALD – The Wood Nymph – signed – watercolour heightened with white – 8¾ x 7in.
(Christie's) **$489** **£324**

JOHN ANSTER FITZGERALD – A Fairy Dance – signed – watercolour heightened with bodycolour – 11 x 17in.
(Sotheby, King & Chasemore) **$458** **£286**

WILLIAM FITZ – A Poacher Sighted – signed – 38 x 64cm.
(Sotheby's) **$614** **£320**

FLEMISH SCHOOL, 18th century – The Adoration Of The Kings – on copper panel – 11 x 9½in.
(Morphets) **$859** **£480**

FLEMISH SCHOOL

FLEMISH SCHOOL, 16th century –
The Personification Of Justice And
Wisdom – on panel – 13½ x 7½in.
(Sotheby's) **$605** **£352 Pair**

EDWARD HENRY FLETCHER – Running For Port – signed – oil on canvas –
20 x 30in.
(Sotheby, King &
Chasemore) **$789** **£506**

EDWIN HENRY EUGENE FLETCHER
– 'Coastal Scene With Fishing Boats' –
oil – 9 x 12in.
(Dacre, Son &
Hartley) **$380** **£200**

EDWIN HENRY EUGENE FLETCHER
– Fishing Boat Off The Coast; and
Towing In – signed – 15½ x 23½in.
(Sotheby's) **$803** **£528 Pair**

EDWIN HENRY EUGENE FLETCHER –
Big Ben From The Thames – signed –
36 x 28in.
(Sotheby Beresford
Adams) **$1,275** **£759**

GOVAERT FLINCK – Portrait Of A Girl
With Two Dogs – bears a signature – 44
x 35in.
(Sotheby's) **$26,400** **£17,600**

SIR WILLIAM RUSSELL FLINT – Scene
From 'The Canterbury Tales' – signed
and dated 1912 – watercolour and bodycolour – 10½ x 8½in.
(Christie's) **$978** **£648**

SIR WILLIAM RUSSELL FLINT –
'Brunette' – signed – sanguine – 7½ x
10¾in.
(Stalker &
Boos) **$350** **£218**

SIR WILLIAM RUSSELL FLINT – The Track Across The Dunes – signed – watercolour – 21¼ x 30¼in.
(Christie's) **$4,892 £3,240**

SIR WILLIAM RUSSELL FLINT – 'A Composition In Archady – Figures At A Country Bath' – signed and inscribed – watercolour – 37 x 56cm.
(Geoff K. Gray) **$10,294 £5,882**

SIR WILLIAM RUSSELL FLINT – Nude With Hoop And Cockerel – signed – watercolour – 12½ x 17in.
(Christie's) **$2,609 £1,728**

SIR WILLIAM RUSSELL FLINT – The Oxcart – signed – watercolour – 10½ x 14¾in.
(Sotheby's) **$1,514 £880**

SIR WILLIAM RUSSELL FLINT – The Swimmer – signed and dated 1914 – 13½ x 20in. *(Sotheby Beresford Adams)* **$5,544 £3,300**

FLINT

WILLIAM RUSSELL FLINT – Mooring
At The Old Mill – signed on the reverse
– watercolour on paper – 13 x 21¾in.
(Butterfield's)   **$7,000   £4,190**

FLORENTINE SCHOOL, circa 1525 –
The Crucifixion With The Three Maries,
St. Francis, St. Jerome And St. John –
on panel – 25¼ x 17¼in.
(Sotheby's)   **$4,347   £2,860**

FRANS FLORIS – The Nurturing Of
Jupiter – on panel – 47½ x 66½in.
(Sotheby's)   **$5,016   £3,300**

FRANS FLORIS – The Virgin And Child
– on panel – 46¼ x 38½in.
(Sotheby's)   **$3,678   £2,420**

HENRY FOLEY – 'Old Houses, Rouen';
'St. Omer, France' – signed and inscribed
on reverse – oil on canvas – 14 x 10in.
(Sotheby, King &
Chasemore)   **$1,057   £594 Pair**

ANDRE DES FONTAINES – Environs De Melun – signed – pastel – 11 x 16½in.
(Sotheby's) **$196** **£110**

ROBERTO FONTANA – A Young Girl Wearing A Black Shawl – signed – 20¼ x 17½in.
(Sotheby's) **$3,678** **£2,420**

FRANCESCO FONTEBASSO – The Adoration Of The Magi – 22 x 29in.
(Sotheby's) **$23,100** **£15,400**

JEAN LOUIS FORAIN – Trois Nus – signed with initial – 28½ x 22in.
(Sotheby's) **$1,772** **£990**

JEAN LOUIS FORAIN – Au Theatre – signed – oil on canvas – 10¾ x 8¾in.
(William Doyle Galleries) **$7,250** **£4,289**

LEYTON FORBES – A Country Cottage – 5½ x 8½in.
(Lawrence) **$88** **£55**

M. STANHOPE FORBES – A Still Life Subject – signed and dated 1906 – oil – 20 x 25in.
(Lawrence) **$211** **£132**

STANHOPE ALEXANDER FORBES – The Leavetaking – oil on canvas – 33 x 24in.
(Christie's) **$1,630** **£1,080**

STANHOPE ALEXANDER FORBES – 'Trevithal', A Farm Lane And Buildings In A Pastoral Landscape – signed – oil on board – 8 x 12in.
(W. H. Lane & Son) **$957** **£550**

FORBES

STANLEY FORBES – 'Thatched Cottages In Landscapes' – watercolour – 14 x 21in.
(Dacre, Son & Hartley) **$155** **£90 Pair**

ARTHUR EWAN FORBES-DALRYMPLE – The Fruit Basket – signed in monogram – en gouache – 32 x 19in.
(Lawrence) **$297** **£187**

R. ONSLOW FORD – The Mill Stream, River Ouse; and The Marshland Near Barmouth – one signed, both inscribed ,and dated 1920 on the reverse – on board – 13 x 16in.
(Sotheby's) **$535** **£352 Pair**

CHARLES ALEX COESSIN DE LA FOSSE – A Garden Luncheon – signed – oil on board – 21½ x 26in.
(Butterfield's) **$5,250 £3,143**

M. B. FOSTER – A Country Stile With Figures – inscribed with monogram – watercolour – 6.7 x 5.2in.
(Woolley & Wallis) **$500** **£300**

MYLES BIRKET FOSTER – A Witley Cottage, 1895 – pen and brown ink and watercolour heightened with white – 3¾ x 4¼in.
(Christie's) **$763** **£486**

MYLES BIRKET FOSTER – Rain's Nest, Near Chiddingfold – signed – watercolour over pencil, heightened with white – 8 x 12in. *(Sotheby's)* **$1,050 £682**

MYLES BIRKET FOSTER – Near Naples – signed with monogram – watercolour over pencil heightened with bodycolour – 6¼ x 9¼in.
(Sotheby's)   **$4,235   £2,750**

MYLES BIRKET FOSTER – Fetching Water – signed with monogram – 30 x 26in.
(Sotheby's)   **$8,893   £5,775**

MYLES BIRKET FOSTER – Evening: Haymakers At A River's Edge – signed with monogram – watercolour heightened with white – 7¼ x 14in.
(Christie's)   **$7,257   £4,320**

MYLES BIRKET FOSTER – Loch Awe – signed, inscribed and dated 1886 – heightened with white – 11½ x 16½in.
(Sotheby's)   **$2,202   £1,430**

MYLES BIRKET FOSTER – View In Hampshire – signed with monogram – watercolour – 5¼ x 9in.
(Sotheby, King & Chasemore) **$3,300   £2,200**

MYLES BIRKET FOSTER – Picking Blackberries – signed with monogram – heightened with bodycolour – 14 x 24in.
(Sotheby's)   **$15,585   £10,120**

FOSTER

MYLES BIRKET FOSTER – Hambledon, Near Witley, Children Playing By A Tree – signed with monogram and inscribed – watercolour – 9 x 7in.
(Christie's)   **$1,793**   **£1,188**

THEODORE FOURMOIS – Cattle In A Stream By A Rustic Cottage – signed – 18 x 24in.
(Sotheby's)   **$1,420**   **£935**

A. MOULTON FOWERAKER – A Continental Street Scene With Figures – 9 x 11in.
(Lawrence)   **$280**   **£176**

A. MOULTON FOWERAKER – The Lantern Carrier – signed – 10½ x 8½in.
(Sotheby Beresford Adams)   **$406**   **£242**

A. MOULTON FOWERAKER – A French River Scene Near St. Antoine – signed – 9 x 13in.
(Lawrence)   **$70**   **£44**

BERTHA FOWLE – Hastings – signed and dated 1939 – watercolour – 6 x 8in.
(John Hogbin & Son)   **$27**   **£16**

ROBERT FOWLER – Summer Morning – signed – 12 x 16in.
(Sotheby's)   **$735**   **£484**

ROBERT FOWLER – Sea Shell – signed – 16 x 30in.
(Sotheby's)   **$702**   **£462**

A. W. FOWLES – Men-o'-War Saluting The Royal Steamship Off The Isle Of Wight – signed and dated 1873 – 23½ x 41½in.
(Christie's)   **$3,866**   **£2,160**

H. C. FOX – At Beccles, Suffolk – dated 1903 – watercolour – 20 x 30½in.
(Norman Hope & Partners)   **$665**   **£380**

H. C. FOX – View Of The Avon – dated 1905 – watercolour – 20 x 30½in.
(Norman Hope & Partners)   **$560**   **£320**

HENRY CHARLES FOX – 'Homewards'
– signed and dated 1896 – watercolour
heightened with bodycolour – 13½ x
20½in.
(Sotheby, King &
Chasemore) **$443** **£253**

HENRY CHARLES FOX – 'A Shepherd And
His Flock Outside Windsor' – signed and
dated 1916 – watercolour with scratching
out – 13¾ x 21in.
(Sotheby, King &
Chasemore) **$1,056** **£704 Pair**

HENRY CHARLES FOX – On The Farm
– signed and dated 1910 and 1911 –
heightened with white – 15 x 22in.
(Sotheby's) **$982** **£638**
JOHN FOX – Breezy Weather – signed
– 15½ x 24in.
(Sotheby Beresford
Adams) **$340** **£198 Pair**

EDWARD REGINALD FRAMPTON –
Flora Of The Fields – signed – tempera
on board – 12 x 12in.
(Sotheby's) **$3,850** **£2,200**

FRAMPTON

EDWARD REGINALD FRAMPTON – Katherine – signed and dated 1920, inscribed on the reverse – tempera on panel – 14 x 11in.
(Sotheby's) **$350** **£242**

EDWARD REGINALD FRAMPTON – Bishopstone, Sussex – 24 x 20in.
(Sotheby's) **$14,437** **£8,250**

CHARLES FRANCE – Shipping At Night – signed and dated 1885 – 23½ x 35½in.
(Sotheby Beresford Adams) **$147** **£88**

FRANCOIS LOUIS FRANCIA – Dutch Fishing Boats Off The Coast – bears signature – on panel – 11 x 14¾in. *(Sotheby, King & Chasemore)* **$686 £440**

THOMAS EDWARD FRANCIS – Lago Di Garda – signed, inscribed on the reverse – 11½ x 15½in.
(Sotheby Beresford Adams) **$135** **£79**

FRANS FRANCKEN, The Younger – Episodes From The Life Of Moses – 21¾ x 28¾in.
(Sotheby's) **$7,231** **£4,180**

FRANS FRANCKEN, Circle of – The Crossing Of The Red Sea – gouache on vellum – 13½ x 18in.
(Sotheby's) **$1,672** **£1,100**

ALBERT JOSEPH FRANKE – The Christening – signed – oil on panel – 15½ x 23½in.
(Butterfield's) **$8,500** **£5,090**

JEAN AUGUSTIN FRANQUELIN – The Young Chimney-Sweep – signed – 12¼ x 15¾in.
(Christie's) **$3,888** **£2,160**

ALEXANDER FRASER – The Oak Tree's Shade – signed, inscribed on a label on the reverse – on board – 9¼ x 11¾in.
(Sotheby Beresford Adams) **$178** **£104**

ALEXANDER FRASER – Women, Children And Cows By A Country Cottage – signed and dated – oil – 7.7 x 11.5in.
(Woolley & Wallis) **$672** **£380**

FRANCIS ARTHUR FRASER – River Landscapes – signed, one with initials – watercolour – 10.5 x 18.2in.
(Woolley & Wallis) **$208** **£125 Pair**

ROBERT WINTER FRASER – 'Oakley' – signed, inscribed and dated 1889 – 17 x 28½in.
(Sotheby, King & Chasemore) **$560** **£374**

ELOISE FRATANI – 'La Promenade', Figures In Edwardian Costume On Promenade With Bandstand Beyond – oil on panel – 8 x 11½in.
(W. H. Lane & Son) **$207** **£120**

GEORGE AUGUSTUS FREEZOR – Hide And Seek – signed and dated '72 – 13¾ x 17¼in.
(Christie's) **$670** **£432**

FRENCH SCHOOL

FRENCH SCHOOL, 1780 – 'The Letter'
– dated – oil – 33 x 51.5in.
(Woolley &
Wallis) $1,858 £1,050

FRENCH SCHOOL, 18th century – The
Shepherd Boy – oil on canvas – 36 x
34½in.
(Sotheby, King &
Chasemore) $1,544 £990

ANNIE FRENCH – A Girl In A Red Dress
Before A Tangle Of Briar – signed – water-
colour – 23 x 17cm.
(Christie's &
Edmiston's) $655 £360

CHARLES FRERE – The Oyster Seller
– signed and dated '74 – 18 x 14½in.
(Sotheby's) $1,378 £770

THEODORE FRERE – Famille Fellah
En Voyage – signed, inscribed and
dated 1879 – on terracotta – 6¾ x 15in.
(Sotheby, King &
Chasemore) $5,490 £3,520

EDOUARD FRERE – Learning To Walk – signed and dated – oil on panel – 18 x 14¾in.
(Woolley & Wallis)   **$3,234   £2,100**

DONALD STUART LESLIE FRIEND – 'Houses At Freshwater' – signed – watercolour and ink – 27 x 35cm.
(Geoff K. Gray)   **$904   £537**

EMILE OTHON FRIESZ – Nu Allonge – signed – charcoal over red chalk – 10¾ x 17¼in.
(Sotheby's)   **$267   £176**

EMILE OTHON FRIESZ – Le Port De Dieppe – signed – oil on canvas – 26.5 x 41.3cm.
(Germann Auktionshaus)   **$9,398   £5,248**

EMILE OTHON FRIESZ – Scene De Port – on paper on canvas – 28¾ x 36in.
(Sotheby's)   **$2,165   £1,210**

HANS GABRIEL FRIIS – An Extensive Danish Landscape – signed and dated 1882 – 36¾ x 60½in.
(Sotheby's)   **$585   £385**

ALFRED DOWNING FRIPP – Peasant Girl Gathering Flowers – signed and dated 1892 – 26 x 18½in.
(Laurence & Martin Taylor)   **$422   £250**

157

FRIPP

ALFRED DOWNING FRIPP – Rome: The Market Place – signed, inscribed and indistinctly dated – watercolour and bodycolour – 10¾ x 17¾in.
(Christie's) **$1,451** **$864**

WILLIAM POWELL FRITH – Brown And Blue Eyes – signed and dated 1874 – 45 x 38in.
(Sotheby's) **$13,475** **£7,700**

WILLIAM POWELL FRITH – A Study For The Two Central Figures Of Derby Day – signed and dated 1860 – 18 x 12in.
(Sotheby's) **$36,575** **£20,900**

ERNEST FROMMHOLD – Square Rigger Under Full Sail – signed – oil – 32 x 57½in.
(Laurence & Martin Taylor) **$865** **£500**

WILLIAM EDWARD FROST – Panope – signed and dated 1862 – 28 x 36in.
(Sotheby's) **$4,620** **£3,080**

JOHN FULLEYLOVE – The Great Gate, Trinity College, Cambridge – signed with monogram and dated 1889 – pencil and watercolour – 6¾ x 5in.
(Christie's) **$388** **£259**

FURINI – Bathsheba – 45½ x 37½in.
(Sotheby's) **$4,948** **£2,860**

FUSELI – Figures Defending A Rocky Promontory, A Battle Being Waged Beyond – oil – 39½ x 52in.
(Lawrence) **$198** **£77**

I. FUSS – Man-O'-War Off The Coast – signed – on canvas – 27 x 41½in.
(Sotheby, King & Chasemore) **$3,432** **£2,200**

BESSIE FYFE – From The Hills Of Dream; Eilidh My Fawn; and Fairies Among The Reeds – signed and one dated 1919 – pen and black ink and watercolour – two 5 x 4½in. and one 5 x 4in.
(Sotheby's) **$440** **£286 Three**

LUIGI M. GALEA – Valetta Harbour; and A Country View – signed on board – 11 x 26in.
(Sotheby, King &
Chasemore) **$704** **£440 Pair**

B. GAEL – Horses And Figures By An Inn – on fruitwood panel – 13¼ x 18in.
(Laurence & Martin
Taylor) **$1,014** **£600**

BARENT GAEL – A Dutch Landscape With A Cottage, Horseman And Figures – signed – oil – 12.7 x 15in.
(Woolley &
Wallis) **$4,779** **£2,700**

JOSE Y ARNOSA GALLEGOS – The Cardinal's Arrival – signed and dated 1891 – on panel – 18 x 24in.
(Christie's S.
Kensington) **$8,690** **£5,500**

THOMAS GAINSBOROUGH – Portrait Of Dorothea, Lady Eden, Wearing A Blue Dress And A Grey Cloak – 29½ x 24½in.
(Sotheby's) **$31,559** **£20,900**

GAINSBOROUGH – A Shepherd And Flock In Wooded Uplands – black and white chalk – on grey paper – 24 x 32cm.
(Sotheby's) **$106** **£60**

ROBERT GALLON – 'Richmond, York-shire' – signed – oil on canvas – 24½ x 40½in.
(Sotheby, King &
Chasemore) **$4,400** **£2,750**

GAMBLE

OTTO GAMPERT – A Summer Landscape – signed with monogram – oil on board – 9 x 10½in.
(Sotheby, King &
Chasemore) **$423** **£242**

HIPPOLYTE JEAN-BAPTISTE GARNEREY – In A Continental Harbour – signed – watercolour heightened with white – 4¾ x 7¼in.
(Christie's) **$652** **£432**

CHARLES GARNETT – Cottage Gardens – signed – 13½ x 19½in.
(Sotheby Beresford
Adams) **$344** **£198 Pair**

JOHN MARSHALL GAMBLE – Moorish Court – signed and dated 1893 – oil on canvas – 26 x 18in.
(Butterfield's) **$700** **£414**

JAN ANTON GAREMYN – A Country Fair – on panel – 10¾ x 14¾in. *(Sotheby Beresford Adams)* **$10,164 £6,050**

OSWALD GARSIDE — 'Mersea Island' — signed and inscribed — watercolour — 11½ x 27½in.
(Sotheby, King & Chasemore)   **$425**   **£250**

GEORGE A. GASKELL — The Lady Godiva — signed and dated 1875 — pencil and watercolour — 18½ x 12¾in.
(Christie's)   **$595**   **£320**

GASTINEAU — View Of Lee, Near Ilfracombe — 9½ x 12in.
(Lawrence)   **$140**   **£88**

HENRY GASTINEAU — A Continental River Landscape — signed and dated 1860 — watercolour — 13¼ x 17¾in.
(Sotheby, King & Chasemore)   **$528**   **£352**

HENRI GAUDIER-BRZESKA — Standing Female Nude — pen and brown ink — 15 x 9½in.
(Christie's)   **$570**   **£378**

HENRI GAUDIER-BRZESKA — Seated Male Nude — signed — pen and black ink — 14 x 9¼in.
(Christie's)   **$292**   **£194**

EDWARD GAY — Pause In The Day — signed and dated 1873 — oil on canvas — 23¼ x 34½in.
(Christie's)   **$1,760**   **£1,173**

HENRI GEGARTHEN — A Winter Landscape At Sunset — indistinctly signed and dated 1888 — on panel — 10¼ x 7¾in.
(Sotheby's)   **$1,098**   **£600**

JOHANN NEPOMUK GELLER — A Market Scene, Ringplatz In Dudweis — signed — 36½ x 54¼in.
(Christie's)   **$6,197**   **£4,104**

JOHANN NEPOMUK GELLER – A Market Scene – signed – on board – 11¼ x 15in.
(Christie's) **$2,511** **£1,620**

BERNARD DE GEMPT – After The Battle – signed – 28 x 50in.
(Sotheby Beresford Adams) **$185** **£110**

JOHN GENDALL – A Rocky Pool With Surrounding Trees – oil on canvas – 39½ x 50in.
(Hy. Duke & Son) **$2,162** **£1,250**

GENOESE SCHOOL, 17th century – The Rest On The Flight Into Egypt – 68½ x 48in.
(Sotheby's) **$29,700** **£19,800**

F. GENUTAT – The Sultan's Favourite – signed and dated 1911 – 66 x 43in.
(Christie's) **$5,832** **£3,240**

JEAN-LOUIS GERARD, After – Portrait Of Napoleon I – 23 x 19in.
(Sotheby Beresford Adams) **$1,663** **£990**

LEON FRANCOIS GERARD – A Riverside Picnic – bears signature and dated 1846 – on panel – 8½ x 16in.
(Sotheby's) $836   £550

THEODORE GERARD – A Mother And Child – signed and dated 1867 – on panel – 12½ x 9¼in.
(Christie's) $2,244   £1,512

CHARLES MARCH GERE – 'Half Portrait Of A Young Woman With Veil And White Blouse' – signed and dated 1891 – oil on canvas – 20½ x 16½in.
(W. H. Lane & Son) $104   £60

GERMAN SCHOOL – The Magic Act – indistinctly signed – oil on canvas – 28½ x 38in.
(Butterfield's) $2,000   £1,184

JEAN LEON GEROME – Mun Chak – 10¼ x 8¼in.
(Sotheby's) $9,240   £5,280

JEAN LEON GEROME – A Portrait Of Marie Gerome, nee Goupil – signed – 21¼ x 14¼in.
(Sotheby's) $78,925   £45,100

CHARLES GERRARD – Still Life, A Vase Of Yellow Roses, A Royal Lancastrian Vase, A Chinese Prunus Pattern Vase, With A William Morris Drape And A Classical Bust – signed and dated 1916 – watercolour – 60 x 51cm.
(Henry Spencer & Sons) $716   £400

GERTLER

MARK GERTLER – Study Of A Nude
Woman – signed and dated '32 – pastel
– 21½ x 17½in.
(Sotheby's)   **$946**   **£550**

PAUL JEAN GERVAIS – Antony And
Cleopatra – signed – 59 x 77½in.
(Sotheby's)   **$3,347**   **£1,870**

HENRY GERVEX – Mother And Child –
signed – pastel – 25¼ x 23½in.
*(Sotheby, King &
    Chasemore)*   **$560**   **£330**

LEO GESTEL – The Promenade –
signed and dated '06 – 77½ x 36½in.
(Christie's)   **$3,240**   **£2,160**

GHEERAERTS – Portrait Of A Gentleman,
Thought To Be John Dudley, Duke Of
Northumberland, Half Length, Wearing
Armour And A Ruff, A Coat-of-Arms Of
Lozenges To His Right – bears date 1594 –
23½ x 19½in.
(Sotheby's)   **$630**   **£420**

GHEERAERTS, The Younger – Portrait
Of Sir Thomas Fleming At The Age Of 64,
Three-Quarter Length, Wearing His Robes Of
Office And Holding A Parchment – dated
1608 – inscribed – on panel – 35¼ x 25¾in.
(Sotheby's)   **$684**   **£480**

GIAN GIANNI – Valetta Harbour –
signed and dated 1881 – 8½ x 26½in.
(Christie's) $1,166   £648

GIAN GIANNI – 'The Temple Of Apollo
Near Ghigoleio, Greece' – signed and
dated 1875, inscribed on the reverse – on
board – 11 x 19¾in.
(Christie's) $680   £378

GIAN GIANNI – Valetta By Moonlight –
signed – 7¼ x 16¼in.
(Sotheby's) $984   £550

GIAN GIANNI – Young Boys Watching
Boats Off Capri – signed and dated 1893
– on panel – 8 x 14½in.
(Sotheby's) $551   £308

GIAN GIANNI – Views In Naples –
signed – gouache – 16 x 17¼in.
*(Sotheby Beresford
   Adams)* $132   £77 Two

MARCUS GHEERAERTS, The Younger
– Portrait Of John Graves Of Beamsley,
Yorkshire – 35¾ x 26¾in.
(Sotheby's) $3,322   £2,200
PETER GHENT – Village Talk – signed
– 80 x 30in.
*(Sotheby Beresford
   Adams)* $114   £66

GIAN GIANNI – An Extensive View Of Valetta From The Sea – signed and dated
1880 – 18½ x 39¾in. *(Sotheby's)*
     $3,344   £2,200

GIAN GIANNI – Valetta At Sunset – signed and dated 1887 – 7¼ x 16¼in.
(Sotheby's)
     $1,063   £594

SANFORD ROBINSON GIFFORD –
Long Branch – signed and dated 1864,
signed and inscribed on the reverse –
oil on canvas – 11 x 19in.
(William Doyle
Galleries)   **$25,000 £14,792**
SIR JOHN GILBERT – The Battle – sig-
ned and dated 1871 – watercolour height-
ened with white – 20¼ x 35½in.
(Christie's)   **$648   £432**
SIR JOHN GILBERT – The Prisoners
– signed and dated 1870 – watercolour
and bodycolour – 16¾ x 26¾in.
(Christie's)   **$544   £324**
GODFREY DOUGLAS GILES – Mares
And Foals – signed, inscribed and dated
1904 – 20 x 24in.
(Sotheby Beresford
Adams)   **$646   £385**
ERIC GILL – Nude – pencil – 8½ x
11½in.
(Sotheby's)   **$143   £99**

WILHELM GIMMI – Nature Morte Aux
Harengs – signed – oil on canvas – 38 x
46cm.
(Germann
Auktionshaus) **$7,514   £4,696**

WILHELM GIMMI – Demi-Nu Au
Peignoir – signed and dated 1924 – oil
on canvas – 46 x 55cm.
(Germann
Auktionshaus) **$9,723   £6,077**

ERNEST GUSTAVE GIRARDOT – 'In
Reverie Sweet' – inscribed – oil on can-
vas – 19 x 15½in.
(Sotheby, King &
Chasemore)   **$1,018   £572**

CAR. FAUST GIUSTO – Girl With Water Jugs – signed and dated '97 – oil on panel – 11 x 7in.
(Butterfield's)   **$425**   **£251**
JOHN HAMILTON GLASS – St. Monance Fife – signed – watercolour – 9½ x 13in.
(Christie's &
Edmiston's)   **$77**   **£48**
JOHN HAMILTON GLASS – A Fishing Village – signed – heightened with bodycolour – 13½ x 20½in.
(Sotheby Beresford
Adams)   **$92**   **£55**

ALFRED AUGUSTUS GLENDENNING – River Landscapes – signed with monogram – oil on board – 12 x 8in.
(Sotheby, King &
Chasemore)   **$892**   **£572**

ARTHUR GLENNIE – On The Tiber, Rome – signed and inscribed – watercolour over pencil with stopping out – 14¾ x 21¼in. *(Sotheby's)*   **$610 £396**

GLOVER

JOHN GLOVER – Landscape, With
Wooded Scene And Cattle At A Pool –
dated 1799 – 6½ x 10in.
(Hall, Wateridge &
Owen)   **$840   £480**

GLUCK – Portrait Of Georgina Cookson
– signed – 11 x 9in.
(Sotheby's)   **$925   £638**

E. R. GOBLET – Springtime – signed –
on panel – 39 x 13½in.
(Sotheby Beresford
Adams)   **$321   £187**

W. C. GODDARD – A View Of Staithes,
Yorkshire – inscribed and signed 1899 –
watercolour – 12 x 19in.
(Hy. Duke &
Son)   **$164   £95**

W. C. GODDARD – An Estuary With Barges In The Foreground – oil on board –
15 x 21in.
(Hy. Duke &
Son)   **$69   £40**

JOHN WILLIAM GODWARD – The
Toilet – signed and dated 1900 – 63½ x
30½in.
(Sotheby's)   **$57,750 £33,000**

JOHN WILLIAM GODWARD – Perilla
– signed and dated 1911 – 20 x 15¾in.
(Christie's)   **$3,180   £2,052**

JOHN WILLIAM GODWARD – The Engagement Ring Or The Betrothal Ring –
signed and dated 1888 – 16 x 18in.
(Sotheby's)   **$23,100 £13,200**

JOHN WILLIAM GODWARD – Contemplation – signed and dated 1922 – 50 x 30in.
(Sotheby's) **$19,250 £11,000**

FREDERICK E. J. GOFF – Norwich – signed and inscribed – watercolour with touches of bodycolour – 6 x 4¼in.
(Sotheby's) **$372 £242**

DAVID GOLDSCHMIDT – Piazza Della Loggia, (Brescia, Italien) – signed and dated 1966 – oil on canvas – 40 x 49.5cm.
(Germann Auktionshaus) **$1,680 £1,050**

GOODALL – A Street Scene – bears monogram and dated '65 – 19½ x 15¾in.
(Christie's) **$1,506 £972**

FREDERICK GOODALL – Sarah And Isaac – signed with monogram and dated 1879 – watercolour – 10 x 6¾in.
(Sotheby, King & Chasemore) **$216 £143**

GOODALL

FREDERICK GOODALL – Sheik Distributing Alms – signed and dated 1865 – watercolour over pencil, heightened with scratching out – 20 x 30in.
(Sotheby's) **$20,625 £13,750**

FREDERICK GOODALL – Ploughing With Oxen Near Gheza – signed with monogram and dated 1874 – watercolour heightened with white – 8½ x 22in.
(Christie's) **$2,283 £1,512**

J. GOODALL – Egyptian Views – signed – heightened with bodycolour – 7¾ x 13¾in.
(Sotheby Beresford Adams) **$71 £41 Pair**

ALBERT GOODWIN – The Citadel, Cairo – signed, inscribed and dated 1909 – 11 x 15½in.
(Sotheby's) **$2,763 £1,760**

ALBERT GOODWIN – San Giorgio Maggiore, Venice, From The Quay At The Arsenale – signed with monogram, inscribed and dated '91, pencil, pen and black ink and watercolour on buff paper – 6¾ x 10½in.
(Christie's) **$1,542 £918**

ALBERT GOODWIN – Fluelen, Lake Lucerne – signed and inscribed – 10¼ x 14½in.
(Christie's) **$4,077 £2,700**

ALBERT GOODWIN – Venice: Sunset – signed, inscribed and dated 1919 – watercolour and bodycolour on grey blue paper – 11¾ x 17½in.
(Christie's) **$4,354 £2,592**

ALBERT GOODWIN – Lucerne, The Rigi Beyond – inscribed – pencil, watercolour and bodycolour on blue paper – 5¼ x 7in.
(Christie's)   **$896**   **£594**

ALBERT GOODWIN – Mont Blanc From Near Geneva – signed and indistinctly inscribed – 10 x 14in.
(Christie's)   **$1,995**   **£1,188**

ALBERT GOODWIN – Grey Weather, Venice: View Along The Molo From The Riva Degli Schiavoni – signed with monogram and dated 1891 – grey ink and watercolour on pale grey green paper – 6¼ x 10½in.
(Christie's)   **$1,632**   **$972**

ALBERT GOODWIN – Hastings – signed and dated 1910 – watercolour heightened with white – 9¾ x 14½in.
(Sotheby, King & Chasemore)   **$1,544**   **£990**

ALBERT GOODWIN – 'A View Of Lake Lucerne' – signed with monogram and dated 1890 – watercolour – 11 x 17½in. *(Sotheby, King & Chasemore)*
$2,552 £1,595

GOODWIN

ALBERT GOODWIN — St. Mark's, Venice: The West Doors And The Piazzetta — signed with monogram and dated '91 — pencil and watercolour — 6¾ x 9¾in.
(Christie's) $4,354   £2,592

ALBERT GOODWIN — Iffley, Near Oxford — signed and dated 1908 — watercolour heightened with bodycolour — 10½ x 14½in.
(Sotheby, King & Chasemore) $1,160   £726

ALBERT GOODWIN — 'A Shepherd And His Flock' — signed with monogram and dated 1886 — watercolour — 13½ x 20in.
(Sotheby, King & Chasemore) $915   £572

ALBERT GOODWIN — The Jesuit Fathers, Palermo — signed and inscribed — watercolour with bodycolour — 7 x 9¾in.
(Sotheby's) $508   £330

ALBERT GOODWIN — 'Bonlac, Cairo' — signed and dated 1918 — 11¼ x 15¼in.
(Sotheby, King & Chasemore) $5,984   £3,740

ALBERT GOODWIN – Fruit Market, Venice – signed with monogram and dated 1872 – pencil and watercolour – 3¼ x 6¾in.
(Christie's)   **$398**   **£237**

ALBERT GOODWIN – Twilight, South Devon – signed and dated '66 – heightened with bodycolour – 8½ x 19¾in.
(Sotheby's)   **$542**   **£352**

ARTHUR CLIFTON GOODWIN – 'Spring Landscape' – signed – pastel on buff paper – 17 x 21in.
(Robert W. Skinner Inc.)   **$400**   **£250**

ARTHUR CLIFTON GOODWIN – 'Gloucester Harbor Scene' – signed – oil on canvas – 30 x 36in.
(Robert W. Skinner Inc.)   **$1,800**   **£1,125**

ARTHUR CLIFTON GOODWIN – 'Autumn Landscape, New Hampshire' – signed – pastel on linen – 18½ x 12½in.
(Robert W. Skinner Inc.)   **$1,050**   **£656**

ARTHUR CLIFTON GOODWIN – 'Tremont Street, Winter' – signed – oil on board – 13¾ x 19½in.
(Robert W. Skinner Inc.)   **$5,500**   **£3,437**

EDWARD GOODWIN – View In The Lakes – signed and dated 1805 – pen and ink with sepia wash – 11¼ x 18½in.
(Sotheby Beresford Adams)   **$52**   **£30**

JAN GOSSAERT, Called Mabuse – Christ Crucified – on panel – 13½ x 9in.
(Sotheby's)   **$23,100**   **£15,400**

SYLVIA GOSSE – Two Women Gossiping – signed – 18¾ x 13in.
(Sotheby's) **$1,475** **£858**

CAROLINE BURLAND GOTCH – 'Fishing Boats On Gwavas Lake' – oil on board – 9½ x 6in.
(W. H. Lane & Son) **$147** **£85**

THOMAS COOPER GOTCH – 'St. Michael's Mount' – signed – watercolour – 5¼ x 8½in.
(W. H. Lane & Son) **$226** **£130**

THOMAS COOPER GOTCH – 'Cottage Interior With Woman Peeling Potatoes' – signed – oil on canvas – 15¾ x 20in.
(W. H. Lane & Son) **$9,048** **£5,200**

THOMAS COOPER GOTCH – 'Coastal Scene – Trefan Head, North Cornwall' – watercolour – 4 x 7½in.
(W. H. Lane & Son) **$52** **£30**

THOMAS COOPER GOTCH – 'Young Girls' – pencil drawings – 9 x 6¾in.
(W. H. Lane & Son) **$522** **£300 Pair**

THOMAS COOPER GOTCH – 'The Reunion' – charcoal drawings – 15½ x 11½in.
(W. H. Lane & Son) **$260** **£150**

FRIEDRICH KARL GOTSCH – Die Rotblonde – monogrammed, signed and dated 1926 – oil on canvas – 80 x 61cm.
(Germann Auktionshaus) **$15,027** **£9,392**

JEAN RICHARD GOUBIE – The Morning Ride – signed and dated 1890 – 21 x 31in.
(Christie's) **$8,970 £5,940**

ANDREW CARRICK GOW – Prepared For Trouble – signed and dated 1911 – watercolour and bodycolour – 10½ x 14½in.
(Christie's) **$423 £280**

A. GOWER – 'Rural Scene With Cottage And River' – signed – oil on canvas – 9¼ x 11½in.
(Bracketts) **$175 £110 Pair**

A. GOWERS – 'Canal Scene With Windmills' – signed – oil on canvas – 9½ x 11¾in.
(Bracketts) **$335 £210**

J. VAN GOYEN – A View Of Arnhem – on panel – 19 x 38in.
(Sotheby's) **$5,328 £3,080**

JAN VAN GOYEN – A Cottage Amid Dunes – signed and dated – on panel – 13 x 21¼in.
(Sotheby's) **$59,400 £39,600**

JAN VAN GOYEN – A River Landscape With A Ferry – signed – on panel – 18 x 27in.
(Sotheby's) **$84,150 £56,100**

GRABER

JOHN WILLIAM GOZZARD – At The
Forge; and A Wayside Inn – signed –
19½ x 29½in.
*(Sotheby Beresford
Adams)* **$1,478** **£880 Two**

OSCAR GRABER – Rustic Courtship
– signed and inscribed – on panel –
16 x 11½in.
*(Sotheby Beresford
Adams)* **$813** **£484**

ALFRED FITZWALTER GRACE – Cattle
Watering By A Stream – signed and dated
1873 – watercolour – 16 x 29in.
*(Sotheby, King &
Chasemore)* **$774** **£484**

ALFRED FITZWALTER GRACE – Horses
Watering By A Stream – signed and dated
1874 – watercolour – 16 x 29in.
*(Sotheby, King &
Chasemore)* **$564** **£353**

JAMES EDWARD GRACE – A Barge –
signed – 13½ x 9½in.
*(Sotheby Beresford
Adams)* **$19** **£11**

COLIN GRAEME – Landscape With
Highland Cattle And A Mallard – signed
and dated – oil – 24 x 36in.
*(Woolley &
Wallis)* **$900** **£540**

GEORGE GRAHAM – A Peaceful
Estuary – signed and dated 1916 – 34
x 45½in.
(Sotheby's) **$1,036** **£715**

WILLIAM GRAHAM – 'Arab Village' –
signed and dated 1881 and inscribed on
the reverse – oil on canvas – 11 x 18½in.
*(Robert W. Skinner
Inc.)* **$700** **£438**

DUNCAN GRANT – Still Life With Flowers In A Vase And A Guitar – signed –
16½ x 28¾in.
(Sotheby's) **$567** **£330**

DUNCAN GRANT – Spring Flowers In
A Vase – signed and dated '41 – 11¾ x
9½in.
(Sotheby's) **$756** **£440**

GORDON GRANT – Clearing After The
Rain – signed, inscribed on the reverse –
oil on masonite – 11¾ x 15¾in.
(Christie's) **$2,860** **£1,906**
WILLIAM GREGORY GRANT – 'Old
Boatshed' – watercolour – 26 x 33cm.
(Geoff K. Gray) **$27** **£16**

DUNCAN GRANT – A Vase Of Flowers
– signed – 26 x 24in.
(Sotheby's) **$1,276** **£880**

DOUGLAS STANNUS GRAY – 'Siesta'
– signed and dated 1924 – oil on canvas
– 22 x 18in.
*(Sotheby, King &
Chasemore)* **$1,122** **£748**

GEORGE GRAY – A Harbour Scene –
signed – oil on board – 8½ x 13¼in.
(Sotheby, King &
Chasemore) **$231** **£132**

KATE GRAY – Mother And Sleeping
Child – signed and dated 1850 – oil on
canvas – 22 x 18½in.
(Sotheby, King &
Chasemore) **$510** **£286**

KATE C. GRAY – A Young Man Seated
Upon A Log Watching A Procession Of
Girls And Young Women Gathering
Flowers On A Woodland Path, The Spire
Of A Church And A Town In The Middle
Distance – signed – 60 x 50in.
(Anderson &
Garland) **$3,006** **£1,800**

PERCY GRAY – Monterey Cypress – signed – watercolour on board – 15½ x 19½in.
(Butterfield's) **$3,250 £1,946**

TOM GRAY – 'Dining Alone' – signed and dated '71 – gouache on board – 18 x 23in.
(Robert W. Skinner Inc.) **$600 £375**

W. GRAY – Venetian Views – signed – 19 x 29in.
(Sotheby Beresford Adams) **$340 £198** Two

ROLAND GREEN – 'Pheasants' – watercolour – 14¼ x 18¾in.
(Hilhams) **$500 £290**

WILLIAM GREEN – A View Across Derwentwater At Dusk, Sailing Boats On The Still Waters Of The Lake – watercolour – 9 x 13¼in.
(Anderson & Garland) **$102 £64**

KATE GREENAWAY – Phyllis And Baby – signed with initials, inscribed and dated 1883 – pencil and watercolour – 4 x 4¼in.
(Christie's) **$2,177 £1,296**

CHARLES EDWIN LEWIS GREEN – 'Swampscott Dories' – signed – oil on canvas – 10 x 14in. *(Robert W. Skinner Inc.)* **$2,000 £1,250**

GREENHAM

ROBERT GREENHAM – Albert Einstein
– signed, inscribed and dated '47 also
inscribed on the reverse – on board – 14
x 12in.
(Sotheby's) **$303** **£209**

EDWARD JOHN GREGORY – A Siesta
– signed – 12½ x 15in.
(Sotheby's) **$508** **£330**

T. GREGORY – A Cottage Garden
– signed – 13 x 11in.
(Sotheby's) **$592** **£385**

JAMES GREIG – 'Old Shrewsbury' –
signed – watercolour – 18¾ x 14½in.
(Olivers) **$17** **£10**
GREUZE, After – 'The Milkmaid' –
39.5 x 32in.
*(Woolley &
Wallis)* **$258** **£155**

**JEAN-BAPTISTE GREUZE, Attributed
to** – A Young Girl With A Dog – on
panel – 18½ x 15¼in.
(Sotheby's) **$1,337** **£880**

ORAZIO GREVENBROECK – Southern
Harbour Scenes – signed – 18¾ x 28¾in.
(Sotheby's) **$4,186** **£2,420 Pair**

CHARLES MACIVOR GRIERSON –
Held By A Thread – signed and dated
1894 – watercolour – 24½ x 31½in.
(Sotheby's) **$542** **£352**

ABEL GRIMMER – A Riverside Village
In Autumn – on panel – 10¼ x 14¼in.
(Sotheby's) **$19,800** **£13,200**

ROBERT GRIFFIER – Estuary Scenes
By Moonlight – signed – 20¾ x 25½in.
(Sotheby's) **$21,450** **£14,300 Pair**

ABEL GRIMMER – The Interior Of A
Gothic Church With A Franciscan Preaching – signed and dated – on panel – 9¾
x 11½in.
(Sotheby's) **$6,270** **£4,180**

GRIMSHAW

JOHN ATKINSON GRIMSHAW – 'Ye Ladye Bountifulle' – signed and dated 1884, inscribed on reverse – oil on canvas – 20 x 30in.
(Sotheby, King & Chasemore) **$6,545 £3,740**

ATKINSON GRIMSHAW – View Of Liverpool By Night – signed, and signed and inscribed on the reverse – 12 x 18in.
(Christie's) **$5,859 £3,780**

JOHN ATKINSON GRIMSHAW – Liverpool Customs House – signed, inscribed on the reverse – 23½ x 35½in.
(Sotheby Beresford Adams) **$21,252 £12,650**

JOHN ATKINSON GRIMSHAW – Blea Tarn – signed – oil on board – 14 x 18in.
(Woolley & Wallis) **$4,004 £2,600**

JOHN ATKINSON GRIMSHAW – Nab Scar – signed and dated 1864 also inscribed on the reverse – on board – 25 x 30in.
(Sotheby's) **$82,500 £55,000**

JOHN ATKINSON GRIMSHAW – St. Paul's From Ludgate Circus – signed and dated 1885 – 36 x 24in.
(Sotheby's) **$32,175** **£21,450**

JOHN ATKINSON GRIMSHAW – An Extensive View Of Leeds Dockland At Evening – signed and dated 1880 – oil – 7¾ x 16¼in.
(Anderson & Garland) **$2,480** **£1,550**

JOHN ATKINSON GRIMSHAW – Greenock By Lamplight – signed, signed and inscribed on the reverse – 24 x 36in.
(Sotheby's) **$34,650** **£23,100**

FERDINAND E. GRONE – A Goose Girl With Her Gaggle In A Landscape On A Summers Day – signed – water-colour – 49 x 33cm.
(Osmond, Tricks) **$585** **£340**

A. DE GROOTE – A Frozen River Land-scape With Skaters By A Village – on panel – 9½ x 12½in.
(Christie's) **$680** **£378**

THE MASTER OF THE VAN GROOTE ADORATION – The Adoration Of The Magi – on panel – 25½ x 21¾in.
(Sotheby's) **$22,455** **£12,980**

ROBERT E. GROVES – In Mazagaw, Morocco – signed – on board – 12 x 9¾in.
(Sotheby's) **$378** **£220**

GRUBACS

GRUBACS – Saint Mark's Square, Venice
– 8 x 11in.
(Christie's)   **$776**   **£432**

MARCEL GRUBAS – Venice By Day
And Night – signed – on board – 10½
x 5½in.
*(Sotheby Beresford
     Adams)*   **$416**   **£242** Two

CHARLES PAUL GRUPPE – Cloudy Day
On The Canal – signed – oil on canvas –
22½ x 33¼in.
(Christie's)   **$3,080**   **£2,053**

M. GRUETZNER – A Split Decision –
signed – oil on canvas – 27 x 20¾in.
*(Sotheby, King &
    Chasemore)*   **$1,527**   **£858**

EDUARD VON GRUTZNER – Delivering
The Daily Provisions – signed and dated
'95 – 20½ x 16½in.
(Sotheby's)   **$26,752** **£17,600**

CHARLES PAUL GRUPPE – Port Scene – signed – oil on canvas – 26 x 30in.
(Butterfield's)   **$3,000 £1,796**

GIACOMO GUARDI – Venice, The Rialto Bridge – 9½ x 13¾in. *(Sotheby's)* **$4,620 £3,080**

ADRIEN DE GRYFF – Farmyard Scenes – signed – on panel – 10½ x 14½in. *(Sotheby's)* **$6,688 £4,400 Pair**

GABRIEL GUAY – Fishing On The Seine – signed and dated 1876 – 15¾ x 20¾in. *(Christie's)* **$16,308 £10,800**

OSWALDO GUAYASAMIN – Dolorosa – signed, signed on the reverse – oil on canvas – 25 x 13in. *(Butterfield's)* **$1,000 £599**

FRANCESCO GUARDI – A Landscape Caprice With Roman Ruins; and A Caprice With A Ruined Arch And A Tempietto – 18½ x 13½in. *(Sotheby's)* **$209,330 £121,000 Pair**

MAX GUBLER – Der Kunstler Und Sein Modell – signed – oil on canvas – 73 x 92cm. *(Germann Auktionshaus)* **$15,028 £9,392**

GUDIN

JEAN ANTOINE THEODORE GUDIN
– 'A Royal Greeting' – signed and
dated 1871 – 45½ x 63in.
(Sotheby, King &
Chasemore) **$2,992** **£1,760**

THEODORE GUDIN – The Boatyard –
signed – on panel – 15½ x 25½in.
(Sotheby's) **$984** **£550**
GUERCINO, After – The Madonna And
Child With A Goldfinch – 30 x 22in.
(Sotheby Beresford
Adams) **$1,256** **£748**

CARL ADOLF GUGEL – A Portrait
Of A Mother With Her Two Sons –
signed – 45½ x 39¼in.
(Sotheby's) **$1,004** **£660**
**JEAN BAPTISTE ARMAND
GUILLAUMIN** – Agay, Au Pied Du
Dramont – signed – oil on canvas – 25¾
x 32in.
(William Doyle
Galleries) **$11,000** **£6,508**

JEAN BAPTISTE ANTOINE GUILLEMET
– Mother And Child Watching A Bird –
signed – oil on panel – 14¼ x 10¾in.
(William Doyle
Galleries) **$1,600** **£946**
JEAN BAPTISTE ANTOINE GUILLEMET
– A River Landscape – signed – 21½ x
29in.
(Christie's) **$4,276** **£2,376**
T. B. GURNELL – A Still Life Study,
Grapes, Peaches, Pears, Melons And
Plums Arranged Upon A Carved Table, A
Landscape Lit By The Setting Sun Visible
In The Background – signed and dated
1862 – 29½in. diam.
(Anderson &
Garland) **$768** **£460**

G. GURNEY – 'Wooded Landscape'; and
'Coastal Landscape' – watercolour – 9½
x 15in. and 12½ x 11¾in.
(Bracketts) **$12** **£8 Pair**

GIUSEPPE GUZZARDI – Musketeers
Keeping Watch – signed and dated
1878 – oil on canvas – 13½ x 9½in.
(Butterfield's) **$800** **£473**

P. GYSELS – Travellers On A Road
Beside A Wood – on metal – 6½ x 8¼in.
(Sotheby's) **$13,320** **£7,700**

WILLIAM FREDERICK DE HAAS –
Strolling At High Tide – signed and dated
'77 – oil on canvas – 15 x 26in.
*(William Doyle
    Galleries)* **$2,500 £1,479**

J. HACKERT – A Hawking Party In A
Wooded Landscape – 27¾ x 24in.
*(Sotheby Beresford
    Adams)* **$2,956 £1,760**

W. HACKSTOUN – 'Figures In A Cornfield Before A Wooded Ruin' – dated
1897 – watercolour – 13¼ x 18¼in.
*(W. H. Lane &
    Son)* **$70 £40**

KARL HAAG – A Romantic Distraction
– signed – 39 x 31¼in.
(Christie's) **$1,546 £864**

REMI VAN HAANEN, Attributed to –
A Watermill In An Extensive Landscape
– 25¼ x 33¾in.
(Sotheby's) **$1,870 £1,045**

TREVOR HADDON – 'The Lady Of The
Manor' – oil on board – 15½ x 23in.
*(Sotheby, King &
    Chasemore)* **$1,144 £715**

PARKER HAGARTY – A Wet Day –
signed – 8 x 15in.
*(Sotheby Beresford
    Adams)* **$267 £154**

**MAURITZ FREDERICK HENDRICK
DE HAAS** – Rowing To Shore By Moonlight – signed and dated '75 – oil on
canvas – 12¼ x 20in.
*(William Doyle
    Galleries)* **$5,000 £2,958**

**MAURITZ FREDERICK HENDRICK DE
HAAS** – Westhampton Beach – oil on
canvas – 18 x 21½in.
(Christie's) **$715 £476**

JOSHUA ANDERSON HAGUE – Two
Children Picking Flowers On A Hill –
signed – oil on canvas – 66 x 92cm.
*(Sotheby, King &
    Chasemore)* **$255 £150**

HAITE

GEORGE CHARLES HAITE – Venice – signed and dated 1903 – 4¼ x 7in. *(Sotheby Beresford Adams)* $124 £71

WILLIAM MATTHEW HALE – Bristol Cathedral With College Green With Trees And Figures In The Foreground, At Sunset – signed and dated 1910 – oil on canvas – 124 x 83cm. *(Osmond, Tricks)* $653 £380

CLIFFORD HALL – Kneeling Nude – signed and dated 1963 – coloured chalks on buff paper – 21½ x 24½in. *(Sotheby Beresford Adams)* $92 £55

G. L. HALL – A Stormy Scene – dated 1878 – 15½ x 27½in. *(Lawrence)* $43 £27

S. E. HALL – The Crest Of The Moor – signed and inscribed – 9½ x 29in. *(Sotheby Beresford Adams)* $18 £11

HARRY HALL – Rataplan A Chestnut Racehorse, With Joseph Dawson On Newmarket Heath – 22½ x 29½in. *(Sotheby's)* $5,980 £3,960

WINIFRED HALL – The Drover's Cart – signed – 8½ x 14in. *(Sotheby Beresford Adams)* $86 £50

KEELEY HALSWELLE – On The Footpath, Sonning – signed and dated – oil – 24 x 13.5in. *(Woolley & Wallis)* $566 £320

DIRCK HALS – An Elegant Company – indistinctly signed – on panel – 12¼ x 15½in. *(Sotheby's)* $10,656 £6,160

KEELEY HALSWELLE – 'Venice' – signed and dated 1873 – oil on canvas – 13½ x 21¼in. *(Sotheby, King & Chasemore)*   **$770 £440**

ANDRE HAMBOURG – Etretat – Les Planches – signed – oil on canvas – 23¼ x 28¼in. *(Sotheby's)*   **$2,090 £1,375**

HAMILTON

EDWARD W. D. HAMILTON – 'Gray Day In France' – signed – oil on canvas – 24 x 20in.
(Robert W. Skinner Inc.) **$2,100** **£1,312**

HAMILTON HAMILTON – Spring Meadow – signed – oil on canvas – 20 x 24in.
(Christie's) **$2,090** **£1,393**

JAMES HAMILTON – Squally Weather – signed, signed, dated '76 and inscribed on the reverse – oil on canvas – 32¼ x 42in.
(Christie's) **$2,640** **£1,760**

JAMES HAMILTON – View Across The Golden Gate – signed – oil on canvas – 7 x 11½in.
(Butterfield's) **$425** **£250**

JOHANN GEORG HAMILTON – Still Lives Of Birds – 15 x 19in.
(Sotheby's) **$2,842** **£1,870 Two**

GERTRUDE E. DEMAIN HAMMOND – Ten Vestal Virgins On Temple Steps – signed and dated 1888 – watercolour – 12 x 31in.
(Edgar Horne) **$1,480** **£980**

T. HAND – A Winter Landscape With Figures Skating By A Cottage – on panel – 12 x 16¼in.
(Christie's) **$699** **£378**

WILLIAM LEE HANKEY — A Spanish
Street — signed — 20 x 24in.
(Sotheby's) **$1,355** **£935**

WILLIAM LEE HANKEY — She Was The
Daughter Of A Cottager — signed — 23½
x 19¼in.
(Sotheby's) **$10,595** **£6,160**

WILLIAM LEE HANKEY — Mother
And Child — signed and dated 1904 —
watercolour over pencil — 11 x 7in.
(Sotheby's) **$1,595** **£1,100**

WILLIAM LEE HANKEY — A Trio — signed — pencil and watercolour — 19½ x
16¼in.
(Sotheby's) **$756** **£440**

A. HANNEMAN — Portrait Of A Young
Girl And A Child — 45½ x 37in.
(Sotheby's) **$5,297** **£3,080**

HANSEN

NIELS CHRISTIAN HANSEN – Copenhagen, Children Playing Near The Town Hall – signed and dated 1916 – 11½ x 15in.
(Sotheby's)   **$1,087   £715**

JAMES DUFFIELD HARDING – Freyberg, Switzerland – signed – on panel – 14½ x 21½in.
(Sotheby's)   **$2,325   £1,540**

CYRIL HARDY – A Spanish Street – signed – 11 x 7¼in.
(Anderson & Garland)   **$120   £75**

DUDLEY HARDY – In The Stocks – signed – grisaille, heightened with white – 14 x 10in.
(Sotheby Beresford Adams)   **$19   £11**

FREDERICK DANIEL HARDY – Stealing Cherries – signed – on panel – 9¼ x 11½in.
(Sotheby Beresford Adams)   **$5,544   £3,300**

DAVID HARDY – Threading A Needle; and A Smoke And A Read – signed and dated 1864 – on panel – 8 x 6in. *(Sotheby's)*   **$702 £462 Two**

FREDERICK DANIEL HARDY – Diamonds Are Trumps – signed and dated 1903 – on panel – 13½ x 18in. *(Christie's)* **$2,678 £1,728**

FREDERICK DANIEL HARDY – The Unexpected Visitor – signed and dated 1888 – 14½ x 20½in. *(Christie's)* **$2,510 £1,620**

FREDERICK DANIEL HARDY – Christmas Visitors – signed and dated 1860 – 24 x 32½in. *(Christie's)* **$14,580 £9,720**

JAMES HARDY – Two Hunting Dogs Sitting Next To A Catch Of Birds And Rabbits – signed and dated '79 – 20¾ x 29in. *(Du Mouchelles)* **$11,000 £6,470**

JAMES HARDY, JNR. – Dead Game In The Larder – signed – watercolour heightened with white – 12¾ x 20¼in. *(Christie's)* **$689 £410**

HARDY

JAMES HARDY, JNR. – 'The Hard Sum', A Poor School Boy Working Out A Sum On His Slate – signed and dated '60 – watercolour – 17.5 x 24cm.
(Osmond,
Tricks) $498 £290

JAMES HARDY, JNR. – Their Masters Glove – signed – oil on canvas – 13¼ x 17¼in.
(Edgar Horne) $906 £600

THOMAS BUSH HARDY – Near Ryde, Isle Of Wight – signed and dated 1891 – watercolour over traces of pencil heightened with bodycolour – 10¼ x 13¾in.
(Sotheby's) $592 £385

THOMAS BUSH HARDY – 'Off Calais' – signed and inscribed – watercolour with scratching out – 19½ x 29½in.
(Sotheby, King &
Chasemore) $759 £506

THOMAS BUSH HARDY – Calais Pier; and Boulogne – signed and dated 1883 – heightened with white – 8 x 18in.
(Sotheby's) **$1,185** **£770 Pair**

THOMAS BUSH HARDY – Dutch Fish Boats, Extensive Estuary Scene With A Group Of Fishing Boats Drawn Up On A Sand Spit – signed, inscribed and dated 1895 – watercolour – 36.5 x 77cm.
(Henry Spencer &
Sons) **$1,074** **£600**

THOMAS BUSH HARDY – Dutch Coast – signed and dated 1895 – heightened with white – 9 x 18in.
(Sotheby's) **$1,105** **£770**

THOMAS BUSH HARDY – 'Nearing Home', Evening On The Grand Canal – signed, dated and inscribed – watercolour – 12 x 29in.
(Woolley &
Wallis) **$584** **£330**

THOMAS BUSH HARDY – 'Off Sheerness'
– signed and inscribed – watercolour with
scratching out – 12¾ x 23¼in.
(Sotheby, King &
Chasemore)   **$445**   **£297**

THOMAS BUSH HARDY – 'The Drudge',
Laden Donkey – initialled – watercolour
– 4 x 6in.
(Hilhams)   **$128**   **£80**

THOMAS BUSH HARDY – 'Clearing A
Wreck, Wissant, Picardy' – signed and
inscribed – watercolour heightened with
bodycolour – 12 x 19in.
(Sotheby, King &
Chasemore)   **$943**   **£539**

THOMAS BUSH HARDY – Entrance
To The Hamoaze, Plymouth – signed
– heightened with white – 9 x 28in.
(Sotheby's)   **$1,863**   **£1,210**

THOMAS BUSH HARDY – Shipping In A Rough Sea – signed – watercolour –
12¾ x 38¼in.   *(Sotheby, King & Chasemore)*
                                            $790 £452

HARFORD

ALFRED HARFORD – Langdale Pikes
– signed – 19½ x 29½in.
*(Sotheby Beresford
Adams)* **$174** **£104**

EDWARD HARGITT – Drovers With
Highland Cattle On A Mountain Road
– signed and dated 1867 – watercolour
heightened with white – 15½ x 23½in.
(Christie's) **$728** **£432**

W. H. HARKER – Trooper Of The 21st
Lancers – signed and inscribed – 12¾ x
9½in.
*(Laurence & Martin
Taylor)* **$118** **£70**

ALEXIS ALEXEIEVICH HARLAMOFF –
Devotion – signed – 21¾ x 17¼in.
(Christie's) **$972** **£540**

HENRI HARPIGNIES – Environs De
Menton, Le Royal – signed and dated
1904 – oil on canvas – 64 x 79.5cm.
*(Germann
Auktionshaus)* **$5,745** **£3,590**

HENRI HARPIGNIES – Paysage Fluvial
– signed – oil on canvas – 81.5 x 122cm.
*(Germann
Auktionshaus)* **$12,375** **£7,735**

HENRI JOSEPH HARPIGNIES – A River
Landscape At Dusk – signed and dated
1910 – 14¾ x 21½in.
(Sotheby's) **$2,424** **£1,595**

HENRI JOSEPH HARPIGNIES – A View In The Campagna – signed and dated 1896 – 25 x 31in.
(Lawrence) **$2,710** **£1,705**

HENRI JOSEPH HARPIGNIES – Cattle In Watermeadows – signed and dated 1882 – 16½ x 31¾in.
(Sotheby's) **$32,725** **£18,700**

CHARLES HARMONY HARRISON – Sailing On The Broads – signed and dated – watercolour – 14 x 22in.
(Sotheby, King & Chasemore) **$789** **£506 Pair**

CHARLES HARMONY HARRISON – Pastoral Scene, Elderly Drover With Cattle And Calf In Landscape – watercolour – 9¾ x 18in.
(Hilhams) **$432** **£250**

CHARLES HARMONY HARRISON – 'Yarmouth Quayside' – watercolour and wash – 18 x 27¾in.
(Hilhams) **$294** **£170**

CHARLES HARMONY HARRISON – 'Blakeney Quay', Moored Sailing Boat And Barge At The Anchor & Hope – watercolour – 14¼ x 20¼in.
(Hilhams) **$432** **£250**

CHARLES HARMONY HARRISON – 'Quiet Backwater' – watercolour – 22 x 35½in.
(Hilhams) **$847** **£490**

H. ST. JOHN HARRISON – Sweden From Meulenborg, Denmark – 9 x 13½in.
(Lawrence) **$70** **£44**

MARY KENT HARRISON – Bedfordshire Village – signed and dated '48 – 19¼ x 27¼in.
(Sotheby's) **$558** **£385**

ALFRED HENRY HART – The Old Town Hall, Bridport – signed – watercolour – 10 x 11in.
(Lawrence) **$148** **£93**

WILLIAM HART – 'Mountainous Landscape' – signed and dated '67 – oil on board – 10in. diam.
(Stalker & Boos) **$2,300** **£1,438**

WILLIAM M. HART – Figures Seated With Rocky Coast Beyond Nahant – signed and dated 1887 – oil on canvas – 13¼ x 21½in.
(Butterfield's)   **$6,500**   **£3,846**

HENRY ALBERT HARTLAND – View Near Dolgellau – signed – 13 x 19in.
*(Sotheby Beresford
        Adams)*   **$160**   **£93**

HAROLD HARVEY – Portrait Of A Young Girl – signed and dated 1909 – black chalk – 19¾ x 14½in.
(Sotheby's)   **$662**   **£382**

HAROLD HARVEY – 'Titbits' – signed and dated 1929 – oil on canvas – 24 x 20in.
*(Sotheby, King &
        Chasemore)*   **$1,480**   **£825**

HAROLD HARVEY – Portrait Of The Artist's Wife, Gertrude, In A Coloured Shawl – signed and dated 1922 – 29½ x 19½in.
(Sotheby's)   **$667**   **£363**

HAROLD HARVEY – 'Coloured Wools'
– signed, dated 1919 and inscribed on a
label on the reverse – 22 x 30in.
(Sotheby, King &
Chasemore) $8,789   £5,170

HAROLD HARVEY – Janie – signed and
dated 1923 – oil on canvas – 20 x 30in.
(Sotheby, King &
Chasemore) $1,958   £1,100

HAROLD HARVEY – A Cornish View
Across A River – signed and dated 1915 –
oil on canvas – 20 x 18¼in.
(Sotheby, King &
Chasemore) $548   £308

HASSAM

FREDERICK CHILDE HASSAM –
Sea And Rocks, Appledore, Isles Of
Shoals – signed, signed with monogram
and dated on the reverse – oil on canvas
– 20 x 14¼in.
(Butterfield's)   **$30,000 £17,964**

ROBERT HAVELL – The Admiral's
Regatta, Greenwich – on board – 11½ x
15in.
(Sotheby's)   **$4,650   £3,080**
W. HAVELL – Thames Scene – bears
signature and dated 1837 – oil – 18 x
24in.
(Woolley &
Wallis)   **$566   £320**
W. HAVELL – Mountain Torrents Land-
scape With Mountain Stream And Figures
– watercolor – 21½ x 16in.
(G. H. Bayley
& Sons)   **$346   £200**

LEWIS WELDEN HAWKINS – Summer
By The River – signed – 24 x 29in.
(Sotheby's)   **$1,515   £1,045**

FREDERICK CHILDE HASSAM – A Walk In The Park – signed – oil on canvas –
10½ x 12½in. *(William Doyle Galleries)*   **$42,000 £24,825**

C. HAYES – 'The Mill, Wareham Common' – watercolour – 21½ x 18in.
(G. H. Bayley
& Sons) **$1,176** **£680**

CLAUDE HAYES – A Rural Landscape With A Figure In A Punt On A River – signed – watercolour – 20½ x 29in.
(Geering &
Colyer) **$379** **£240**

CLAUDE HAYES – Landscape With A Figure On Horseback – signed – watercolour – 6.5 x 9.7in.
(Woolley &
Wallis) **$267** **£160**

CLAUDE HAYES – A Moorland Pond – signed – heightened with bodycolour – 10 x 17½in.
(Sotheby Beresford
Adams) **$249** **£143**

JESSICA HAYLLAR – Autumn Sunlight – signed and dated 1891 – 21 x 14½in.
(Sotheby's) **$48,125** **£27,500**

SIR GEORGE HAYTER – Portrait Of A Young Woman – signed and dated 1843 – oil on canvas – 30 x 24½in.
(Sotheby, King &
Chasemore) **$567** **£319**

JOHN HAYTER – Study Of A Nude – pencil heightened with red and white chalk – 11 x 12¼in.
(Sotheby's) **$72** **£40**

MARTIN JOHNSON HEADE – 'Golden Marguerites' – signed – oil on canvas – 24 x 15in.
(Robert W. Skinner
Inc.) **$45,000** **£28,125**

HEADE

MARTIN JOHNSON HEADE – Magnolia – signed – oil on canvas – 12 x 20in.
(Christie's)   **$66,000   £44,000**

WILLEM CLAESZ. HEDA, Follower of –
Still Life With A Coffee Pot, A Lemon And A Crab – bears signature and dated 1651 – on panel – 21½ x 23¾in.
(Sotheby's)   **$4,347   £2,860**

RALPH HEDLEY – A Good Book – signed and dated '97 – 24 x 29½in.
(Sotheby Beresford Adams)   **$628   £374**

RALPH HEDLEY – 'Autumn Leaves', An Elderly Gardener Shovelling Leaves Into A Wheelbarrow – signed with initials and dated '04 – pastel – 26¾ x 20½in.
(Anderson & Garland)   **$440   £275**

RALPH HEDLEY – Dr. Parker's First Sermon, An Open Air Prayer Meeting, Figures Gathered Round A Crude Timber Podium – inscribed on the reverse – 13½ x 11½in.
(Anderson & Garland)   **$120   £72**

CORNELIS DE HEEM – A Still Life With Grapes And Apples – signed – 14 x 10¼in.
(Sotheby's)   **$38,775   £25,850**

202

CORNELIS DE HEEM, Follower of —
A Still Life Of A Roemer, Fruits On A
Silver Plate; and A Still Life Of Fruits, A
Pipe And A Crab, All On A Table — 11¾
x 16½in.
(Sotheby's)   **$20,900 £13,750 Pair**

JAN DAVIDSZ. DE HEEM — A Still Life
With Roses And A Nautilus Shell — 21 x
24¾in.
(Sotheby's)   **$8,564 £4,950**

HEEMSKERK — Peasants Playing Cards —
9¾ x 11in.
(Sotheby's)   **$1,985 £1,050**

EGBERT VAN HEEMSKERK,
Follower of — A Girl Performing To An
Assembly — 23¾ x 17¾in.
(Sotheby's)   **$1,672 £1,100**

HEEMSKERK

HEEMSKERK – An Interior Of An Inn With Musicians And Other Figures – 20 x 22½in.
(Lawrence)   **$1,574**   **£990**

GERRIT VAN HEES – A Wooded Landscape With Cottages – 26 x 36in.
(Sotheby's)   **$6,090**   **£3,520**

KARL HEFFNER – Dusk Over A Wooded Lake – signed and inscribed – 5¾ x 10in.
(Sotheby's)   **$1,280**   **£715**

PAUL CESAR HELLEU – Symphonie En Blanc, A Portrait Of Yvonne Paulmier – signed – pastel – 62¼ x 70¼in.
(Sotheby's)   **$71,225**   **£40,700**

WILLEM DE HAAS HEMKEN – A Busy Dutch Street Scene – signed – on panel – 17 x 28in.
(Sotheby's)   **$4,680**   **£3,080**

WILLEM DE HAAS HEMKEN – Haarlem – signed – 30½ x 25¾in.
(Christie's)   **$2,138**   **£1,188**

WILLIAM HEMSLEY – The New Besom
– signed – pencil and watercolour heightened with white – 14¾ x 10¾in.
(Christie's)   **$1,054**   **£702**

WILLIAM HEMSLEY – Young Carol
Singers – signed – oil on canvas – 16
x 12in.
(Butterfield's)   **$1,600**   **£946**

BERNARD BENEDICT HEMY – The
Castle And Priory At Tynemouth
Viewed From The Beach Below, A Tug
Towing A Sailing Ship In The Middle
Distance – signed – watercolour – 16¼
x 28½in.
(Anderson &
Garland)   **$160**   **£100**

CHARLES NAPIER HEMY – 'Returning
Home After A Day's Fishing' – signed
with monogram – oil on canvas – 30 x
19½in.
(Sotheby, King &
Chasemore)   **$330**   **£220**

CHARLES NAPIER HEMY – 'Portrait
Of A Fisherman', Study For The
'Wrecker' – initialled and dated 1899 –
watercolour – 26½ x 17½in.
(W. H. Lane &
Son)   **$191**   **£110**

CHARLES NAPIER HEMY – Old Fisherman In Boat Catching A Mackerel – signed –
watercolour – 19 x 28in.
(Chrystals)   **$957**   **£520**

**THOMAS MARIE MADAWASKA
HEMY** – Steamers And Barges At The
Docks – signed and dated 1889 –
watercolour over pencil heightened
with bodycolour – 9¾ x 13¾in.
(Sotheby's)   **$270**   **£176**

C. C. HENDERSON – The Welleyn To London Stagecoach – oil on canvas – 21 x 30in.
(Sotheby, King & Chasemore) **$2,406** **£1,375**

CHARLES COOPER HENDERSON – At The Coach House Gates – signed – 16½ x 20¾in.
(Sotheby's) **$946** **£550**

CHARLES COOPER HENDERSON – 'The Stage Coach'; and 'A Horse-Drawn Wagon' – signed with monogram – watercolour – 5½ x 9in.
(Sotheby, King & Chasemore) **$346** **£231 Pair**

CHARLES COOPER HENDERSON – A French Coaching Scene – signed with monogram – watercolour – 13 x 19½in.
(Sotheby, King & Chasemore) **$360** **£226**

CHARLES COOPER HENDERSON –
Pulling Up To Un-Skid The Gloucester-
Hereford Mail On The Road – 17¾ x
26½in.
(Sotheby's)   **$1,661   £1,100**

CHARLES COOPER HENDERSON –
Changing Horses, The Louth-London
Royal Mail – 17¾ x 26½in.
(Sotheby's)   **$1,661   £1,100**

CHARLES COOPER HENDERSON –
Waking Up, The Chester-London Royal
Mail Travelling At Speed – 17¾ x 26½in.
(Sotheby's)   **$1,661   £1,100**

CHARLES COOPER HENDERSON –
Coaching Scenes, Departing From An
Inn; Changing Horses; In Open Country-
side; and Changing Horse In The Evening
– three signed and initials – oil – 26¾
x 35¼in.
*(Anderson &
   Garland)*   **$24,800   £15,000 Four**

CHARLES COOPER HENDERSON – All
Right, The Exeter-London Royal Mail
Pulling Up Outside A Coach House – 17¾
x 26½in.
(Sotheby's)   **$1,661   £1,100**

HENDERSON

CHARLES COOPER HENDERSON –
Behind Schedule, A Diligence On The
Open Road – 16½ x 20¾in.
(Sotheby's) **$1,337** **£880**

G. HENDRIKS – A Still Life With Finches
– signed, signed and inscribed on the
reverse – on panel – 15¼ x 11½in.
(Sotheby's) **$920** **£605**

W. HENLEY – Anglers On A River –
signed – oil on canvas – 24 x 42in.
*(Sotheby, King &
Chasemore)* **$969** **£570**

JEAN JACQUES HENNER – Artist
Model – signed – oil on canvas – 10 x
7½in.
(Butterfield's) **$1,000** **£591**

ADOLF HENNING – 'Play Time' – signed
and dated 1831 – oil on canvas – 18½ x
15½in.
*(Sotheby, King &
Chasemore)* **$2,062** **£1,375**

J. HENRY – Seaside Rides – one
indistinctly signed – heightened with
white – 7 x 9¾in.
*(Sotheby Beresford
Adams)* **$574** **£330 Pair**

FREDERICK HENRY HENSHAW –
Bolton Abbey, Yorkshire – signed –
14½ x 23½in.
*(Sotheby Beresford
Adams)* **$605** **£352**

T. HENWOOD – Study Of A Greyhound
– signed and dated 1854, inscribed on
reverse – oil on canvas – 18 x 22in.
*(Sotheby, King &
Chasemore)* **$1,193** **£683**

ALFRED HERBERT – Shipping In
Harbour – signed and dated 1854 –
pencil and watercolour – 8½ x 20½in.
(Christie's) **$325** **£194**

AUGUSTE HERBIN – OM – signed and
dated 1945 – oil on canvas – 80 x 60cm.
*(Germann
Auktionshaus)* **$10,386** **£6,490**

G. HEPPER – Kitchen Interior With Figures And Dogs – signed and dated –
oil – 28.2 x 36in. *(Woolley & Wallis)* **$1,102 £600**

HERDMAN

INNES HERDMAN – St. Luke's, Liverpool – signed and dated 1870 – heightened with bodycolour – 11¾ x 9¼in.
*(Sotheby Beresford
  Adams)*   **$154**   **£88**

W. P. HERDMAN – Watergate Street, Chester – signed – 10¾ x 14¾in.
*(Sotheby Beresford
  Adams)*   **$220**   **£132**

WILLIAM GAWIN HERDMAN – View From St. Augustine's Reach To St. Augustine's Church, With Bristol Cathedral Beyond – signed, inscribed and dated 1846 – 20 x 27in.
(Christie's)   **$1,546**   **£864**

FRANCISCO HERRERA – St. Peter – 21½ x 28½in.
(Sotheby's)   **$2,473**   **£1,430**

HERRING, After – Flying Dutchman, Winner Of The Derby In 1849 – inscribed – 19½ x 27in.
*(Sotheby Beresford
  Adams)*   **$333**   **£198**

BENJAMIN HERRING – A Lady Riding On A Coastal Path – signed and dated 1870 – grisaille – 12¼ x 10¼in.
(Christie's)   **$1,450**   **£810**

J. F. HERRING – A Hunting Scene – 'Full Cry' – 24 x 30in.
(Lawrence)   **$1,400**   **£880**

J. F. HERRING, JNR. – Two Shire Horses – signed and dated 1849 – oil on canvas – 42 x 36in.
*(Sotheby, King &
  Chasemore)*   **$2,805**   **£1,650**

J. F. HERRING, JNR. – 'Stable With Horse, Ducks And Chickens' – signed – oil on canvas – 14½ x 19½in.
*(Stalker &
  Boos)*   **$2,100**   **£1,363**

JOHN FREDERICK HERRING, JNR.,
After – 'Farmyard Scene' – oil on canvas
– 16 x 24in. .
(Sotheby, King &
Chasemore) **$739** **£462**

JOHN FREDERICK HERRING, JNR. –
Farmhorses Watering At A Pond; and
Horses and Pigs In A Farmyard – signed
– pencil and watercolour heightened
with white on grey paper – 8 x 11¾in.
(Christie's) **$725** **£432 Pair**

JOHN FREDERICK HERRING, SNR. –
A Bay Carriage Horse In A Stable Interior
– signed and dated 1843 – 27¼ x 35¾in.
(Sotheby's) **$15,136** **£8,800**

JOHN FREDERICK HERRING, JNR.,
Attributed to – 'Hounds In An Interior'
– oil on board on panel – 6 x 8in.
(Sotheby, King &
Chasemore) **$1,496** **£935**

JOHN FREDERICK HERRING, SNR. –
Merry Monarch, A Bay Racehorse, In A
Stable Interior – signed, inscribed and
dated 1845 – 27½ x 35½in.
(Sotheby's) **$26,488** **£15,400**

HERRING

JOHN FREDERICK HERRING, SNR. –
Slane, A Bay Racehorse With Davis Up –
24½ x 29¼in.
(Sotheby's)   **$7,475   £4,950**

JOHN FREDERICK HERRING, SNR.,
Attributed to – A Chestnut Pony, A
Dark Bay Coach Horse And A Dog In A
Stable – 27¼ x 35in.
(Sotheby's)   **$1,329   £880**

JOHN FREDERICK HERRING, .
Follower of – Horses And Poultry In
A Farmyard – 27¼ x 35¼in.
(Sotheby's)   **$1,254   £825**

OTTO HERSCHEL – A Portrait Of
A Young Dutch Girl – signed – 20¼ x
16in.
(Sotheby's)   **$585   £385**

HERMAN HERZOG – On The Maine
Coast – signed – oil on canvas – 18 x
25in.
(William Doyle
Galleries)   **$2,000   £1,183**

FRIEDRICH-JOSEPH-NICOLAI
HEYDENDAHL – A Winter Landscape
With Peasants At The Entrance To A
Village – signed – 26¾ x 38½in.
(Christie's)   **$7,776   £4,320**

SIR HANS HEYSEN – 'South Australia Landscape' – signed – pencil and wash – 12 x 20cm.
(Geoff K. Gray) **$768** **£456**

SIR HANS HEYSEN – 'A Town In Europe' – signed – pastel – 22 x 37cm.
(Geoff K. Gray) **$540** **£322**

F. HIDER – View In Killarney – 9 x 13in.
(Lawrence) **$74** **£46**

JESSE JEWHURST HILDER – 'The Northern Road' – signed – watercolour – 18.5 x 22.5cm.
(Geoff K. Gray) **$1,806** **£1,075**

RICHARD HILDER – A Wooded Landscape With A Herdsman And Cattle By A Pond – on panel – 14½ x 21in.
(Christie's) **$1,865** **£1,188**

RICHARD HILDER – A Cottage By A Stream, With A Woman Crossing A Bridge – signed – 12 x 16in.
(Christie's) **$2,706** **£1,512**

ROWLAND HILDER – The Journey To Town – signed and inscribed on the reverse – 20 x 24in.
(Phillips) **$225** **£120**

J. HIGHMORE – A Group Portrait Of A Gentleman And A Lady, Seated With Their Family, By A Fountain In A Park – 33 x 42¼in. *(Christie's)* **$5,594** **£3,024**

JAMES JOHN HILL – 'After A Long Walk' – signed – oil on canvas – 20 x 16in. *(Sotheby, King & Chasemore)* **$510** **£286**

KATE E. HILL – Self Portrait – signed with initials and dated 1894 – 16 x 11in. *(Sotheby's)* **$270** **£176**

JUSTUS HILL – 'Well-Fed' – signed – oil on board – 10 x 8in. *(Sotheby, King & Chasemore)* **$442** **£260**

LEONARD RAVEN HILL – 'The Ambush' – signed and dated 1887 – oil on canvas – 43¼ x 51½in. *(Sotheby, King & Chasemore)* **$334** **£209**

ROWLAND HENRY HILL – A Lake In Co. Galway – signed – oil – 12 x 16.5in. *(Woolley & Wallis)* **$208** **£125**

ROBERT HILLS – Studies Of Reapers Going To Work – inscribed – pencil and watercolour – 9 x 7½in. *(Christie's)* **$260** **£172**

W. HILTON – 'Southampton Paddle Boats At The Quay' – signed – watercolour – 14 x 23in.
(W. H. Lane & Son) $52   £30

HENRY GEORGE HINE – Seaford Bay – signed, inscribed and dated 1860 – watercolour – 11¼ x 17½in.
(Sotheby, King & Chasemore) $652   £418

WILLIAM EGERTON HINE – A Country Cottage – signed and dated 1876 – watercolour – 11 x 17¾in.
(Sotheby, King & Chasemore) $404   £253

FREDERICK HINES – Milkmaid In An Orchard, Apple Blossom And Ducks By A Pond – signed and dated – watercolour – 14¾ x 21¼in.
(Woolley & Wallis) $630   £410

FREDERICK HINES – Minding The Flock – signed,– gouache – 10 x 13½in.
(Sotheby Beresford Adams) $90   £52

M. HINES – Fishermen On A Beach Below Chalk Cliffs – signed – watercolour – 10½ x 7in.
(Anderson & Garland) $5   £3

THEODORE HINES – Pangbourne Weir On The Thames – signed, inscribed on the reverse – 15½ x 23½in.
(Sotheby Beresford Adams) $406   £242

THEODORE HINES – A Young Woman Seated Below A Tree At The Edge Of A Field Watching Reapers At Work, The Spire Of A Church On The Horizon Beyond – signed and dated '79 – watercolour – 15 x 21¾in.
(Anderson & Garland) $384   £240

E. HODGES – Oast House And Barn In A Landscape – oil – 15½ x 21½in.
(Lawrence) $78   £49

CARL HOFER – Sitzende Dame – signed and dated '43 – oil on canvas – 22 x 11½in.
(Sotheby's) $4,013   £2,640

HOGARTH

WILLIAM HOGARTH, Circle of –
Portrait Of Gustavus Hamilton, 2nd Viscount Boyne – 20¼ x 14½in.
(Sotheby's) **$1,245** **£825**

WILLIAM HOGARTH, Manner of –
'The Cook' – oil on canvas – 18 x 14in.
(Sotheby, King &
Chasemore) **$660** **£440**

WILLIAM HOGGATT – Belle Abbey Farm, Colby, Isle Of Man – signed – 15 x 19in.
(Chrystals) **$570** **£330**

WILLIAM HOGGATT – Old Kewaigue, Isle Of Man, Showing The Steam Train With Six Coaches – signed – watercolour – 18 x 22in.
(Chrystals) **$900** **£520**

WILLIAM HOGGATT – A Sunny Afternoon, Port St. Mary, Isle of Man – signed – 12 x 18in.
(Chrystals) **$544** **£340**

WILLIAM HOGGATT – On The Shore – signed – heightened with white – 9½ x 13½in.
(Sotheby Beresford
Adams) **$258** **£154**

WILLIAM HOGGATT – Silverburn, Isle Of Man – signed – watercolour – 15 x 22in.
(Chrystals) **$830** **£480**

HANS HOLBEIN, The Elder, Attributed to – Portrait Of A Man In A Black Cap, On A Blue Ground – inscribed – on panel – 8 x 6¼in.
(Sotheby's) **$72,600** **£48,400**

HOLBEIN, After – Portrait Of Mary Tudor – 30 x 24in.
(Sotheby Beresford Adams)   **$370**   **£220**

J. HOLDEN – Coming Into Harbour – signed and dated 1896 – coloured chalks – 24 x 38in.
(Sotheby's)   **$644**   **£418**

JOHN HOLDING – Near Crummock Water, Cumberland – signed – 9½ x 13in.
(Sotheby Beresford Adams)   **$240**   **£143**

JOHN HOLDING – Woodland View – signed – grisaille, heightened with white – 10 x 13½in.
(Sotheby Beresford Adams)   **$22**   **£13**

RANSOME G. HOLDREDGE – Indians With Wigwams In Wooded Landscape At Sunset – signed, inscribed on verso – oil – 30 x 51in.
(Woolley & Wallis)   **$1,062**   **£600**

HOLESWORTH – 'Ship At Dock' – signed – watercolour – 25 x 21cm.
(Geoff K. Gray)   **$135**   **£90**

HOLLAND – Flower Studies – signed – watercolour – 20 x 16in.
(Elliott & Green)   **$692**   **£400 Pair**

FRANCIS HOLMAN – A British Man Of War, H.M.S. Britannia, Firing A Salute – 21½ x 17¼in.
(Sotheby's)   **$2,080**   **£1,210**

FRANK HOLL – Her First Born – signed and dated 1877 – on board – 13¼ x 19¾in. *(Sotheby's)*   **$4,620**   **£3,080**

F. HOLMAN – British Men Of War In Line Off The Coast – 25 x 43in. *(Sotheby's)* **$1,135 £660**

LAURITS HOLST – Icebound – signed and dated 1889 – 29½ x 49¾in. *(Sotheby's)* **$1,254 £825**

NATHANIEL HONE – Portrait Of Dr. John Hinchliffe, Bishop of Peterborough – 29¼ x 24¼in. *(Sotheby's)* **$5,647 £3,740**

SCHOOL OF HONDECOETER – Study Of Pheasant, Turkey, Chicken And Wildfowl By A River Landscape – oil on canvas – 29 x 52½in. *(Edgar Horne)* **$5,889 £3,900**

BERNARD DE HOOG – 'Friendly Gossips' – signed – 24 x 22in.
(Christie's)   **$5,054   £2,808**

BERNARD DE HOOG – Mother And Children After Supper – signed – oil on canvas – 39½ x 31½in.
(Butterfield's)   **$3,750   £2,245**

JOHN HORACE HOOPER – The Watermill – signed and inscribed – oil on canvas – 24 x 42in.
(Sotheby, King & Chasemore)   **$1,887   £1,210**

ARTHUR HOPKINS – 'An Afterthought' – signed – watercolour – 18 x 12in.
(Lawrence)   **$332   £209**

EDWARD HOPPER – Study Of A Woman Knitting – pencil on paper – 9½ x 7¾in.
(Christie's)   **$4,400   £2,933**

JOHN HOPPNER – Portrait Of The Hon. Mary Rycroft – 29¼ x 24in.
(Sotheby's)   **$6,644   £4,400**

JAN JOSEPH HOREMANS, The Elder – 'Under The Mistletoe' – 18 x 21½in.
(Sotheby's)   **$1,371   £902**

HORLOR

GEORGE W. HORLOR – Ready For Sport – signed and dated 1861, inscribed on the reverse – 32 x 45½in.
(Sotheby Beresford
Adams)   **$4,343   £2,585**

GEORGE W. HORLOR – Waiting For Master – signed and dated 1881 – oil on canvas – 18 x 24in.
(Sotheby, King &
Chasemore)   **$1,347   £770**

EDWARD ATKINSON HORNEL – Weaving A Chaplet – signed and dated 1919 – 24 x 20in.
(Christie's &
Edmiston's)   **$5,440   £3,400**

EDWARD ATKINSON HORNEL – Burning Leaves – signed and dated 1906 – 21 x 8½in.
(Christie's &
Edmiston's)   **$6,400   £4,000**

EDWARD ATKINSON HORNEL – Girl Among Lambs In A Wood – signed and dated 1917 – canvas on panel – 16 x 19½in. *(Christie's & Edmiston's)*
$4,160 £2,600

EDWARD ATKINSON HORNEL – The Butterfly – signed and dated 1916 – 20 x 24in.
*(Christie's &
 Edmiston's)* **$4,800 £3,000**

EDWARD ATKINSON HORNEL – Two Girls Paddling By A Flowering Tree – signed and dated 1919 – 20 x 24in.
*(Christie's &
 Edmiston's)* **$4,800 £3,000**

JOHN CALLCOTT HORSLEY – 'Detected' – signed and dated 1868 – 28 x 36½in.
(Christie's) **$3,673 £2,052**

JOHN CALLCOTT HORSLEY – Cupboard Love – signed – 36 x 28in.
(Sotheby's) **$10,588 £6,050**

HORTON

GEORGE HORTON – 'Jarrow Rocks, South Shields' – signed – pencil sketch – 7 x 10in.
(Anderson & Garland)   **$28**   **£18**

GEORGE HORTON – 'On Shields Sands, Durham' – pencil sketch – 7 x 10in.
(Anderson & Garland)   **$42**   **£26**

GEORGE HORTON – 'On The Bents, South Shields' – signed – pencil sketch – 7 x 10in.
(Anderson & Garland)   **$26**   **£16**

ELMYR DE HORY, After Renoir – Jeune Fille Coussante – bears signature – 24 x 20in.
(Christie's S. Kensington)   **$1,800**   **£1,200**

GEORGE HOUSTON – Still Life With Peonies In A Blue Vase – signed – 24 x 20in.
(Christie's & Edmiston's)   **$120**   **£75**

JOHN ADAM HOUSTON – Wahabee Scheikh – signed and inscribed on an old label on the reverse – 24¼ x 18¼in.
(Christie's)   **$4,687**   **£3,024**

ROBERT HOUSTON – Loch Venacher And Ben Venue – signed – 15½ x 19in.
(Christie's & Edmiston's)   **$384**   **£240**

F. VAN DEN HOVE – Venice, A View Across The Lagoon Towards The Dogana – signed – 11½ x 19½in.
(Sotheby's)   **$602**   **£396**

WILLIAM HOWARD – 'Eel Pie Island' – signed and inscribed – oil on canvas – 24 x 42½in.
(Sotheby, King & Chasemore)   **$1,316**   **£748**

EDWIN HOYER – A Sailing Vessel And Steamship In Choppy Seas – signed and dated 1870 – oil on canvas – 20 x 30in.
(Hy. Duke & Son)   **$147**   **£85**

JAN VAN HUCHTENBERG – A Cavalry Skirmish Between Turks And Christians – signed with monogram and dated – 20 x 24in.
(Sotheby Beresford Adams)   **$4,065**   **£2,420**

ROBERT HUDSON, JNR. – The Village Of Edwinstowe On The Border Of The Dukeries, Nottinghamshire – signed and dated 1880 – oil on canvas – 33 x 48in.
(Hy. Duke & Son)   **$1,003**   **£580**

ARTHUR HUGHES – Poll The Milkmaid – signed and inscribed – 18½ x 34in.
(Sotheby's) **$4,950 £3,300**

WILLIAM HUGGINS – 'Cheshire Cattle' – signed and inscribed on reverse, and dated 1857 – 30 x 25in.
(Sotheby, King & Chasemore) **$4,576 £2,860**

EDWARD HUGHES – A First Visit To The Dentist – signed and dated 1866 – 24 x 20in.
(Christie's) **$12,960 £8,640**

ARTHUR HUGHES – The Home Quartette, Mrs Vernon Lushington And Children – signed and dated 1883, inscribed on the reverse – 40 x 52in.
(Sotheby's) **$34,650 £23,100**

HUGHES

EDWARD ROBERT HUGHES – Midsummer Eve – signed, inscribed on a label on the reverse – watercolour heightened with bodycolour – 44½ x 29½in.
(Sotheby's) **$34,650** **£19,800**

J. TALBOT HUGHES – Anaradapura, Ceylon – signed and dated '91 – 14 x 20½in.
(Sotheby Beresford Adams) **$84** **£49**

WILLIAM HUGHES – Still Life Of Game And Fruit – signed and dated 1864 – on board – 14 x 18in.
(Sotheby's) **$535** **£352**

SIR HERBERT EDWIN PELHAM HUGHES-STANTON – A Normandy Landscape – signed and dated 1906 – pencil and watercolour on card – 7¼ x 14½in.
(Christie's) **$288** **£172**

SIR HERBERT HUGHES-STANTON – Suffolk Vale – 19½ x 26½in.
(Sotheby Beresford Adams) **$924** **£550**

SIR HERBERT HUGHES-STANTON – Morning On The Thames – signed and dated 1921 – 30½ x 36in.
(Sotheby's) **$2,073** **£1,430**

ABRAHAM HULK, SNR. – Fishing Boats Off The Coast – signed – 15½ x 23½in.
(Sotheby's) **$3,344** **£2,200**

ABRAHAM HULK, SNR. – Fishing Boats Returning Home – signed – on panel – 7 x 10in.
(Sotheby's) **$1,378** **£770**

ABRAHAM HULK, SNR. – Sailing Barges Becalmed On A River – signed – 14 x 21¼in.
(Sotheby, King &
Chasemore) **$2,244** **£1,320**

ABRAHAM HULK, SNR. – Fishing Boats Off The Coast At Dusk – signed – on panel – 11½ x 17¼in.
(Sotheby's) **$2,756** **£1,540**

ABRAHAM HULK, SNR. – Fishing Vessels Off The Coast – 22 x 33½in.
(Sotheby's) **$1,772** **£990**

ABRAHAM HULK, SNR. – 'Off The Dutch Coast' – signed – oil on panel – 6½ x 10in.
(Sotheby, King &
Chasemore) **$3,300** **£2,200**

ABRAHAM HULK – A Coastal Landscape With A Beached Fishing Vessel – signed – on panel – 6 x 8in. *(Christie's)* **$2,176** **£1,404**

HULK

ABRAHAM HULK, SNR. – Fishing Boats Off The Coast – signed – on panel – 12 x 16in.
(Sotheby's) **$7,598 £4,840**

ABRAHAM HULK – Shipping In An Estuary In A Calm; and Dutch Shipping In A Stiff Breeze – both signed – on panel – 6¾ x 10in.
(Christie's) **$1,846 £1,026 Pair**

ABRAHAM HULK – Fishing Vessels Beside A Jetty Under A Stormy Sky – signed – oil on panel – 8½ x 11in.
(Hy..Duke & Son) **$2,682 £1,550**

HENDRIK HULK – Dutch Sailing Barges In A Calm – signed – on panel – 9¼ x 14in.
(Christie's) **$972 £540**

EDWARD HULL – A French Farmyard; and A Haycart Outside A Glass Factory – signed and one dated 1838 – pencil and watercolour with touches of white heightening – 12 x 17¼in.
(Christie's) **$1,815 £1,080 Pair**

EDWARD HULL – Harnessing A Phaeton In A Stable-Yard – signed – pencil and watercolour heightened with white – 5¾ x 8¾in.
(Christie's) **$544 £324**

FREDERICK HULK – The Hague, Holland – signed – 15 x 12¼in. *(Sotheby Beresford Adams)* **$1,000 £595 Pair**

FREDERICK WILLIAM HULME – A Lakeside Scene With A Punt Moored In The Reeds With A Distant Town, At Sunset – signed – oil on canvas – 33 x 30cm.
(Osmond, Tricks) **$430** **£250**

EDITH HUME – By The Shore – signed with initials, inscribed on the reverse – on board – 4 x 6¾in.
(Sotheby Beresford Adams) **$628** **£374**

THOMAS H. HUNN – Primulas – signed, inscribed and dated 1908 – pencil and watercolour – 10½ x 14¾in.
(Christie's) **$398** **£237**

CHARLES HUNT – 'Making Love' – signed and dated 1874 – oil on panel – 7½ x 5¼in.
(Sotheby, King & Chasemore) **$1,548** **£968**

CHARLES HUNT – A Boy With Poultry And A Goat In A Farmyard – signed and dated 1903 – 19½ x 29½in.
(Christie's) **$6,696** **£4,320**

EDGAR HUNT – Rabbits And Pigeons – signed – on board – 10 x 8in.
(Sotheby, King & Chasemore) **$3,960** **£2,640**

EDGAR HUNT – Farmyard Friends – signed and dated 1934 – 19½ x 29½in.
(Christie's) **$14,230** **£9,180**

EDGAR HUNT – 'Timidity' – signed and dated 1908, inscribed on reverse – oil on canvas – 18 x 14in.
(Sotheby, King & Chasemore)   **$3,328**   **£1,870**

EDGAR HUNT – Best Of Friends – signed – on board – 11 x 15in.
(Christie's)   **$3,682**   **£2,376**

W. HUNT – The Village Pond – signed – 8 x 10½in.
(Sotheby Beresford Adams)   **$29**   **£17**

WILLIAM HENRY HUNT – The Russian Game Seller – signed – heightened with bodycolour – 14½ x 10½in.
(Sotheby's)   **$762**   **£495**

REUBEN HUNT – 'Disputing The Way'; and 'Friends Or Enemies' – signed and dated – oil – 10.2 x 14in. *(Woolley & Wallis)*   **$1,133**   **£640 Pair**

WILLIAM HENRY HUNT — A Farm Hand
Resting On A Pile Of Straw In A Barn —
on panel — 12 x 10in.
(Sotheby's) **$3,986 £2,640**

WILLIAM HENRY HUNT — Still Life
With Plums And Cherries — signed —
watercolour heightened with white and
gum arabic — 7½ x 10in.
(Sotheby's) **$320 £209**

WILLIAM HENRY HUNT — Fruit And
Nuts — 5 x 8in.
(Sotheby's) **$762 £495**

WILLIAM HOLMAN HUNT — Portrait
Of Mrs George Waugh, In A Black Dress
With A White Lace Collar — signed with
monogram and dated 1868 — 34 x 26in.
(Christie's) **$29,160 £19,440**

WILLIAM HOLMAN HUNT — Portrait
Of John Blount Price, Esq., J.P. — signed
with monogram — canvas on board —
24½ x 19¾in.
(Sotheby's) **$12,375 £8,250**

WILLIAM MORRIS HUNT — 'Governor's
Creek, Florida' 1873 — monogrammed —
oil on canvas — 10 x 16in.
*(Robert W. Skinner
Inc.)* **$5,000 £3,125**

PETER HURD — Pecor Valley — signed,
inscribed on the reverse — pen and brush
and black ink on paper — 11 x 15½in.
(Christie's) **$715 £476**

HUTCHINSON

SYBIL HUTCHINSON – A Portrait Of The Horse 'Marlow' – signed with initials, dated and inscribed – oil – 20 x 24in.
(Woolley & Wallis) $192 £115

ROBERT GEMMELL HUTCHISON – Shore At Machrihanish – signed – on canvas board – 8 x 10in.
(Christie's & Edmiston's) $1,408 £880

ROBERT GEMMELL HUTCHISON – 'The Faggot Gatherer' – signed – oil on canvas – 9 x 6in.
(Sotheby, King & Chasemore) $793 £495

THOMAS S. HUTTON – A Fishing Village – signed and indistinctly inscribed – 16 x 24in.
(Sotheby Beresford Adams) $154 £88

WILLIAM HENRY FLORIO HUTCHISSON – Buffalo Shooting From Elephants; and Sand Grouse Shooting From Elephants – signed and dated 1837 – 25 x 30in.
(Christie's) $10,989 £5,940 **Pair**

JAN VAN HUYSUM – Flowers In A Vase – signed – on metal – 19¼ x 16in.
(Sotheby's) $49,500 £33,000

IBBETSON – Travellers Crossing A Mountain Bridge – bears signature and date – 23 x 25in.
(Sotheby Beresford Adams) **$462** **£275**

JULIUS CAESAR IBBETSON – Children At A Stone Bridge – signed and dated 1809 – oil on canvas – 24 x 31in.
(William Doyle Galleries) **$1,200** **£710**

JOSEPH MURRAY INCE – A Steamer Leaving A Town On A Continental Lake – signed and dated 1839 – pencil and watercolour – 8 x 13¼in.
(Christie's) **$456** **£302**

JOSEPH MURRAY INCE – St. Georges Chapel, Windsor – signed and dated 1845 – oil on board – 16 x 12in.
(Butterfield's) **$1,500** **£898**

A. INGRAM – Durham Cathedral; and Windsor Castle – one signed – cork and watercolour – 3¼ x 5¼in.
(Sotheby Beresford Adams) **$22** **£13 Two**

GEORGE INNESS – Late Autumn In The Country – signed – oil on canvas – 22 x 27in.
(William Doyle Galleries) **$5,000** **£2,958**

THOMAS TAYLOR IRELAND – Trees In Autumn – signed – 20 x 13in.
(Sotheby Beresford Adams) **$227** **£132 Pair**

THOMAS TAYLOR IRELAND – Misty Days – signed – 12½ x 20in.
(Sotheby Beresford Adams) **$227** **£132 Two**

WALTER IRELAND – Autumn View – signed – 15½ x 23½in.
(Sotheby Beresford Adams) **$103** **£60**

WILSON IRVINE – Winter Thaw – signed – oil on board – 11¼ x 13¼in.
(Christie's) **$1,045** **£596**

ROLF ISELI – Komposition – oil on canvas – 35.5 x 27cm.
(Germann Auktionshaus) **$1,325** **£828**

ITALIAN SCHOOL

ITALIAN SCHOOL – Religious Scene –
oil – 72 x 45in.
*(Capes, Dunn
& Co.)*   **$960**   **£600**

PAUL IVANOVITCH – On Guard –
signed – 25 x 17in.
(Christie's)   **$9,720**   **£6,480**

A. JACKSON – 'Sheep And Goats In Barn
Interior' – oil on board – 10 x 16in.
*(Dacre, Son &
Hartley)*   **$344**   **£200**

FREDERICK WILLIAM JACKSON –
Windmill On A Hill – signed – oil on
canvas – 24 x 30in.
*(Sotheby, King &
Chasemore)*   **$390**   **£220**

G. JACKSON – A Black And White
Spaniel In A Landscape – signed – 10 x
12in.
(Christie's)   **$1,198**   **£648**

G. JACKSON – 'Well Over' – signed –
on board – 7¾ x 10in.
(Christie's)   **$520**   **£280**

JAMES RANALPH JACKSON – 'Spanish
Border Town' – signed – oil on board –
50 x 60cm.
(Geoff K. Gray)   **$90**   **£54**

SAMUEL JACKSON – An Extensive Landscape Showing Harvesters Lunching In The Foreground With Portbury Church And The Channel And The Welsh Hills In The Distance – inscribed – watercolour – 32.5 x 25cm.
(Osmond, Tricks)   **$1,032**   **£600**

SAMUEL PHILLIPS JACKSON – 'Wreck On The Coast Of Gower', The Rescue Of A Brig On The Rocks – signed – watercolour – 24 x 23cm.
(Osmond, Tricks)   **$430**   **£250**

SAMUEL PHILLIPS JACKSON – 'Par Harbour', A Harbour Scene At Low Tide Showing Fishing Boats Beached, The Harbour Wall And Cliff Tower – signed – watercolour – 58 x 36cm.
(Osmond, Tricks)   **$292**   **£170**

SAMUEL PHILLIPS JACKSON – 'Oslyermouth Castle, Swansea Bay'; and 'St. Michael's Mount, Cornwall' – signed and dated – 9 x 12½in.
(Morphets)   **$2,356**   **£1,550 Pair**

SAMUEL PHILLIPS JACKSON – 'Mullion', A Coastal Sea Scape With A Fisherman On The Beach Amongst Rocks And Sand – signed and dated 1881 – watercolour – 54.5 x 31cm.
(Osmond, Tricks)   **$258**   **£150**

WILLIAM JACKSON – Lake Conniston – dated 1914 – watercolour – 11 x 17in.
(John Hogbin & Son)   **$17**   **£10**

MAX JACOB – Maison Au Bord Du Lac – signed and dated '20 – gouache – 10¼ x 13¼in.
(Sotheby's)   **$886**   **£495**

JACOBSEN

ANTONIO JACOBSEN – The Steamsailer St. Louis – signed and dated '31 – oil on canvas – 21¾ x 35¾in.
(Christie's)   **$2,860**   **£1,906**

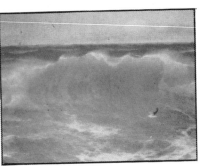

DAVID JAMES – An Atlantic Roll – signed and dated '93 – 23½ x 48in.
(Sotheby Beresford Adams)   **$2,772**   **£1,650**

CHARLES EMILE JACQUE – Shepherdess And Flock In A Farmyard – signed – oil on panel – 18½ x 14½in.
(William Doyle Galleries)   **$4,000**   **£2,366**

DAVID JAMES – The Incoming Tide – signed – 30 x 50in.
(Christie's)   **$3,673**   **£2,052**

WILLIAM JAMES – Venice, The Grand Canal: San Geremia And The Entrance To The Cannaregio – 43¼ x 46½in. *(Sotheby's)* **$11,798 £6,820**

ALEXANDER JAMIESON – Spring, Weston Turville – signed, inscribed on the reverse – 30 x 40in. *(Sotheby's)* **$368 £242**

F. E. JAMIESON – 'Nr. Whistleford, Argyllshire' – signed and inscribed – oil on canvas – 16 x 24in. *(Sotheby, King & Chasemore)* **$77 £44**

MATHURIN JANSSAUD – Paysages – one signed – pastel – one 10¾ x 8¼in., the other 9 x 11¾in. *(Sotheby's)* **$315 £176 Pair**

ABRAHAM JANSSENS – The Musical Contest Between Apollo And Pan – on panel – 37 x 49in. *(Sotheby's)* **$16,500 £11,000**

FRANZ JASCHKE – Vue De L'Isle De Marie – signed and dated 1824 – watercolour and gouache on paper – 18¼ x 27½in. *(Butterfield's)* **$500 £295**

A. JEGOROV – A Troika Ride – signed, inscribed on the reverse – on board – 16 x 24in.
(Sotheby Beresford Adams) $517 £308

DAVID JENKINS – A Summers Day By The River – signed – 72 x 48in.
(Sotheby's) $1,914 £1,320

BLANCHE JENKINS – The Flower Girl – signed and dated 1873 – 20½ x 14in.
(Sotheby Beresford Adams) $440 £262

GEORGE H. JENKINS – Fishing Smacks Off The Coast – signed – 18 x 30in.
(Sotheby Beresford Adams) $590 £352

JOSEPH JOHN JENKINS – A Dutch Fisher-girl – signed and dated 1855 – watercolour heightened with bodycolour – 16 x 10¼in.
(Sotheby's) $322 £209

WILLIAM JENNER – Running A Cutter
Into Shoreham Harbour In A South
Westerly – signed and inscribed on the
reverse – oil on canvas – 12 x 18in.
(Sotheby, King &
Chasemore) **$343** **£220**

AUGUSTUS JOHN – Going Shrimping
– pen and black ink on beige paper –
9½ x 12in.
(Christie's) **$423** **£280**

AUGUSTUS JOHN – Self Portrait With
A Pipe – oil on panel – 34¾ x 23¾in.
(Christie's) **$26,092 £17,280**

AUGUSTUS JOHN – Seated Nude –
pencil – 13½ x 11in.
(Christie's) **$390** **£259**

AUGUSTUS JOHN – Studies Of A Young
Girl – pencil – 11½ x 7½in.
(Sotheby's) **$670** **£462**

AUGUSTUS JOHN – Seated Nude With
Feet Resting On A Ledge – pencil –
12 x 13¾in.
(Christie's) **$978** **£648**

J. JEUM – A Dutch Landscape With Cattle
And A Drover In The Foreground –
indistinctly signed – oil on canvas – 20¾ x
35½in.
(Sotheby, King &
Chasemore) **$495** **£330**

ROBERT JOBLING – A Harbour Scene – watercolour with scratching out – 10½
x 17½in. *(Sotheby, King & Chasemore)* **$166 £104**

JOHN

AUGUSTUS JOHN – Standing Girl, Hitching Her Skirt – signed – pencil – 15½ x 8in.
(Christie's) **$1,630** **£1,080**

AUGUSTUS JOHN – Girl With Eyes Closed – oil on canvas – 22 x 15in.
(Christie's) **$3,260** **£2,160**

AUGUSTUS JOHN – Standing Girl In A Long Dress – signed – pencil – 14¾ x 8¾in.
(Christie's) **$733** **£486**

AUGUSTUS JOHN – Galway Peasants – signed – pen and ink – 7¾ x 4½in.
(Christie's) **$816** **£540**

AUGUSTUS JOHN – Standing Nude – signed – pen and ink and wash – 17½ x 8¾in.
(Sotheby's) **$567** **£330**

GWEN JOHN – Interior Of A Church, France – pencil – 10 x 8in.
(Christie's) **$815** **£540**

CORNELIUS JOHNSON – Portrait Of A Lady – signed – oval 28¼ x 21½in.
(Sotheby's) **$3,322** **£2,200**

DAVID JOHNSON – On The Wallkill – signed, also signed, dated 1874 and inscribed – oil on canvas – 4¼ x 6¼in.
(Christie's) **$2,860** **£1,906**

EDWARD KILLINGWORTH JOHNSON
— The New Ring — signed and dated
1883 — watercolour and bodycolour —
13¾ x 7½in.
(Christie's)   **$729   £486**

EDWARD KILLINGWORTH JOHNSON
— The Old Home — signed and dated
1878 — heightened with bodycolour —
14½ x 9½in.
(Sotheby's)   **$1,863   £1,210**

MARSHALL JOHNSON — The Constitution Under Sail — signed and dated '84 —
oil on canvas — 28 x 48in. *(Robert W. Skinner Inc.)*   **$1,000 £625**

JOHNSON

SIDNEY YATES JOHNSON – Shore
Scene With Figures And Boats – signed
– 12 x 24in.
(Laurence & Martin
Taylor) **$169** **£100**

GEORGE WHITTON JOHNSTON –
Cramond Island, On The Forth, Near
Edinburgh – signed, inscribed on the
reverse – 11½ x 15½in.
(Sotheby Beresford
Adams) **$287** **£165**

G. JOLLEY – An Italian Girl Carrying An
Urn On Her Head – signed – oil – 15 x
7in.
(Lawrence) **$228** **£143**

C. R. JONES – The Sailing Ship 'Rambler'
– 14½ x 18½in.
(Lawrence) **$157** **£99**

REGINALD JONES – 'Children In A
Meadow' – signed – watercolour – 7 x
9¾in.
(Sotheby, King &
Chasemore) **$495** **£330**

LUDOLF DE JONGH – A Sportsman
Seated On A Rock – inscribed – on panel
– 25 x 20¼in.
(Sotheby's) **$4,948** **£2,860**

FRANCIS COATES JONES – Picking
Wild Flowers – signed – oil on canvas –
26¼ x 19¼in.
(Christie's) **$16,500** **£11,000**

J. C. JONES – A Mountainous Landscape
– signed and dated 1890 – 8 x 16½in.
(Lawrence) **$95** **£60**

OENE ROMKES DE JONGH – A Village
Canal In Winter – signed – oil on canvas
– 34 x 28in.
(William Doyle
Galleries) **$3,000** **£1,775**

CARL HENRICK JONNEVOLD – Mt. Tamalpais – signed – oil on canvas – 12½ x 14in.
(Butterfield's)   **$300**   **£177**

J. JORDAENS – An Allegory With Time And Youth Personified – on copper – 9 x 6¾in.
(Sotheby Beresford Adams)   **$740**   **£440**

CHRIS JORGENSEN – Yosemite Valley – signed – watercolour on paper – 4¾ x 7in.
(Butterfield's)   **$275**   **£162**

JULES JOYANT, Attributed to – A View Of The Admiralty., St. Petersburg – pen and brown ink and wash – 11¾ x 17in.
(Sotheby's)   **$502**   **£330**

ADOLPHE JOURDAN – The Necklace – signed and dated 1867 – oil on canvas – 30 x 24in.
(Butterfield's)   **$1,300**   **£770**

JOHN JOWITT – A Still Life Subject – oil – 22½ x 18in.
(Lawrence)   **$20**   **£13**

JEAN MARIE AUGUSTE JUGELET – Vessels Entering A Port – signed – on panel – 9 x 11in.
(Sotheby Beresford Adams)   **$406**   **£242**

H. JUTSUM – Landscape With Figures And A Dog – oil on canvas – 35 x 21½in.
(G. H. Bayley & Sons)   **$3,028**   **£1,750**

WILLIAM JOY – A British Man Of War With Other Shipping Off The Coast – signed – 20 x 29in. *(Sotheby's)*   **$24,915 £16,500**

ADRIAEN VAN DER KABEL – Bandits Attacking Travellers In A Rocky Cavern – signed – on panel – 16 x 21in.
(Sotheby's) **$3,806 £2,200**

BELA KADAR – Portrait Of A Girl – signed – on board – 21½ x 16½in.
(Sotheby's) **$945 £528**

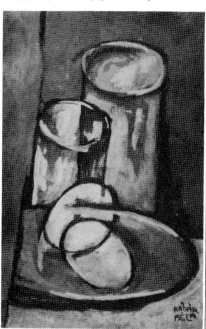

BELA KADAR – Still Life With Glasses – signed – gouache – 17 x 12¼in.; and Portrait Of A Man In A Hat – gouache – 16¾ x 12in.
(Sotheby's) **$315 £176 Two**

GEORGES KARS – Seated Nude Woman – signed – oil on canvas – 24 x 15in.
(Sotheby's) **$1,672 £1,100**

KATZ – On The Rhine – inscribed on the reverse – oil on canvas – 55 x 40½in.
(Sotheby, King & Chasemore) **$969** **£570**

WILHELM VON KAULBACH – Lohengrin's Departure From Elsa – signed and dated 1866 – pencil – 56¾ x 45¾in.
(Sotheby's) **$9,625** **£5,500**

MARTIN KAVEL – Portrait Of A Lady Wearing A Pink Band Round Her Blonde Curly Hair, a Pink Dress With Velvet Bodice – signed – oil – 98 x 70cm.
(Henry Spencer & Sons) **$1,309** **£850**

ARCHIBALD KAY – A Highland Stream – signed – 14 x 17in.
(Christie's & Edmiston's) **$448** **£280**

ARCHIBALD KAY – The River Leny – signed – 20 x 30in.
(Christie's & Edmiston's) **$544** **£340**

C. J. KEATS – A View In Rouen – signed and dated 1885 – 19 x 12½in.
(Lawrence) **$77** **£49**

JEAN KEIFFER – 'The Last Supper' – signed – oil on canvas – 39 x 51½in.
(Stalker & Boos) **$100** **£65**

ELIZABETH KEITH – Still Life Of Tazza And Fruit – signed – oil on canvas – 24 x 20in.
(Butterfield's) **$3,000** **£1,796**

WILLIAM KEITH – Early San Francisco – signed – oil on canvas – 23 x 33in.
(Butterfield's) **$13,000** **£7,784**

ROBERT GEORGE KELLY – Waiting
For The Boat, A Fisherman's Daughter
– signed, inscribed on a label on the
reverse – 22 x 17½in.
*(Sotheby Beresford
     Adams)*   **$740**   **£440**

ROCKWELL KENT – Embrace – signed
and dated 1920 and inscribed – pencil
on paper – on board – 20.3 x 24.7cm.
(Christie's)   **$1,650**   **£1,000**

ROCKWELL KENT – Man And Mush-
rooms – pen, brush and black ink and
pencil – on board – 12.3 x 14.7cm.
(Christie's)   **$605**   **£400**

HARRY KERNOFF – A Street Scene – pencil and watercolour – 19¾ x 28¼in.
(Sotheby's)   **$757 £440**

FERDINAND VAN KESSEL – A Monkey
Feast – on panel – 19 x 25in.
(Sotheby's) **$7,524** **£4,950**

T. KETTLE – Portrait Of A Lady, Half
Length, In A White Dress, Leaning On A
Ledge, In A Landscape – 36 x 28in.
(Christie's) **$1,102** **£702**

W. KIDD – Three Boys Playing Marbles
On A Path By A Cottage, Watched By A
Small Girl – bears signature – 7½ x 9½in.
*(Anderson &
Garland)* **$600** **£360**

ALEXEI ALEXEYEVICH KHARLAMOV
– Young Girl With A Bouquet Of Flowers
– signed – watercolour – 18 x 12in.
(Sotheby's) **$3,344** **£2,200**

WILLIAM KIDD – Fast Asleep – 10 x
7½in.
*(Sotheby Beresford
Adams)* **$382** **£220**

WILLIAM KIDD – The Fisherman's Tale – signed – 11½ x 15½in.
(Sotheby's) $969   £638

PETRUS KIERS – A Young Couple Conversing At A Window – signed – on board – 17 x 13½in.
(Sotheby Beresford Adams) $6,283   £3,740

GEORGE GOODWIN KILBURNE – Reverie – watercolour heightened with white – 13 x 10in.
(Sotheby, King & Chasemore) $500   £295

GEORGE EDWARD KILBURNE – The Hunters Return – signed – watercolour heightened with white – 5½ x 6½in. *(Sotheby, King & Chasemore)* $510 £286

GEORGE GOODWIN KILBURNE – Vanity – signed – watercolour – 10½ x 14½in.) *(Christie's)* **$1,956 £1,296**

GEORGE GOODWIN KILBURNE – Snowballing – signed – watercolour heightened with white – 3 x 4½in. *(Sotheby's)* **$677 £440**

GEORGE GOODWIN KILBURNE – Peeling Apples – signed – watercolour – 26.5 x 36cm. *(Henry Spencer & Sons)* **$2,363 £1,320**

GEORGE GOODWIN KILBURNE – The King's Armchair – signed and inscribed – watercolour heightened with white – 5¾ x 7½in. *(Christie's)* **$307 £183**

GEORGE GOODWIN KILBURNE – A Girl With Her Book In A Garden, Tennis Racquets By Her Chair – signed and dated '80 – pencil and watercolour heightened with white – 10¾ x 8¼in. *(Christie's)* **$4,354 £2,592**

GEORGE GOODWIN KILBURNE – A
Game Of Tennis – signed and dated '82
– 13½ x 20in.
(Sotheby's)   **$5,082**   **£3,300**

GEORGE GOODWIN KILBURNE –
'Morning Call' – signed – oil on panel –
7½ x 11½in.
(Sotheby, King &
Chasemore)   **$962**   **£550**

GEORGE GOODWIN KILBURNE –
'Come And Look' – signed – watercolour
– 7½ x 6in.
(Sotheby, King &
Chasemore)   **$1,057**   **£594**

GEORGE GOODWIN KILBURNE –
The Squire – signed – 13½ x 19¾in.
(Sotheby Beresford
Adams)   **$1,052**   **£605**

GEORGE GOODWIN KILBURNE – The Picnic – signed – watercolour – 35 x 52cm.
(Henry Spencer & Sons)　　**$4,296**　**£2,400**

GEORGE GOODWIN KILBURNE – Hearts Are Trumps – signed – 40¼ x 30¼in.
(Christie's)　　**$6,156**　**£4,104**

ADELE KINDT – Paul Et Virginie – signed – 50¼ x 37¼in.
(Sotheby's)　　**$1,575**　**£880**

HAYNES KING – Fisher Girl – signed – on panel – 12½ x 9in.
(Sotheby, King & Chasemore)　**$1,063**　**£682**

KIKOINE

MICHEL KIKOINE – Autoportrait – signed, and signed on the reverse – oil on canvas – 9½ x 7½in.
(Christie's)   **$813**   **£518**

HENRY JOHN YEEND KING – On A Garden Seat – signed – heightened with bodycolour – 14 x 10in.
(Sotheby's)   **$678**   **£440**

HENRY JOHN YEEND KING – Gathering Poppies – signed – heightened with bodycolour – 10¼ x 17¼in.
(Sotheby Beresford Adams)   **$459**   **£264**

HENRY JOHN YEEND KING – Hanging Out The Washing – signed – on board – 14½ x 10¼in.
(Christie's)   **$1,160**   **£648**

PAUL KING – 'The Old Barn' – signed, signed and dated 1910 on the reverse – oil on panel – 5½ x 8in.
(Robert W. Skinner Inc.)   **$600**   **£375**

W. KING – 'Rural Landscapes' – oil – 20 x 30¼in.
(Dacre, Son & Hartley)   **$86**   **£50 Pair**

GERALD KINNAIRD – A New Button – signed and dated 1867 – 36 x 28in.
(Sotheby's)   **$920**   **£605**

HENRY J. KINNAIRD – A Cornfield Near Arundel – signed and inscribed – watercolour heightened with white – 10 x 14¾in.
(Christie's)   **$816**   **£486**

HENRY JAMES KINNAIRD – A Sunny Cornfield – signed and inscribed – watercolour – 15 x 10in.
(Woolley & Wallis)   **$602**   **£340**

HENRY JOHN KINNAIRD – 'On The Ouse, Sussex' – signed and inscribed – watercolour heightened with white – 13 x 20in.
(Sotheby, King &
Chasemore) **$594** **£396**

JAMES KINNEAR – Gathering Firewood – signed – 19½ x 24½in.
(Sotheby Beresford
Adams) **$287** **£165**

FRANK L. KIRKPATRICK – Italian Nobility And Clergy Before The Palace – signed and dated 1882 – oil on canvas – 29¼ x 60in.
(Butterfield's) **$2,000** **£1,197**

JOSEF KINZEL – Interior Scene With Three Men Drinking – signed and inscribed – oil on panel – 20 x 15¼in.
(Sotheby, King &
Chasemore) **$2,349** **£1,320**

JOSEPH KIRKPATRICK – By The Cottage Door – signed – heightened with bodycolour – 13½ x 9½in.
(Sotheby's) **$711** **£462**

KIRKPATRICK

JOSEPH KIRKPATRICK – Gathering Primroses – signed – watercolour – 5¾ x 9¼in.
(Christie's) $307   £183

GUSTAV KISPERT – Lesson Time – signed and dated '83 – on panel – 11½ x 8¼in.
(Christie's) $2,592   £1,728

A. KLEYN – Dutch Marine Scenes With Fishing Boats In An Estuary – signed – oil on panel – 15 x 19in.
(Hall, Wateridge & Owen)   **$11,200**   **£6,400 Pair**

H. KNAPPING – 'A Fishing Smack Anchored Off The Coast' – oil on canvas – 11½ x 9½in.
(W. H. Lane & Son) $31   £18

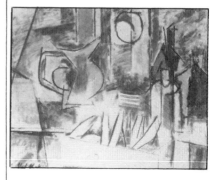

KARL KNATHS – Bananas – signed, inscribed and dated 1964 – oil on canvas – 30¼ x 36in.
(Christie's) $6,050   £4,006

CHARLES W. KNAPP – Landscape With Farmhouse – signed – oil on canvas – 20 x 36in. *(Robert W. Skinner Inc.)*   **$900 £562**

KNELL – A Rising Storm – on board –
11 x 14in.
*(Sotheby Beresford
Adams)* **$76** **£44**

KNELL – Shipping Off The Coast – 13 x
17¼in.
*(Sotheby Beresford
Adams)* **$406** **£242**

KNELL – Shipping Scenes – on board
– 12 x 18in.
*(Sotheby Beresford
Adams)* **$208** **£121 Two**

ADOLPHUS KNELL – Shipping At
Sunset – signed – on board – 6¼ x 9in.
*(Sotheby Beresford
Adams)* **$590** **£352**

WILLIAM ADOLPHUS KNELL – A Moonlight Shipping Scene – signed – oil on
board – 5½ x 13½in.
*(Sotheby, King &
Chasemore)* **$957** **£638 Pair**

WILLIAM ADOLPHUS KNELL –
Shipping At Sunset In A Choppy Sea˙
– signed – 16 x 21in.
(Christie's) **$966** **£540**

WILLIAM CALLCOTT KNELL – Fishing Boats – signed – oil on canvas – 12
x 20in.
*(Sotheby, King &
Chasemore)* **$578** **£340**

SIR GEOFFREY KNELLER, Follower of –
Robert Harley, 1st Earl of Oxford, In Garter
Robes – oil on canvas – 3¼ x 25in.
*(Sotheby, King &
Chasemore)* **$1,056** **£704**

SIR GODFREY KNELLER – Portrait
Of Sir William Twisden, Bt., Wearing A
Brown Cloak – 30 x 25in.
(Christie's) **$1,499** **£810**

KNELLER

SIR GODFREY KNELLER, Studio of —
Portrait Of Sarah, Duchess Of Marlborough
— 48½ x 38¾in.
(Sotheby's) **$2,325 £1,540**

GEORGE KNIGHT — Shipping Scenes
— signed — oil on canvas — 24 x 16in.
(Edgar Horne) **$770 £510 Pair**

HAROLD KNIGHT — Grief — inscribed
on the reverse — watercolour — 16 x
16in.
(Sotheby's) **$319 £220**

JOSEPH KNIGHT — Morning Light —
signed and dated 1901, inscribed on the
reverse — watercolour and bodycolour —
19 x 23½in.
(Sotheby's) **$287 £187**

DAME LAURA KNIGHT — Hop Picking
— signed — oil on canvas — 30 x 25in.
(Christie's) **$1,630 £1,080**

DAME LAURA KNIGHT — Miss Ele-
gance — signed — pencil and watercolour
— 31 x 19in.
(Sotheby's) **$1,324 £770**

DAME LAURA KNIGHT – Waiting To Go On – signed – oil on canvas – 30 x 25in.
(Christie's) **$2,120** **£1,404**

DAME LAURA KNIGHT – The Dancing School – signed – pencil and charcoal – 13¼ x 9¼in.
(Christie's) **$130** **£86**

DAME LAURA KNIGHT – Taking A Bow – signed – watercolour and soft pencil – 12 x 9½in.
(Christie's) **$734** **£486**

LOUIS ASTON KNIGHT – Spring River By A Thatched Cottage – signed – oil on canvas – 26 x 32¼in.
(Butterfield's) **$1,600** **£946**

ARTHUR KNOWLES – One Of Britain's Watchdogs – signed and inscribed on a label – heightened with white – 11 x 14½in.
(Sotheby Beresford Adams) **$41** **£24**

DAVIDSON KNOWLES – 'A Winter's Walk' – signed – 13½ x 10in.
(Christie's) **$810** **£453**

J. KNOX – A Regatta On The Clyde At Glasgow Green, In The Background The Cathedral And Necropolis – 16½ x 21in. *(Christie's & Edmiston's)* **$2,560 £1,600**

KNOX

SUSAN RICKER KNOX – 'Woman With A Parasol' – signed – oil on canvas – 30¼ x 25in.
(Robert W. Skinner Inc.)   **$700**   **£438**

KOBELL – A Peasant Directing Soldiers To A Ruined Castle – pen and grey ink, brown wash – 30.7 x 46.8cm.
(Christie's)   **$100**   **£60**

HENDRIK KOBELL – Men-O'-War Off A Coast With A Tower – pen and brown ink, brown wash – 14 x 16.8cm.
(Christie's)   **$265**   **£175**

JOHANN BAPTISTE KOBELL – Travellers On A Road At The Edge Of A Road – signed – grey and brown wash – 20.3 x 27.4cm.
(Christie's)   **$155**   **£100**

JOSEPH ANTON KOCH – Heroische Landschaft Mit Regenbogen – 28½ x 23in.
(Christie's)   **$46,980**   **£31,320**

KOEKKOEK – Winter Landscape With Figures On A Frozen River – oil on panel – 6 x 7.7in.
(Woolley & Wallis)   **$500**   **£300**

BAREND CORNELIS KOEKKOEK – A River Landscape With A Ruined Castle – signed and dated 1855 – on panel – 9½ x 11¾in.
(Christie's)   **$13,565**   **£8,640**

M. A. KOEKKOEK – A Woodland Walk – bears signature – on panel – 13½ x 7¼in.
(Sotheby Beresford Adams)   **$287**   **£165**

HENDRIK PIETER KOEKKOEK – Figures On A Country Lane – signed – 11 x 17in.
(Sotheby's)   **$826**   **£462**

HERMANUS KOEKKOEK, JNR. – The Entrance To A Busy Harbour – signed and dated '69 – 21¼ x 33in.
(Sotheby's)   **$6,695**   **£3,740**

HERMANUS KOEKKOEK – Dutch Shipping In An Estuary – signed – on panel – 12½ x 17¾in.
(Christie's)   **$7,828   £5,184**

W. KOEKKOEK – A Dutch Town Scene With Numerous Figures – bears signature – 31 x 26½in.
(Christie's)   **$2,176   £1,404**

JOHANNES H. B. KOEKKOEK – A Dutch River Scene With Boys Fishing – oil on canvas – 17 x 27¾in.
(Sotheby, King & Chasemore)   **$1,200   £770**

JOHAN PHILIP KOELMAN – An Italian Family By The Coast; and An Artist Sketching Italian Peasants – signed – on board – 10 x 14in.
(Sotheby's)   **$2,090   £1,375 Two**

JOHANNES HERMANUS KOEKKOEK – Landing The Catch Near The Zuyder Zee – signed and dated 1821 – on panel – 7½ x 10in.
(Sotheby's)   **$3,176   £2,090**

WALTER KOENIGER – The Old Deserted Mill – signed, inscribed and dated – oil on canvas – 35 x 37¼in.
(Christie's)   **$1,320   £880**

WILLIAM HENRY DETHLEF KOERNER
– City Man On Vacation – signed – oil on
canvas – 22 x 36½in.
(Butterfield's)   **$2,700   £1,646**

CARL R. KRAFFT – Sleighride With
Rivertown Beyond – signed – oil on canvas – 27 x 36in.
(Butterfield's)   **$3,250   £1,946**

PIERRE KREMER – Escape From The
Battle – signed and inscribed – on panel
– 34¾ x 28in.
(Sotheby's)   **$669   £440**

FRANZ KRISCHKE – 'Still Life With
Tea Pot, Tea Cup And Saucer And Mantel Clock' – signed – oil on canvas – 23½
x 19½in.
*(Stalker &
Boos)*   **$475   £296**

SIPKE KOOL – Domestic Scene With
Mother And Baby In Cradle – oil on
panel – 13¾ x 18¾in.
*(Dacre, Son &
Hartley)*   **$800   £520**

FRANZ KORWAN – Sailing Boats At
Sunset – signed – 27¾ x 38¾in.
(Sotheby's)   **$1,204   £792**

CHRISTIAN KROHG – Fishermen
Watching A Steamer – signed – 17½
x 16in.
(Sotheby's)   **$2,340   £1,540**

REINHOLD KUNDIG – Horgenerberg – signed and dated 1942 – oil on canvas – 65.5 x 80.5cm.
(Germann Auktionshaus) **$2,650   £1,658**

C. KUWASSEG – 'Stormy Coastal Scene' – signed and dated 1867; verso 'Port De Kermank, Brettagne' – oil on canvas – 12½ x 18in.
(Bracketts) **$1,600   £1,000**

CHARLES EUPHRASIE KUWASSEG, JNR. – French Coastal Towns With Boats Moored Off Shore – signed and dated 1869 – 12 x 17½in.
(Sotheby's) **$8,846   £5,820 Pair**

CHARLES EUPHRASIE KUWASSEG – In The Bay Of Naples – signed and dated 1869 – 22¼ x 39¼in.
(Christie's) **$4,536   £3,024**

WILHELM KUHNERT – Laufender Loewe – signed – oil and gouache on canvas – 41 x 64in.
(Christie's) **$13,860   £9,180**

CHARLES J. DE LACY – Tugs Bringing A Ship Into Harbour – signed and dated 1892 – on canvas – 31½ x 41½in.
(Sotheby, King & Chasemore) **$755   £484**

ROBERT LADBROOKE, Attributed to – Landscape With A Pond And Distant Cottages – 6 x 10in.
(Sotheby's) **$702   £462**

EDWARD LADELL, Attributed to – Still Life With Rhenish Jug – oil on canvas – 17 x 14in.
(Sotheby, King & Chasemore) **$1,496   £935**

LEV FELIXOVICH LAGORIO – The Neva With The Fortress Of St. Peter And St. Paul At Dusk – signed and dated 1900 – oil on canvas – 17¼ x 25in.
(Sotheby's) **$6,688   £4,400**

LAMBE

WILLIAM LAMBE – Portrait Of A Gentleman Seated In A Chair – signed and dated 1843 – watercolour – 11½ x 9in.
(Hy. Duke & Son) $28 £16

B. LAMBERT – Winter And Summer Forests – signed – 10½ x 18½in.
(Sotheby Beresford Adams) $340 £198 Two

TED R. LAMBERT – Fishcamp On The Yukon – signed and dated 1937 and signed and dated on the reverse – oil on board – 9½ x 14in.
(Butterfield's) $3,750 £2,245

TED R. LAMBERT – Native Fishcamp At Anvik, Alaska – signed and dated 1937 and signed and dated on the reverse – oil on board – 28½ x 38½in.
(Butterfield's) $13,000 £7,785

EMILE CHARLES LAMBINET – A French River Landscape – signed – on panel – 15 x 24in.
(Sotheby, King & Chasemore) $4,662 £3,630

WILLIAM BLAKE LAMOND – A Corner Of The Farmyard – signed – 9 x 11in.
(Christie's & Edmiston's) $152 £95

AUGUSTUS OSBORNE LAMPLOUGH – In The Desert; and Egyptian Views – signed, one inscribed – 9 x 23in.
(Sotheby Beresford Adams) $813 £484 Three

JAIME LANA, Attributed to – Saint James The Great Baptizing The Magus Hermogenes – on panel – 61 x 26¾in.
(Sotheby's) $8,250 £5,500

PERCY LANCASTER – Wharfdale – signed – 9½ x 13in.
(Sotheby's) $338 £220

GEORGE LANCE – Still Life Of Dead
Mallard, Grapes, Apples And Other Fruit
In A Basket – signed – 30 x 40in.
(Christie's) **$4,640 £2,592**

CHARLES ZACHÁRIE LANDELLE –
La Recolte Des Citrones – signed – 33
x 23in.
(Christie's) **$1,590 £1,026**

J. LANDER – A Primitive Study Portrait
– signed and dated 1835 – oil on canvas
– 9½ x 7½in.
(Sotheby, King &
Chasemore) **$629 £370**

LANDSEER, After – 'The Sentinel';
and 'Laying Down The Law' – oil –
19.7 x 28in. the other 24 x 26.5in.
(Woolley &
Wallis) **$785 £470 Two**

LANDSEER

LANDSEER – A Study Of Three Bloodhounds – oil on canvas – 46 x 72in.
(Sotheby, King &
Chasemore) **$4,420** **£2,600**

LANDSEER – A Hound – oil sketch –
29½ x 33½in.
(Laurence & Martin
Taylor) **$2,595** **£1,500**

LANDSEER – Waiting For Master – 32
x 40in.
(Heathcote Ball
& Co.) **$188** **£105**

LANDSEER – A Horse Eating Hay From
A Wooden Box, A Goat And A Pigeon
Nearby; and Three Horses And Two
Pigeons In A Field – bears another signature and date 1867 – oil on board – 12¾
x 10in.
(Anderson &
Garland) **$80** **£48 Pair**

SIR EDWIN LANDSEER – Portrait Of
William, 2nd Baron Alvanley, Wearing A
Black Coat – signed and inscribed on a
label – 10¼ x 8¼in.
(Sotheby's[1] **$2,658** **£1,760**

WALTER LANGLEY – A Study Of
Fisherfolk – signed – watercolour – 6½
x 19in.
(Lawrence) **$857** **£539**

WILLIAM LANGLEY – Cattle In The Highlands – signed – 11½ x 19½in.
(Sotheby Beresford
Adams) **$354** **£200 Pair**

MARK W. LANGLOIS – The Old Tinker
– signed – 30 x 25in.
(Sotheby's)   **$535**   **£352**

ANDRE LANSKOY – Composition –
signed – gouache – 60 x 44cm.
*(Germann
    Auktionshaus)* **$2,650**   **£1,657**

THE LANINI, Studio of – The Virgin
And Child – on panel – 21 x 14¾in.
(Sotheby's)   **£3,406**   **£1,980**

ANDRE LANSKOY – Composition –
signed – oil on canvas – 60 x 73cm.
*(Germann
    Auktionshaus)* **$3,535**   **£2,210**

**GEORGE HENRY LAPORTE, Attributed
to** – Officers Of The 2nd Life Guards; and
Royal Horse Guards Before Parade Near
Hyde Park Barracks – dated 1829 – 15½
x 20½in.
(Sotheby's)   **$4,983**   **£3,300 Pair**

LASSALLE

LOUIS LASSALLE – A Mother With Children – signed – oil on canvas – 16 x 12½in.
(Du Mouchelles) $4,000   £2,222

LOUIS-SIMON LASSALLE – The Wood Gatherer – signed – on panel – 11 x 9in.
(Christie's) $1,088   £702

R. S. LAUDER – Undine By The Pool – oil – 21½ x 18½in.
(Lawrence) $275   £154

MARIE LAURENCIN – Tete De Fillette – signed – oil on board – 13 x 9½in.
(William Doyle Galleries) $27,000 £15,976

AUGUST LAUX – 'Still Life With Strawberries And Blackberries' – signed – oil on canvas – 10 x 18in.
(Robert W. Skinner Inc.) $1,100   £688

FLORENCE H. LAVEROCK – Country Cousins – signed and dated 1906, inscribed on the reverse – watercolour – 17¼ x 12¼in.
(Sotheby, King & Chasemore) $528   £330

SIR JOHN LAVERY – Portrait Of Mrs T. C. Owen – signed, also signed, inscribed and dated 1916 on the reverse – 29½ x 24½in.
(Sotheby's) $1,702   £990

SIR JOHN LAVERY — Portrait Of A Girl With A Fur Wrap, Seated In Profile — signed and dated 1886 and signed and dated on the reverse — oil on canvas — 21¾ x 18in.
(Christie's)　**$1,549**　**£1,026**

SIR JOHN LAVERY — Zachra — signed and inscribed and dated 1914 on the reverse — 29 x 20in.
*(Christie's &
Edmiston's)*　**$24,000**　**£15,000**

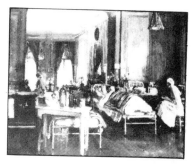

SIR JOHN LAVERY — A London Drawing Room In War Time; Sister Juliet — signed, signed, inscribed and dated 1918 on the reverse — oil on canvas — 25 x 30in.
(Christie's)　**$8,184**　**£4,400**

HAROLD LAWES — A Cottage Near Hasle-mere, Surrey; A Devonshire Cottage; and Boating At Stratford-Upon-Avon — signed and inscribed — watercolour — 10 x 14½in.
(Sotheby's)　**$1,050**　**£682 Three**

HAROLD LAWES — Milton's Cottage, Chalfont St. Giles, Buckinghamshire — signed and inscribed — watercolour over pencil — 13¼ x 20¾in.
(Sotheby's)　**$847**　**£550**

GEORGE FEATHER LAWRENCE — 'Landscape' — signed — oil on board — 17 x 24cm.
(Geoff K. Gray)　**$450**　**£268**

LAWRENCE

GEORGE FEATHER LAWRENCE – 'Boats At Anchor, Sydney Harbour' – signed – oil on board – 61 x 76cm. *(Australian Art Auctions)* **$2,866 £1,666**

SIR THOMAS LAWRENCE – Portrait Of A Gentleman, Wearing A Dark Green Coat – 29 x 24in.
(Sotheby's) **$2,823 £1,870**

ALICIA LAWRENSON – 'Cyclamen' – pastel – 15 x 10¼in.
(W. H. Lane & Son) **$16 £9**

CECIL GORDON LAWSON – Twilight – signed and dated 1881 – 24 x 36in. *(Sotheby Beresford Adams)* **$517 £308**

F. LAWSON – Street Scene With Buildings And Figures – signed and dated 1911 – watercolour – 9¾ x 11¾in. *(W. H. Lane & Son)* **$34 £20**

FRANCIS WILFRED LAWSON – Solace – signed – 6 x 4in. *(Sotheby's)* **$336 £180**

LEA – Sleeping Beauties – 28 x 36in.
(Sotheby's) **$362** **£198**

BENJAMIN WILLIAMS LEADER –
The End Of The Day – signed and
dated 1898 – 12 x 18in.
(Sotheby's) **$836** **£550**

BENJAMIN WILLIAMS LEADER – A
View In The Lake District, With Figures
And A Dog In The Foreground – bears
signature – oil on canvas – 20 x 30in.
(Sotheby, King &
Chasemore) **$742** **£495**

BENJAMIN WILLIAMS LEADER – 'A
Beech Wood' – signed and dated 1859 –
oil on canvas – 18 x 26in.
(Sotheby, King &
Chasemore) **$3,910** **£2,300**

BENJAMIN WILLIAMS LEADER – The Wye At Tintern, Moonlight – signed and
dated 1872 – 30 x 50in. *(Christie's)* **$1,757 £1,134**

BENJAMIN WILLIAMS LEADER – Entering The Lock – signed and dated 1885 – oil on canvas – 16 x 23½in. *(Sotheby, King & Chasemore)*   **$8,925 £5,250**

LEAR – Rock Of Gibralter With Soldiers – watercolour – 6½ x 10in. *(Laurence & Martin Taylor)*   **$95   £55**

EDWARD LEAR – Nileboats Near Deir El Kadige, Noon – signed with monogram also signed and dated 1871 – 9½ x 18in. *(Sotheby's)*   **$11,550   £7,700**

CHARLES HUTTON LEAR – A Glimpse Of The Fairies – 23 x 29½in. *(Sotheby's)*   **$8,580   £5,720**

CHARLES LEAVER – A Meeting In The Snow – 21 x 28in. *(Sotheby Beresford Adams)*   **$1,294   £770**

NOEL HARRY LEAVER – Robin Hood's Bay, Yorkshire – signed and inscribed – watercolour – 11¼ x 17½in.
(Christie's) $1,386 £918

NOEL HARRY LEAVER – The Valley Of Chamonix – signed, and inscribed on the reverse – watercolour – 10 x 14½in.
(Christie's) $288 £172

WILLIAM LEAVER – A Summer Landscape – signed – 19½ x 29½in.
(Sotheby Beresford Adams) $170 £99

VICTOR LECOMTE – Lovers In A Dark Salon – signed and inscribed on a label on the reverse – 9½ x 13in.
(Sotheby, King & Chasemore) $670 £395

BERTHA STRINGER LEE – California Coast – signed and dated 1910 – oil on board – 11½ x 16½in.
(Butterfield's) $375 £220

FREDERICK RICHARD LEE – Cattle Watering From A Stream – oil on canvas – 26 x 40in. *(Sotheby, King & Chasemore)* $792 £495

JOHN LEECH – A Windy Day By The Sea – oil – 14 x 23in.
(Capes, Dunn & Co.) **$1,024** **£640**

JOHN LEECH – Inspecting The Volunteers – pen and black ink and watercolour – 4¾ x 7in.
(Christie's) **$194** **£129**

CORNELIS VAN LEEMPUTTEN – Feeding The Chickens – signed – on panel – 9½ x 6¾in.
(Christie's) **$1,422** **£918**

ALEXIS DE LEEUW – The Timber Wagon – signed – 29¼ x 49½in.
(Sotheby's) **$80** **£45**

FERNAND LEGER – L'Homme Au Chandail – signed – watercolour, brush and black ink over pencil on paper – 8½ x 11¼in.
(Christie's) **$44,085** **£28,080**

ALEX. LEGGETT – The Parting Glance – signed, inscribed and dated 1880 on the reverse – 11¾ x 9¼in.
(Sotheby, King & Chasemore) **$510** **£330**

EDMUND BLAIR LEIGHTON – The Charity Of Saint Elizabeth Of Hungary – signed and dated 1895 – 65 x 47¼in.
(Christie's)   **$6,480   £4,320**

FREDERIC, LORD LEIGHTON – Miss Dene – 24 x 20in.
(Sotheby's)   **$16,500   £11,000**

FREDERIC, LORD LEIGHTON – Melpomene, Muse Of Tragic And Lyric Poetry: Terpsichore, Muse Of Dance: Thalia, Muse Of Comedy – a triptych – 65½ x 27½in., 65½ x 43¾in., 65½ x 27½in.
(Sotheby's)   **$211,750 £121,000**

FREDERIC, LORD LEIGHTON – A North African Alley – 8¼ x 5in.
(Christie's)   **$1,440   £864**

SCOTT LEIGHTON – 'A Mountain Pasture' – signed – oil on canvas – 36 x 47in.
(Robert W. Skinner Inc.)   **$2,500   £1,562**

LEITCH

RICHARD PRINCIPAL LEITCH – 'Houses By The Bay' – watercolour – 9 x 13in.
(Sotheby, King &
Chasemore)   **$352**   **£220**

LEITZENS – Angels In A Landscape – signed – oil on board – 5½ x 14¼in.
(Stalker &
Boos)   **$850**   **£508**

ALEXANDRE-LOUIS LELOIR – Grecian Interior With Maiden And Attendants – signed – oil on canvas – 21½ x 25¾in.
(Butterfield's)   **$5,000**   **£2,994**

LELONG, Circle of – Kitchen Still Lives – canvas on panel – 6½ x 8½. and 7 x 8¾in.
(Sotheby's)   **$1,338**   **£880 Two**

SIR PETER LELY, Follower of – Portrait Of Lady Mary Graham – oil on canvas – 43 x 39½in.
(Sotheby, King &
Chasemore)   **$1,287**   **£825**

LOUIS-NICOLAS LEMASLE – Portrait Of A Young Gentleman – signed, dated and inscribed – 86 x 56in.
(Sotheby's)   **$870**   **£506**

CHARLES ROBERT LESLIE – Ladies At Their Toilet – 24¼ x 19¾in. *(Christie's)* **$1,506** **£972**

PRUDENT LOUIS LERAY – The New Gown – signed – on panel – 13¾ x 10½in. *(Sotheby's)* **$1,673** **£935**

GEORGE DUNLOP LESLIE – Morning Coffee – inscribed – oil on canvas – 32¾ x 44in. *(Sotheby, King & Chasemore)* **$2,545** **£1,430**

PAULUS LESIRE – Portrait Of Reynier Johansz Strik; and Portrait Of Alida Pietersdr. Van Scharlaken – signed and inscribed, also inscribed on the reverse – on panel – 33 x 25in. *(Sotheby's)* **$9,240 £6,160 Pair**

LETHERBROW

THOMAS LETHERBROW – Short Millgate, Manchester In 1840 – signed, inscribed and dated on the reverse – 7½ x 15½in.
(Sotheby Beresford Adams) $48   £28

THOMAS LETHERBROW – The Sun Inn, Poets' Corner, Millgate, Manchester – signed and inscribed on the reverse – on board – 14 x 19in.
(Sotheby Beresford Adams) $19   £11

RICHARD HALEY LEVER – 'Fishing Boat' – signed – oil on canvas on board – 12 x 16in.
(Robert W. Skinner Inc.) $200   £125

RICHARD HAYLEY LEVER – Small Sailing Boats In A Port – signed – oil on canvas laid down – 8½ x 11½in.
(Sotheby, King & Chasemore) $646   £363

REYNAUD LEVIEUX, Circle of – The Virgin And Child – 22in. diam.
(Sotheby's) $2,508   £1,650

S. LEVINSEN – A Market – signed – on board – 25½ x 30in.
(Sotheby's) $530   £308

MAURICE LEVIS – Bords De La Mayenne – signed – 17¾ x 31¼in.
(Sotheby's) $3,347   £1,870

MAURICE LEVIS – La Vielle Gare A Etaples – signed and signed on the reverse – on board – 10¾ x 13½in.
(Sotheby's) $501   £330

MAURICE LEVIS – Bords De La Seine, Ile De France – signed – 17¾ x 31¼in.
(Sotheby's) $3,740   £2,090

RUDOLF LEVY – Stilleben Mit
Ananas – signed – 19¾ x 25½in.
(Sotheby's) **$4,922 £2,750**

LEWIS – Shipping In A Harbour – 14 x
23in.
*(Sotheby Beresford
Adams)* **$19 £11**

CHARLES H. LEWIS – A Skiff Offshore – signed – heightened with bodycolour – 12 x 19¾in.
*(Sotheby Beresford
Adams)* **$51 £30**

T. LEWIS – A View On The Rhine –
26 x 38in.
*(Sotheby Beresford
Adams)* **$314 £187**

ANDRE LHOTE – Le Village De
Mirmande Le Haut – signed – watercolour over pencil on paper laid down
on paper – 12½ x 19¾in.
(Sotheby's) **$2,340 £1,540**

PIETRO LIBERI – The Three Graces –
46 x 67in.
(Sotheby's) **$10,656 £6,160**

PIETRO LIBERI – Mercury Masking
Justice – inscribed on the reverse – 37¾ x
51¼in.
(Sotheby's) **$5,709 £3,300**

J. D. LIDDELL – On The Northumber-
land Coast – signed – 16 x 24in.
*(Sotheby Beresford
Adams)* **$277 £165**

JOHN D. LIDDELL – A Steamer
Wrecked By St. Mary's Island – signed
– oil – 11½ x 23½in.
*(Anderson &
Garland)* **$256 £160**

CHARLES SILLEM LIDDERDALE –
The Picnic Basket – signed with mono-
gram and dated 1890 – 25 x 16in.
*(Sotheby Beresford
Adams)* **$1,186 £682**

JONAS LIE – The Inner Harbor – oil on canvas – 30 x 45in.
(William Doyle Galleries) **$4,750 £2,810**

MAX LIEBERMANN – Children Eating Apples By A Doorway – signed – on panel – 14¾ x 10¼in.
(Sotheby's) **$19,250 £11,000**

ADOLF LIER – Full Cry – signed – 9½ x 16½in.
(Christie's) **$3,240 £2,160**

W. LIFTON – A Lakeland Landscape With Shepherd And Sheep – oil – 20 x 24in.
(Woolley & Wallis) **$267 £160**

RICHARD LINDERUM – Prelates Studying A Map – signed – oil on panel – 21 x 27½in.
(Butterfield's) **$6,000 £3,592**

LIONEL LINDSAY – 'The Dancer' – signed – aquatint – 19 x 14cm.
(Geoff K. Gray) **$204 £120**

SIR LIONEL LINDSAY – 'Tropical Birds In A Figtree' – signed – woodcut – 14 x 19.5cm.
(Geoff K. Gray) **$135 £80**

SIR LIONEL LINDSAY – 'Still Life With Egg Plant, Melon And Grapes' – signed – woodcut – 10 x 13cm.
(Geoff K. Gray) **$90 £54**

NORMAN ALFRED WILLIAMS LINDSAY – 'Delighted Captive' – signed with initials – pen and pencil – 24 x 23cm.
(Geoff K. Gray) **$495 £295**

NORMAN ALFRED WILLIAMS LINDSAY – 'Torso Study' – signed – oil on canvas – 60 x 52cm.
(Geoff K. Gray) **$12,352 £7,058**

WILLIAM LINELL – Asking The Way – signed and dated 1859 – 21 x 29½in.
(Sotheby Beresford Adams) **$1,135 £660**

WILLIAM LINELL – Asking The Way –
signed and dated 1859 – 21 x 29½in.
*(Sotheby Beresford
Adams)* **$1,148 £660**

LINTON – View Across A Lake; Figures
On A Balcony – oil on panel – 8 x 12in.
*(Sotheby, King &
Chasemore)* **$1,468 £825 Pair**

JOHN LINNELL, Follower of – Portrait
Of Alderman John Hall, J.P. – oil on
canvas – 15 x 12in.
*(Sotheby, King &
Chasemore)* **$140 £93**

EGIDIUS LINNIG – Ship Repairers
Working In An Estuary – signed and
dated 1847 – on panel – 18½ x 26in.
(Sotheby's) **$4,922 £2,750**

SIR JAMES DROMGOLE LINTON –
The Pet – signed with initials and
dated '93 – 33 x 23in.
(Christie's) **$773 £432**

LINTON

SIR JAMES DROMGOLE LINTON –
'Portia' – signed with monogram –
oil on canvas – 24 x 18in.
(Sotheby, King &
Chasemore) **$627** **£418**

HENRIETTA LISTER – A Footbridge
Over The River Cover, Woodale – signed
– 13½ x 17½in.
(Anderson &
Garland) **$5** **£3**

IDA LITHERLAND – Still Lives –
signed – 8 x 16in.
(Sotheby Beresford
Adams) **$29** **£17 Pair**

PHILIP LITTLE – 'A Summer Day' –
signed on reverse – oil on canvas board
– 22 x 27in.
(Robert W. Skinner
Inc.) **$550** **£343**

PHILIP LITTLE – 'Stream In The Woods'
– signed on the reverse – oil on canvas
board – 26 x 22in.
(Robert W. Skinner
Inc.) **$700** **£438**

HENRY LIVINGS – Glyn Garnwydd,
Afternoon – indistinctly signed and
inscribed on reverse – 29½ x 39½in.
(Sotheby's) **$803** **£528**

WALTER STUART LLOYD – The Arun
– signed – heightened with bodycolour
– 19 x 28½in.
(Sotheby Beresford
Adams) **$445** **£264**

WALTER STUART LLOYD – Sunny Morning, Isle Of Wight; and St. Anthony, Devon – signed – heightened with body-colour – 13 x 9¼in.
(Sotheby Beresford Adams) **$765** **£440** Two

R. LOARON – Two Ladies In An Open Carriage, With An Escort Travelling Through A Wood At Dusk – signed – oil – 22 x 26.7in.
(Woolley & Wallis) **$234** **£140**

ANTON LOCK – A Man On Horseback Drinking – 33½ x 22½in.
(Sotheby's) **$567** **£330**

WILLIAM EWART LOCKHART – 'Aberdeen' – signed and inscribed and dated 1898 – watercolour – 14½ x 20in.
(Sotheby, King & Chasemore) **$230** **£154**

H. J. LOCKLEY – Bluebell Wood With Figures – signed – watercolour – 6½ x 9in.
(Laurence & Martin Taylor) **$114** **£66**

GEORGE EDWARD LODGE – Lenex Kestrels – signed – heightened with bodycolour – 11 x 9in.
(Sotheby's) **$2,202** **£1,430**

GEORGE EDWARD LODGE – A Hoopoe – signed – heightened with bodycolour – 11 x 8½in.
(Sotheby's) **$1,016** **£660**

LODGE

GEORGE EDWARD LODGE – An American Goshawk – signed – heightened with bodycolour – 12 x 9½in.
(Sotheby's) **$2,202** **£1,430**

MARIANNE LOIR, Attributed to – Portrait Of A Lady In A Yellow Dress – 32 x 26in.
(Sotheby's) **$1,672** **£1,100**

JOHN ARTHUR LOMAX – 'Before Publication' – signed – on panel – 11¾ x 17¾in.
(Christie's) **$2,514** **£1,404**

JOHN ARTHUR LOMAX – 'At Your Service' – signed – on panel – 11½ x 17¾in.
(Christie's) **$2,126** **£1,188**

JOHN ARTHUR LOMAX – Home Brewed – signed inscribed on the reverse – on board – 12 x 9½in.
(Sotheby's) **$1,420** **£935**

JOHN ARTHUR LOMAX – The Elopement Discovered – signed – 24½ x 36¼in.
(Christie's) **$7,733** **£4,320**

JOHN ARTHUR LOMAX – The Tale Of A Fox – signed, and signed and inscribed on a label on the reverse – on panel – 11½ x 18in.
(Christie's) **$3,480** **£1,944**

EDWIN LONG – The Easter Vigil – signed, and signed and inscribed – 52 x 80¾in.
(Christie's) **$3,240** **£2,160**

SYDNEY LONG – 'Barges On The Thames' – signed – watercolour – 26 x 33cm.
(Geoff. K. Gray) **$990** **£590**

RAOUL M. DE LONGPRE – 'Roses And Plums On A Ledge' – signed – gouache on paper – 21 x 28in.
(Robert W. Skinner Inc.) **$1,300** **£812**

EDWIN LONG – Raising The Veil – signed and dated 1879 – 23½ x 18in.
(Sotheby's) **$702** **£462**

LONGSTAFFE

EDGAR LONGSTAFFE – Sunset View
– signed on the reverse – 23 x 35in.
*(Sotheby Beresford
   Adams)*   **$132**   **£77**

CARLE VAN LOO, Follower of –
Portrait Of Maria Leczinska – 82 x 54in.
(Sotheby's)   **$3,009**   **£1,980**

CARLOS LOPEZ – Still Life With Fruit –
signed – watercolour – 6¾ x 10in.
*(Stalker &
   Boos)*   **$55**   **£32**

FRANCIS WILLIAM LORING – 'Morning
Conversation' – signed and dated 1891 –
oil on canvas – 18 x 25¼in.
*(Robert W. Skinner
   Inc.)*   **$600**   **£375**

HEINRICH LOSSOW – The Shepherdess
– signed – 39 x 31in.
(Sotheby's)   **$2,756**   **£1,540**

JOHANN CARL LOTH, Studio of – Ecce
Homo – 46½ x 36½in.
(Sotheby's)   **$836**   **£550**

PHILIP JAMES DE LOUTHERBOURG
– A Wooded Landscape And River
Scene With Ruined Church, Figures And
Cattle – signed and dated 1810 – 18 x
25in.
(Lawrence)   **$787**   **£495**

CHARLES LOW – Barge People With Horses And A Dog By A Lock – signed – watercolour – 9 x 15in.
(Sotheby, King &
Chasemore) **$1,232** **£770**

WILHELM LOWITH – Atelierbesuch – signed – oil on wood – 30 x 25.5cm.
(Germann
Auktionshaus) **$6,629** **£4,143**

LAURENCE STEPHEN LOWRY – Walking In The Park In Winter – signed – pencil – 7 x 10in.
(Sotheby's) **$1,595** **£1,100**

LAURENCE STEPHEN LOWRY – Three Figures With Umbrellas – signed and dated 1953 – oil on canvas – 9 x 6½in.
(Christie's) **$3,913** **£2,592**

LAURENCE STEPHEN LOWRY – Poole Harbour – signed, inscribed and dated 1970 – brown felt tip pen and soft pencil – 9¾ x 14in.
(Christie's) **$1,228** **£660**

LAURENCE STEPHEN LOWRY – The Canal – signed and dated 1912 – oil on canvas – 10¼ x 14in.
(Christie's) **$2,610 £1,728**

LAURENCE STEPHEN LOWRY – Figures In The Rain – signed and dated 1953 – oil on panel – 8¾ x 6½in.
(Christie's) **$2,772 £1,836**

EDWARD GEORGE HANDEL LUCAS – Should Auld Acquaintance Be Forgot? – signed and dated 1880, inscribed on the reverse – oil on canvas – 12 x 10in.
(Sotheby, King & Chasemore) **$2,350 £1,320**

MAXIMILIEN LUCE – Le Chiffonier – signed – oil on canvas – 46 x 38cm.
(Germann Auktionshaus) **$4,199 £2,624**

MAXIMILIEN LUCE – Scene De Port – pencil and pen and ink – 5¾ x 8¾in.
(Sotheby's) **$315 £176**

MAXIMILIEN LUCE — Le Chiffonier —
signed — oil on canvas — 46 x 38cm.
*(Germann
Auktionshaus)* **$15,910 £9,944**

MAXIMILIEN LUCE — Bateaux De
Peche Sur La Plage — signed — pencil
on paper on board — 8 x 12in.
(Sotheby's)   **$315   £176**

MAXIMILIEN LUCE — Scene De Rue
— indistinctly signed — on panel — 8¾
x 11in.
(Sotheby's)   **$984   £550**

MAXIMILIEN LUCE — Vue De
Treport — signed — 11¾ x 14¾in.
(Sotheby's)   **$2,559   £1,430**

LUCEBERT — Gefangene — signed and
dated '61 — oil on canvas — 100 x 150cm.
*(Germann
Auktionshaus)*   **$2,872   £1,795**

MAX LUDBY — In A Harvest Field —
signed and dated 1902 — watercolour
over pencil, heightened with bodycolour
— 21¼ x 15¾in.
(Sotheby's)   **$287   £187**

ALBERT LUDOVICI – Rotten Row –
signed – on panel – 10 x 14in.
*(Sotheby Beresford
   Adams)*   **$1,848   £1,100**

ALBERT LUDOVICI, JNR. – The
Umbrella – signed – 6 x 8½in.
(Sotheby's)   `**$762   £495**

EMIL LUGO – A Mediterranean Town
Scene – signed and dated 1896 – 47¼
x 38in.
(Christie's)   **$9,331   £5,184**

THOMAS LUNY – Shipping In A Swell;
and Rescuing Mariners In Distress –
signed and dated – on panel – 10 x 14in.
(Sotheby's) ⁵   **$1,672   £1,100 Pair**

THOMAS LUNY – A Vessel On The Rocks Off Scarborough By Moonlight – signed and dated 1829 – oil on panel – 14½ x 19½in.
(Hy. Duke & Son)   **$726**   **£420**

THOMAS LUNY – Two Sailing Vessels In Rough Seas – signed – oil on panel – 10 x 14in.
(Hy. Duke & Son)   **$432**   **£250**

ANTONI DE LUST – Flowers In A Vase – 22½ x 18in.
(Sotheby's)   **$9,900**   **£6,600**

LUTI – Head Of Young Man – pastel – 17 x 13in.
(Lawrence)   **$35**   **£22**

THOMAS LUNY, Attributed to – A Coastal Scene With Figures Unloading A Rowing Boat In The Foreground – oil on canvas – 18 x 24in. *(Sotheby, King & Chasemore)*
$3,604 £2,310

LUTZENS

LUTZENS – Cherubs – signed – oil –
20 x 30in.
*(Woolley &
Wallis)* $600   £360

ARTHUR C. H. LUXMOORE – Homeward Serenely She Walked With God's
Hand Upon Her – signed and dated
1873 – watercolour heightened with
white – 17½ x 13in.
(Sotheby's) $372   £242

FRANCIS LYMBURNER – 'Children On
The Beach' – signed – oil on board –
26 x 35cm.
(Geoff K. Gray) $1,354   £806

MICHAEL LYNE – In The Berkeley Hill
Country – signed – oil on canvas – 20 x
30in.
(Christie's) $781   £420

MICHAEL LYNE – Derby Day, The
Parade Ring – signed, dated and inscribed
– watercolour – 11.5 x 15in.
*(Woolley &
Wallis)* $534   £320

MICHAEL LYNE – The Quorn, New Plantation – signed – en gouache – 11 x 16in.
(Lawrence) $367   £231

H. S. LYNTON – Arab Street Scene
With A Man Riding On A Camel And
Numerous Other Figures Among Moorish
Buildings, The Domes And Spires Of A
Mosque Beyond – signed and dated (18)99
– watercolour – 79 x 54cm.
*(Henry Spencer &
Sons)* $860   £480

CORNEILLE DE LYON – Portrait Of
A Man – on panel – 7½ x 5½in.
(Sotheby's) $39,600   £26,400

WILLIAM McALPINE – Coastal Scenes, With Sailing Vessels In Choppy Seas – oil on canvas – 7½ x 20in.
(Hy. Duke & Son) $605   £350 **Pair**

McARTHUR – Two Small Girls Carrying Pails Of Milk On A Track By A Herd Of Cattle – signed and dated '83 – 13½ x 21in.
(Anderson & Garland) $272   £170

SAMUEL McCLOY – The First Science Lesson – signed – 14 x 18in.
(Sotheby Beresford Adams) $861   £495

ARTHUR DAVID McCORMICK – A Nautical Enthusiast – signed and dated '36 – 21 x 15in.
(Sotheby's) $406   £264

JOHN BLAKE MACDONALD – 'The Broken Pitcher' – signed and dated 1861, inscribed on the reverse – oil on panel – 15½ x 11¼in.
(Sotheby, King & Chasemore) $1,090   £682

JOHN McDOUGAL – Early Morning On The Anglesey Coast – signed and dated 1908 – 12 x 19in.
(Sotheby Beresford Adams) $115   £66

JOHN McDOUGAL – Trearddur Bay – signed and dated 1926 – heightened with bodycolour – 13½ x 20in.
(Sotheby Beresford Adams) $134   £77

JOHN McDOUGALL – A Surrey Cornfield – signed and dated 1883, inscribed on a label – heightened with white – 21½ x 35in.
(Sotheby Beresford Adams) $382   £220

MACDUFF

WILLIAM MACDUFF – Making Waves –
signed and dated 1876 – 20 x 16in.
(Sotheby's) **$418** **£275**

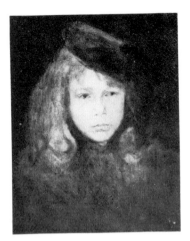

AMBROSE McEVOY – Head Of A Girl
Wearing A Hat – oil on panel – 10½ x 8
8½in.
(Christie's) **$2,772** **£1,836**

AMBROSE McEVOY – Child In A
Ballet Dress – oil on canvas – 62½ x 40in.
(Christie's) **$1,305** **£864**

AMBROSE McEVOY – Lady In Blue,
Mrs How Brown – oil on canvas – 42¾
x 31in.
(Christie's) **$1,793** **£1,188**

MARY McEVOY – Interior With A Girl
Sewing – oil on canvas – 19 x 17in.
(Christie's) **$1,630** **£1,080**

JOHN McGHIE – A Fishergirl Knitting By
The Shore – signed – watercolour and
bodycolour – 13½ x 9½in.
(Christie's &
Edmiston's) **$416** **£260**

JOSEPH WRIGHTSON McINTRYE — Winter Sunset — signed — 17 x 29in. *(Sotheby Beresford Adams)* **$420** **£242**

ROBERT FINLEY McINTYRE — 'The Workshop' — signed, inscribed on verso — oil on panel — 16 x 10.7in. *(Woolley & Wallis)* **$407** **£230**

JOHN McKAY — Resting In The Haystack — signed and dated 1904 — 5½ x 9in. *(Sotheby Beresford Adams)* **$462** **£275**

WILLIAM DARLING MACKAY — Ploughing The Fields — signed — 11 x 14in. *(Christie's & Edmiston's)* **$272** **£170**

FRANK McKELVEY — Coastal Landscape, Ulster — signed — oil on canvas — 18 x 24in. *(Christie's)* **$2,610** **£1,728**

JOHN HAMILTON MACKENZIE — Kirkcudbright High Street — signed — 20 x 26in. *(Christie's & Edmiston's)* **$672** **£420**

PERCY THOMAS MACQUOID — Children Playing By A Gate — signed and dated 1883 — pencil — 9½ x 13½in. *(Sotheby, King & Chasemore)* **$396** **£264**

WILLIAM McTAGGART — The Fisherman's Story — signed and dated '76 — 20 x 30in. *(Christie's & Edmiston's)* **$3,200** **£2,000**

JOHN MacWHIRTER — Venice, From The Gardens — signed — watercolour and bodycolour over pencil — 8¼ x 13½in. *(Sotheby's)* **$338** **£220**

MacWHIRTER

JOHN MacWHIRTER – In The Tyrol –
signed – watercolour with touches of
white heightening – 7½ x 10½in.
(Christie's) $181   £108

GEORG MACCO – A Street Market –
signed and dated 1903 – 19¼ x 14in.
(Sotheby's) $1,673   £935

PETER R. M. MACKIE – Street Scene,
Skye – signed – 14 x 11in.
*(Christie's &
     Edmiston's)* $1,520   £950

CHARLES HODGE MACKIE - View In Venice, The Doge's Palace At Night-
signed – 33x 45in.
(Christie's & Edmiston's) $3,840   £2,400

ELISEE MACLET – Bateaux – signed – watercolour – 8½ x 10¾in.
(Sotheby's) **$334** £220

NICHOLAS MAES, After – Benediction – oil on canvas – 54 x 47in.
(Butterfield's) **$1,500** £888

DANIEL MACLISE – The Time I've Lost In Wooing – 25 x 21in.
(Sotheby's) **$13,860** £7,920

NICOLAES MAES – Portrait Of A Gentleman In A Landscape – 21 x 18in.
(Sotheby's) **$4,730** £2,750

THE MASTER OF THE MAGDALENE LEGEND, Circle of – The Virgin And Child – on panel – 11 x 7½in.
(Sotheby's) **$5,016** £3,300

MAGGS

JOHN CHARLES MAGGS, Follower of – The York Coach – 11 x 14½in.
(Sotheby's) **$335** **£220**

MAGNASCO – Extensive Landscape With Waterfall, Trees, Ruins And Peasants In The Foreground – oil on canvas – 46 x 66in.
(Dreweatt Watson & Barton) **$8,250** **£5,500**

CAMILLE MAGNUS – Landscape – signed – oil on panel – 7 x 9¾in.
(Butterfield's) **$500** **£295**

BEN MAILE – Chester Cathedral – signed, inscribed and dated 1971 on the reverse – 30 x 40in.
(Sotheby Beresford Adams) **$155** **£90**

WILLIAM MALHERBE – Poppies In A Green Vase – signed and dated 1946 – oil on canvas – 35¾ x 24in.
(Christie's) **$1,430** **£953**

J. C. L. MALPASS – 'Chaffinches And Their Young Midst Apple Blossom' – watercolour and gouache – 10½ x 7¼in.
(Dacre, Son & Hartley) **$104** **£60**

LEOPOLD MALEMPRE – The Token; and Idle Moments – signed – 23½ x 15½in.
(Sotheby's) **$669 £440 Two**

K. VAN MANDER – St. John The Baptist Preaching – 50¼ x 36in. *(Sotheby's)* **$2,648** **£1,540**

J. MANDIN – 'Bejewelled Lady In Silk Dress Carrying A Dish Of Fruit And Flowers' – signed on reverse – oil on canvas – 30 x 28in. *(W. H. Lane & Son)* **$190** **£110**

J. H. S. MANN – The First Earrings – 17 x 14in. *(Sotheby Beresford Adams)* **$425** **£253**

WILLIAM MANNERS – On The River Aire – signed and dated 1891 and inscribed – 20 x 30in. *(Sotheby's)* **$1,107** **£605**

MANNERS

WILLIAM MANNERS – Near Kendal – signed – heightened with bodycolour – 11¼ x 16in.
(Sotheby Beresford Adams)   **$497**   **£286**

WILLIAM MANNERS – 'Sunday' – signed – watercolour – 15 x 11½in.
(Sotheby, King & Chasemore)   **$412**   **£275**

JEAN MANNHEIM – 'Meadow Brook' – signed – oil on canvas – 20 x 24in.
(Robert W. Skinner Inc.)   **$500**   **£313**

GEORGE MANSON – 'Gypsy Girl' – signed with monogram – watercolour – 11¼ x 8½in.
(Sotheby, King & Chasemore)   **$462**   **£308**

JAMES BOLIVAR MANSON – August At Hooe, Sussex – signed, and inscribed and dated 1933 on the reverse – oil on panel – 13 x 17in.
(Christie's)   **$652**   **£432**

JAMES BOLIVAR MANSON – Flowers In A Vase – signed – oil on canvas – 24 x 20in.
(Christie's)   **$1,794**   **£1,188**

JAMES BOLIVAR MANSON – Mrs E. R. Workman In Her House At Seamore Place, W.1 – signed – 19½ x 24in.
(Sotheby's)   **$1,276**   **£880**

LOUIS MARCOUSSIS – Vue D'Une Ville – signed – gouache – 13½ x 13½in.
(Sotheby's)   **$3,248**   **£1,815**

S. MARESCA – Kissing Baby – signed – 14 x 9½in.
(Sotheby Beresford Adams)   **$159**   **£93**

GIACOMO MANTEGAZZA – Gypsy Dancers – signed – oil – 21 x 15½in.
(Woolley & Wallis)   **$1,694**   **£1,100**

FLORENCE E. MAPLESTONE – The Armourer's Tale – signed and dated 1881 – watercolour heightened with white – 5¾ x 7¾in.
(Christie's)   **$162**   **£97**

ANDRE MARCHAND – Marque, Animals Grazing – signed, inscribed and dated 1912 – 10 x 13¼in.
(Sotheby Beresford Adams)   **$240**   **£143**

M. MARIESCHI – Piazza San Marco – oil – 34 x 42in.
(Woolley & Wallis)   **$12,936**   **£8,400**

DOMENICO DEI MARCHIS, Called Tempestino – A Southern Landscape – 49¾ x 65½in.
(Sotheby's)   **$8,695**   **£5,720**

LOUIS MARIESTRA – 'An Impression Of Spain' – signed – oil on board – 9 x 13in.
(Sotheby, King & Chasemore)   **$440**   **£275**

MARIS

JACOB MARIS – A Portrait Of A Young Girl – signed – on panel – 8 x 6in. *(Sotheby's)* **$630** **£352**

GEORGE MARKS – When Lengthening Shadows Mark The Sun's Decline – signed and dated 1889 – 11½ x 17½in. *(Sotheby's)* **$847** **£550**

HENRY STACY MARKS – A Purple Gallinule, New Zealand, On A Pad Of Lilies – signed with initials – watercolour heightened with white – 5 x 12¾in. *(Christie's)* **$763** **£486**

WILLIAM MARLOW – The Ruins Of The Pantheon In Oxford Street After The Disastrous Fire Of 14th January, 1792 – 37¼ x 46in. *(Sotheby's)* **$4,983** **£3,300**

PAUL MARNY – 'Rouen Cathedral' – signed and inscribed on a label – watercolour – 32 x 23in. *(Sotheby, King & Chasemore)* **$412** **£275**

PAUL MARNY – Street Scene – watercolour drawing – 44 x 30cm. *(Reeds Rains)* **$298** **£170**

THOMAS FALCON MARSHALL – At
The Spring – signed and dated 1846 –
on panel – 18 x 14in.
*(Sotheby Beresford
    Adams)* $997   £594

HENRI MARTIN – Orphee – signed
and indistinctly dated – 29½ x 48¾in.
(Sotheby's)   **$3,150   £1,760**

F. MARONY – Feeding The Chickens;
and A Wayside Rest – signed – oil on
canvas – 10 x 7¼in.
*(Sotheby, King &
    Chasemore)* $704   **£440 Pair**

HERBERT MENZIES MARSHALL –
Loches – signed – watercolour – 8¼
x 12¼in.
(Christie's) $520   £345

JOHN MARTIN, In The Manner Of –
'Moses Calling The Plague Into Egypt'
– oil on panel – 29 x 43in.
*(Stalker &
    Boos)* $350   £227

WILLIAM MARTIN – Seascapes With Shipping – signed – on board – 8¾ x 13¾in.
(Sotheby, King & Chasemore)   **$618**   **£396 Pair**

F. H. MASON – The Pyramids From Cairo – signed – 4 x 6in.
(Lawrence)   **$49**   **£31**

FRANK HENRY MASON – Low Tide, Scarborough – signed, and inscribed and dated 1923 on the reverse – watercolour heightened with white – 9½ x 13½in.
(Christie's)   **$760**   **£453**

WILLIAM SANFORD MASON – Nymph Of Music – signed and dated 1858 – oil on canvas – 13¾ x 17in.
(Christie's)   **$1,760**   **£1,173**

QUENTIN MASSYS, Follower of – The Virgin And Child Enthroned With St. Joseph And An Angel – on panel – 42 x 29½in.
(Sotheby's)   **$6,811**   **£3,960**

G. MAST – Landscape – signed and dated '34 – pencil and watercolour – 9½ x 14in.
(Stalker & Boos)   **$90**   **£53**

J. MATHAUSER – Peasants In Horses And Carts – signed and one dated 1895 – 28¼ x 38¾in.
(Christie's)   **$2,678**   **£1,728 Pair**

MAURICE

WILLIAM MATHEWSON – 'A Quiet Stream' – signed – oil on board – 59 x 73cm.
(Geoff K. Gray)   **$180**   **£107**

ALEXIS MATHONAT – A Courtesan With A Fan – signed – 28¼ x 23¼in.
(Sotheby's)   **$668**   **£440**

CAMILLE MATISSE – Still Life With A Vase Of Flowers – signed and inscribed – oil – 19 x 17½in.
(Woolley & Wallis)   **$400**   **£260**

T. MATTLINGS – Scenes In Newcastle, The Railway Bridge Crossing Dean Street; and Figures In The Street Beside St. Nicholas' Cathedral – signed – oil on panel – 9 x 7in.
(Anderson & Garland)   **$68**   **£41 Pair**

JAN MATULKA – Cows In A City Landscape – signed – oil on canvas – 29½ x 35¾in.
(Christie's)   **$3,300**   **£2,200**

JAMES MAUBERT, Attributed to – Portrait Of Elizabeth, Wife Of Richard Graves, Wearing A Red Dress, Seated Beside A Fountain And Holding A Scallop Shell – inscribed on a label – 49½ x 39½in.
(Sotheby's)   **$1,410**   **£935**

J. MAURICE – View Near Esher, Surrey, With Church And Figures – oil – 20 x 30in.
(Lawrence)   **$352**   **£220**

MAXENCE

EDWARD MAXENCE – Vase De Fleurs – signed – oil on board – 17½ x 21¼in.
(Sotheby's) **$920 £605**

JAMES EDWIN MEADOWS – A Wayside Inn – signed and dated 1885 – 18 x
32¼in. *(Sotheby, King & Chasemore)* **$1,958 £1,100**

ARTHUR JOSEPH MEADOWS — Dutch
Boats Running For Shelter, Stormy
Weather — signed and dated 1873 — 14
x 24in.
(Sotheby Beresford
Adams)   **$2,679**   **£1,595**

ARTHUR JOSEPH MEADOWS — 'Calais
Boats At Anchor' — signed, inscribed and
dated 1890 — oil on canvas — 30¼ x
40in.
(Sotheby, King &
Chasemore)   **$2,430**   **£1,430**

ARTHUR JOSEPH MEADOWS — Sailing
Boats At The Entrance To Shields Har-
bour With North And South Shields
Beyond — signed and dated 1875 — 24 x
42in.
(Christie's)   **$4,639**   **£2,592**

GORDON A. MEADOWS — Maidenhead
Bridge — signed — heightened with white
— 10 x 14in.
(Sotheby's)   **$372**   **£242**

WILLIAM MEADOWS — Venetian
Capriccios — signed, inscribed and dated
1925 on the reverse — 18 x 32in.
(Sotheby's)   **$1,505**   **£990 Pair**

WILLIAM MEADOWS — Venetian Canal
Scenes — signed — oil on canvas — 12 x
20in.
(Edgar Horne)   **$528**   **£350 Pair**

JOHN MEDINA — Portrait Of Sir Robert
Menzies Of Menzies — signed, inscribed
on the reverse — oil — 50 x 41in.
(Woolley &
Wallis)   **$693**   **£450**

CAMPBELL MELLON – November, Gorleston – signed, inscribed on the reverse – on panel – 8¾ x 12in.
(Sotheby's) **$718** **£418**

CAMPBELL A. MELLON – Corton Denes 1926 – oil – 9¾ x 15¾in.
(Hilams) **$337** **£195**

SIR JOHN BAPTIST MEDINA – Portrait Of Mrs Mary Cholmley And Her Children – 84¼ x 54½in.
(Sotheby's) · **$4,152** **£2,750**

WALTER MEEGAN – Scarborough, Yorkshire – signed – 10 x 14in.
(Sotheby Beresford Adams) **$220** **£132**

WALTER MEEGAN – Ruins By Moonlight – signed – on board – 30.5 x 47cm.
(Sotheby's) **$99** **£60**

WILHELM MELBYE – Sailing Boats In A Swell At Sunset – signed and dated 1853 – 28 x 43in.
(Christie's) **$1,088** **£702**

WILLIAM MELLOR – 'Ingleton' – oil – 36 x 28in.
(Dacre, Son & Hartley) **$1,634** **£950**

WILLIAM MELLOR – On The Dee, Ingleton – oil – 24 x 36in.
(Dacre, Son & Hartley) **$1,386** **£900**

WILLIAM MELLOR – 'Bolton Woods' – oil – 36 x 28in.
(Dacre, Son & Hartley) **$1,634** **£950**

WILLIAM MELLOR – 'On The Burbage, Derbyshire' – signed and inscribed on the reverse – oil on canvas – 20 x 30in.
(Sotheby, King & Chasemore) **$1,020** **£600**

WILLIAM MELLOR – 'Derwentwater'; and 'Windermere' – oil – 12 x 18in.
(Dacre, Son & Hartley) **$2,666** **£1,550 Pair**

WILLIAM MELLOR – Sheep Grazing On The Pasture By A River With Cliffs Rising Above And Heather Covered Hills In The Distance – signed – 19½ x 29¼in.
(Anderson & Garland) **$968** **£580**

WILLIAM MELLOR – On The Wharf, Bolton Woods – signed and inscribed on the reverse – oil on canvas – 20 x 30in.
(Sotheby, King & Chasemore) **$1,496** **£880**

ANDREW MELROSE – Fishing On Lake Placid – signed – oil on canvas – 40 x 29¾in.
(Christie's) **$3,300** **£2,200**

MELVILLE

ARTHUR MELVILLE – Preparing For A Sorti – signed, inscribed and dated 1882 – watercolour – 13¾ x 19¾in.
(Sotheby, King & Chasemore)   **$8,250**   **£5,500**

ARTHUR MELVILLE – Banderilleros A Cheval – signed, inscribed and dated '94 –watercolour and bodycolour – 15½ x 25in.
(Christie's & Edmiston's)   **$3,840**   **£2,400**

ARTHUR MELVILLE – Apple Blossom – signed and dated 1879 – watercolour – 26 x 16½in.
(Christie's & Edmiston's)   **$1,184**   **£740**

ARTHUR MELVILLE – The Alhambra, Granada – watercolour and bodycolour – 25 x 38in.
(Christie's & Edmiston's)   **$4,480**   **£2,800**

HARDEN SIDNEY MELVILLE – The Wood Gatherers – signed and dated 1879 – 24 x 36in.
(Sotheby's)   **$969**   **£638**

BERNARD MENINSKY – Portrait In Green – signed – 20 x 16in.
(Sotheby's)   **$797**   **£550**

BERNARD MENINSKY – Flowers In A Jug – signed – 35½ x 27½in.
(Sotheby's)   **$1,196**   **£825**

MORTIMER MENPES – The Porta Della Carta, Venice – signed – watercolour – 10½ x 8¼in.
(Sotheby, King & Chasemore)   **$858**   **£572**

MORTIMER MENPES – Two Japanese Children In A Street – signed – on panel – 10¼ x 7¾in.
(Sotheby's)   **$605**   **£352**

MORTIMER MENPES – Children In A Boat, Cashmere – signed – pencil and oil on board – 12¾ x 16¼in.
(Sotheby's)   **$340**   **£198**

MENTIAGNIE – A Tyrolean Lake Scene – indistinctly signed – oil on canvas – 15 x 20in.
(Sotheby, King & Chasemore)   **$969**   **£570**

MENZEL

ADOLPH VON MENZEL – Two Men – signed and dated '93 – charcoal and graphite heightened with white – 8¾ x 12in.
(William Doyle Galleries)   **$5,500**   **£3,254**

ADOLPH VON MENZEL – The Visitor – signed – pen and ink on paper – 6½ x 7¼in.
(William Doyle Galleries)   **$1,800**   **£1,065**

BERTHA S. MENZLER-PEYTON – 'Blackie And Company' – signed – oil on canvas – 30 x 40in.
(Robert W. Skinner Inc.)   **$2,300**   **£1,438**

WILLIAM MEREDITH – The Cockle Women Of Pen Clawdd, Wales – signed and dated 1893 – 23 x 35in.
(Sotheby Beresford Adams)   **$2,105**   **£1,210**

DANIEL MERLIN – Caught In The Trap – signed – oil on canvas – 12¾ x 16in.
(Butterfield's)   **$400**   **£236**

P. MESDAG – A Venetian Waterway; and An Old Dutch Town – signed – 16 x 24in.
(Sotheby Beresford Adams)   **$406**   **£242 Pair**

WILLARD LEROY METCALF – Hillside Dwellings, Pelago, Italy – signed – oil on canvas – 26 x 29in.
(William Doyle Galleries)   **$18,000**   **£10,650**

SIDNEY HAROLD METEYARD – Eros,
Love In Idleness, Or Icarus – 34 x 41½in.
(Sotheby's)   **$30,800 £17,600**

GABRIEL METSU – Christ Healing
Peter's Mother-In-Law – indistinctly
signed and dated 166? – 16½ x 13½in.
(Sotheby's)   **$16,830 £11,220**

J. METZINGER – Jeune Fille Au
Plateau De Fruits – dated 1921 – 36½ x
25½in.
(Sotheby's)   **$1,870 £1,045**

MEULENAER

PIETER MEULENAER – A View Of Hemiksem Castle – 32¾ x 45¾in.
(Sotheby's) **$18,078 £10,450**

T. H. MEW – Racehorse 'Thormanby' In A Stable – dated 1860 – 16 x 31in.
(Lawrence) **$193 £121**

WILHELM ALEXANDER MEYERHEIM – A Coastal Town At Dusk – signed – 26¾ x 37½in.
(Sotheby's) **$4,681 £3,080**

ALBERT MEYERING – Figures In A Classical Landscape – oil on canvas – 27 x 23½in.
(Butterfield's) **$3,250 £1,946**

T. MICHAU – A River Landscape With Many Figures – 32¾ x 41in.
(Sotheby's) **$7,189 £4,180**

ARTURO MICHELENA – Portrait Of A Young Girl – signed, inscribed and dated 1888 – 22 x 18in.
(Sotheby Beresford Adams) **$2,838 £1,650**

JAN MIEL – A Peasant Family; and A Beggar With A Pretzel-Seller Both In Southern Landscapes – 9¼ x 12¼in.
(Sotheby's) **$3,678 £2,420 Two**

S. MICHELL – A View Of Penzance, Cornwall From Lezingey – signed and inscribed – 17½ x 31½in.
(Sotheby's) **$535** **£352**

PIERRE MIGNARD – Cupid – 49¼ x 37in.
(Sotheby's) **$12,370** **£7,150**

MIGNON – Wooded Scene – oil – 25 x 21.5in.
(Woolley & Wallis) **$450** **£270**

LOUIS REMY MIGNOT – On The Orinoco, Venezuela – signed and dated 1857 – oil on board – 11¾ x 18¼in.
(Christie's) **$30,800** **£20,533**

THOMAS ROSE MILES – Colwyn Bay – signed, inscribed on a label on the reverse – on board – 12½ x 16½in.
(Sotheby Beresford Adams) **$38** **£22**

SIR J. E. MILLAIS – The Duet – bears monogram – 20 x 17½in.
(Christie's) **$702** **£453**

SIR JOHN EVERETT MILLAIS – Master Hugh Cayley Of Wydale – signed with monogram, inscribed on the reverse – 28½ x 18½in.
(Sotheby's) **$26,400 £17,600**

RAOUL MILLAIS – David And Goliath – signed – 20 x 24in.
(Sotheby's) **$1,754** **£1,210**

FREDERICK MILLER – 'The Old Chain Pier – Brighton', Boats On The Beach Before The Pier – signed – watercolour – 10¼ x 14½in.
(W. H. Lane & Son) **$108** **£62**

MILLER

RALPH DAVIDSON MILLER – In Hopi Village – oil on canvas – 22 x 28in. *(Butterfield's)*   **$2,500**   **£1,497**

FRANCIS DAVID MILLET – 'Fra Fillipo Lippi And Lucrezia Butti' – signed – oil on canvas – 28¼ x 20½in. *(Robert W. Skinner Inc.)*   **$1,200**   **£750**

J. FRANCISQUE MILLET – Idyllic Landscape With Figures And Temple – oil – 19 x 25¼in. *(Laurence & Martin Taylor)*   **$1,400**   **£810**

S. F. MILLS – On The Lookout – signed and dated 1878 – heightened with bodycolour – 16½ x 21in. *(Sotheby Beresford Adams)*   **$702**   **£418**

WILLIAM WATT MILYNE – 'Haughton Village, Hunts.', Cottages Around The Village Pond With Figures And Trees – signed – oil on canvas – 9¾ x 13½in. *(W. H. Lane & Son)*   **$592**   **£340**

HENDRIK VAN MINDERHOUT – A British Man-O'-War Assaulted By Barbary Pirates Off Gibraltar – signed and dated 1682 – 21¾ x 33in. *(Sotheby's)*   **$6,688**   **£4,400**

BENJAMIN EDWIN MINNS – 'Bondi Beach' – signed and dated 1925 – watercolour – 38 x 50cm. *(Geoff K. Gray)*   **$4,967**   **£2,956**

J. MIRO – The Carnival – signed – oil on canvas – 16½ x 20½in. *(Sotheby, King & Chasemore)*   **$1,650**   **£1,100**

JOAN MIRO – 'Composition T' – signed – pencil – 17¾ x 24¼in. *(Du Mouchelles)*   **$1,100**   **£647**

ANTON MIROU – A Wooded Landscape – bears traces of a signature – on metal – 10¼ x 14in.
(Sotheby's)   **$15,605   £9,020**

MARGARET MOCHELES – Venetian Canal Scene – signed and inscribed – oil on canvas – 15 x 22in.
(Sotheby, King & Chasemore)   **$288   £165**

JOHN MOGFORD – A Break In The Clouds – signed – oil on canvas – 18 x 30in.
(Sotheby, King & Chasemore)   **$670   £395**

JOHN MOGFORD – 'Crab Baiting' – signed and dated 1863 – watercolour – 12¾ x 20¾in.
(Sotheby, King & Chasemore)   **$360   £231**

HENRY MOHRMANN – The Olga, A Three-Masted Square Rigger – signed – 24¾ x 39in.
(Sotheby's)   **$2,675   £1,760**

MOLE

JOHN HENRY MOLE – Two Small Girls Shrimping On A Beach – signed and dated 1850 – watercolour – 6¾ x 15¼in.
(Anderson & Garland)   **$64**   **£40**

PIETER DE MOLIJN – A Winter Landscape With Cottages By A Frozen River – signed and dated 1657 – on panel – 17¼ x 29¼in.
(Sotheby's)   **$47,575** **£27,500**

PAOLO MONALDI – Several Peasants Outside An Inn Drinking, Others Seated At A Table, In The Distance Are Trees And Mountains – 39.5 x 31cm.
(Phillips)   **$1,930**   **£1,000**

MONAMY – In Distress – bodycolour – 10¾ x 18in.
(Christie's)   **$260**   **£172**

P. MONAMY – The Catherine And The Royal Caroline In A Storm – oil – 27.5 x 38.5in.
(Woolley & Wallis)   **$774**   **£420**

P. MONAMY – Sailing Vessels Under A Stormy Sky – oil on canvas – 18 x 26½in.
(Hy. Duke & Son)   **$1,003**   **£580**

PETER MONAMY – An English Man Of War Firing A Salute – signed – 7½ x 11in.
(Sotheby's)   **$4,162**   **£2,420**

JAN MONCHABLON – Farm Scene – signed – oil on canvas – 23½ x 32in.
(Du Mouchelles) **$4,000**   **£2,352**

J. B. MONNOYER – Flowers In A Wicker Basket – 18½ x 21¼in.
(Sotheby's)   **$14,757**   **£8,580**

J. B. MONNOYER – Still Lives Of Mixed Flowers In Baskets Upon Stone Ledges – 19 x 25½in.
(Sotheby's)   **$1,142**   **£660 Pair**

CLIFFORD MONTAGUE – A Continental River View – signed – on board – 12 x 15in.
(Sotheby Beresford Adams)   **$203**   **£121**

ALBERT JOSEPH MOORE – Day Dreams
– signed and dated 1874 – 9 x 5¾in.
*(Christie's &
    Edmiston's)*   **$6,400   £4,000**

HENRY MOORE – Vessels Off The
Coast – signed – 16 x 26in.
*(Sotheby Beresford
    Adams)*   **£480   £286**

NELSON AUGUSTUS MOORE – Lake
George, New York – inscribed and
dated 1879 – oil on canvas – 30¼ x 52in.
*(William Doyle
    Galleries)*   **$1,800   £1,065**

RUFUS A. MOORE – Porlock, Somerset,
A Sunlit Scene With Figures In A Colour-
ful Old English Garden – signed – oil on
board – 7½ x 10¾in.
(Neales)   **$1,072   £620**

FRANCIS LUIS MORA – The Matador
– signed and dated 1909 – oil on canvas
– 72¼ x 36in.
*(William Doyle
    Galleries)*   **$2,500   £1,479**

MORA

EDWARD PERCY MORAN – The Gleaners – signed – oil on canvas – 24½ x 18in.
(Butterfield's)   **$1,100**   **£558**

FRANCIS LUIS MORA – Spectators At A Bullfight – signed and dated – oil on canvas – 72 x 36in.
*(William Doyle
    Galleries)*   **$3,200**   **£1,893**

MATIAS MORENO – Arranging The Flowers – signed and dated 1882 – 26 x 16¾in.
(Christie's)   **$3,180**   **£2,052**

EDWARD MORAN – Storm Along The Coast – signed – oil on canvas – 14¾ x 21in.
*(William Doyle
    Galleries)*   **$2,500**   **£1,477**

H. J. MORGAN – Steam And Sailing Ships Off The Coast – signed – oil – 24 x 36in.
*(Woolley &
    Wallis)*   **$443**   **£250**

WALTER JENKS MORGAN – A Midday Rest – signed – 10 x 14in.
(Sotheby Beresford Adams) $813 £484

WILLIAM MORGAN – Bubbles – signed – oil on canvas – 34½ x 28in.
(Butterfield's) $3,250 £1,946

MORLAND – Farmers Conversing Outside An Inn – bears signature – on panel – 14¾ x 11¾in.
(Christie's) $699 £378

AIME MOROT – A Horse And Trainer In A Paddock – signed and dated 1888 – on panel – 9½ x 7¼in.
(Sotheby's) $1,279 £715

A. MORRIS – Sheep In Winter – signed and dated '78 – 29½ x 49½in.
(Sotheby Beresford Adams) $443 £264

SIR CEDRIC MORRIS – Carpet Factories, Isle of Djerba – signed and dated '26 – oil on canvas – 21¼ x 25½in.
(Christie's) $782 £518

CHARLES MORRIS – Rustic Views – three, two signed – various sizes; and an oil on board.
(Sotheby Beresford Adams) $132 £77 Four

GARMAN MORRIS – 'An Essex Creek' – signed – watercolour – 10½ x 27½in.
(Bracketts) $96 £60

P. R. MORRIS – 'Behold I Bring You Good Tidings' – oil on panel – 8 x 11in.
(G. H. Bayley & Sons) $173 £100

PHIL MORRIS – Watering The Shire Horse – signed – oil on canvas – 38 x 51in.
(Sotheby, King & Chasemore) $1,963 £1,155

ALEXANDER MORTIMER – Coming Into Harbour, Newhaven – signed and dated '96 – 20 x 30in.
(Sotheby Beresford Adams) $322 £192

MOSCHELES

MARGARET MOSCHELES – Beach
Scene, Nordwijk – signed and inscribed
– on panel – 9 x 12½in.
*(Sotheby Beresford
Adams)* **$554** **£330**

FORREST K. MOSES – Yellow Store –
signed and dated 1969, also signed,
inscribed and dated on the reverse – oil
on masonite – 15½ x 24in.
(Christie's) **$2,200** **£1,456**

JAN MOSTAERT, Circle of – The Conversion Of Saint Paul – on panel – 17 x
21¼in.
(Sotheby's) **$39,600** **£26,400**

GEORGE WILLIAM MOTE – Near
Guildford – signed and dated 1881 – oil
on canvas – 40½ x 56½in.
*(Sotheby, King &
Chasemore)* **$1,030** **£660**

GEORGE WILLIAM MOTE – Surrey
Landscapes – one signed and dated – oil
on canvas – 20 x 24in.
*(Sotheby, King &
Chasemore)* **$7,820** **£4,600 Pair**

MOTTRAM – 'Sailing Ships And Tugs
On A Calm Sea' – oil on canvas – 23 x
36½in.
*(W. H. Lane &
Son)* **$226** **£130**

FREDERICK DE MOUCHERON – A
Stag Hunt In An Extensive Landscape –
signed – 38¾ x 54in.
(Sotheby's) **$15,675** **£10,450**

FREDERICK DE MOUCHERON –
Elegant Figures Beside A Fountain –
signed – on panel – 16 x 21¾in.
(Sotheby's) **$5,775** **£3,850**

I. DE MOUCHERON – Figures At A Fountain In A Southern Landscape – 23½ x 18¾in.
(Sotheby's)   **$5,709   £3,300**

ANTOINE EDOUARD JOSEPH MOULINET – Priere Avant Le Diner – signed and dated 1867 – oil on wood – 33.5 x 25cm.
(Germann Auktionshaus)   **$2,210   £1,380**

WILLIAM MOUNCEY – The Lower Thames – signed – 34 x 43in.
(Christie's & Edmiston's)   **$2,560   £1,600**

NICHOLAES MOYAERT – Christ And The Women Taken In Adultery – on panel – 39½ x 56¼in.
(Sotheby's)   **$4,540   £2,640**

MOZART – A Watermill In A Mountainous Landscape – on copper – 7 x 9in.
(Sotheby's)   **$946   £550**

MUCKLEY

JAMES MUDD – The Thames At Sunset – signed and dated 1880 – heightened with bodycolour – 16 x 24in.
(Sotheby Beresford Adams) $48   £28

JULES ALEXIS MUENIER – A Rural Scene With A Horse And Cart In The Foreground – signed – oil on canvas – 19¾ x 24in.
(Sotheby, King & Chasemore) $463   £297

PIETER MULIER, Called 'Tempesta' – A Pastoral Landscape – 18 x 28in.
(Sotheby's) $1,892   £1,100

PIETER MULIER – Fishing Boats On The Shore – oil – 22 x 27.5in.
(Woolley & Wallis) $796   £450

LOUIS FAIRFAX MUCKLEY – Autumn – 80½ x 32¼in.
(Christie's) $14,580   £9,720

WILLIAM JABEZ MUCKLEY – Daffodils And Other Flowers In A Vase – signed – 26¾ x 22¾in.
(Christie's) $1,339   £864

WILLIAM JAMES MULLER – Two Figures On A Country Path – signed and dated 1840 – 15½ x 25½in.
(Sotheby's) $1,702   £990

WILLIAM JAMES MULLER – A Coastal Scene With Two Windmills On A Quay; and A Canal Scene With Barges Before A Cottage With Figures – signed – watercolour – 32 x 12.5cm. *(Osmond, Tricks)*   **$620**   **£360 Pair**

WILLIAM JAMES MULLER – Arab Merchants On A Quay In Alexandretta – signed and dated 1843 – 30¼ x 23in. *(Christie's)*   **$8,910**   **£5,940**

WILLIAM JAMES MULLER – An Italian Street Hawker – signed and dated '42 – 30 x 19in. *(Sotheby Beresford Adams)*   **$924**   **£550**

FRITZ MULLER-SANDECK – 'Snow Covered Landscape' – signed and inscribed – oil on canvas – 27½ x 39½in. *(Sotheby, King & Chasemore)*   **$545**   **£341**

MULREADY

AUGUSTUS E. MULREADY –
Uncared For – signed and signed and
inscribed on the reverse – 21½ x 15½in.
(Christie's)   **$1,865**   **£1,188**

PAUL SANDBY MUNN – On The Mou-
dach, North Wales – signed and dated
1832 – watercolour – 7 x 13½in.
(Sotheby, King &
Chasemore)   **$816**   **£480**

HERMAN DUDLEY MURPHY – Along
The Venetian Canal – signed – oil on
canvas – 20 x 28¼in.
(Christie's)   **$7,700**   **£5,133**

HERMAN DUDLEY MURPHY – 'The
Guidecca' – signed on a label – oil on
panel – 9½ x 12½in.
(Robert W. Skinner
Inc.)   **$500**   **£312**

SIR ALFRED JOSEPH MUNNINGS –
The Artist's Wife – signed and dated
1903 – oil on canvas – 16 x 12in.
(Sotheby, King &
Chasemore)   **$1,801**   **£1,012**

MURILLO – The Mystical Marriage Of
St. Catherine – 28 x 20½in.
(Sotheby Beresford
Adams)   **$1,330**   **£792**

MURILLO – Beggar Boys – oil – 21 x
14½in.
(Lawrence)   **$187**   **£66**

CHRISTOPHER MURPHY, JNR. –
Dock Workers – oil on board – 20 x
24in.
(Butterfield's)   **$450**   **£266**

SIR DAVID MURRAY – Roadside Calvary
– signed – 14¾ x 19½in.
(Christie's &
Edmiston's)   **$608**   **£380**

SIR DAVID MURRAY – A Military
Review On The Banks Of The River Forth
– signed and dated 1877 – watercolour
– 9 x 13½in.
(Christie's &
Edmiston's)   **$320**   **£200**

SIR DAVID MURRAY – Beached Boats At Sunset – signed and dated 1898 – oil on canvas – 17½ x 23in.
(Sotheby, King & Chasemore) **$1,733 £1,155**

SIR DAVID MURRAY – 'Storm Coming On' – signed – oil on canvas – 10 x 17¾in.
(Sotheby, King & Chasemore) **$211 £132**

AUGUSTE MUSIN – A Dutch Fishing Smack – signed – on panel – 7½ x 4¾in.
(Sotheby's) **$752 £492**

FRANCOIS MUSIN – Figures In A Storm On A Seafront Promenade – signed – oil on panel – 16 x 28in.
(Woolley & Wallis) **$3,006 £1,800**

THOMAS MURRAY – Portrait Of A Lady Of The Graves Family – oval 29 x 24½in.
(Sotheby's) **$1,578 £1,045**

HENDRIK AARNOT MYIN – Horses And Cattle In A River Landscape – signed and dated 1798 – on panel – 14¾ x 19in.
(Sotheby's) **$3,027 £1,760**

N

CHARLES CHRISTIAN NAHL – Lion In Pursuit Of Two Arabian Horsemen – signed – oil on canvas – 22 x 28in. *(Butterfield's)* **$3,250   £1,946**

JOHN NASH – A Quarry – watercolour over pencil – 17 x 22in. *(Sotheby's)* **$1,515   £1,045**

PAUL NASH – 'Spring Woods' – signed and dated 1923 – pencil and watercolour – 19½ x 13¾in. *(Sotheby, King & Chasemore)* **$380   £253**

PAUL NASH – The Pond At Souldern – signed and dated 1926 – watercolour and coloured chalks – 14½ x 18½in. *(Christie's)* **$2,283   £1,512**

TOM NASH – Descent From The Cross – signed and dated 1934 – oil on paper – 14½ x 10½in. *(Sotheby's)* **$239   £165**

ALEXANDER NASMYTH – A View Of A Castle, Possibly Powis Castle – signed – 18 x 24in. *(Christie's)* **$3,196   £1,728**

PATRICK NASMYTH – A Landscape Near Godstone, Surrey With Sportsmen – signed – 18¾ x 24½in. *(Sotheby's)* **$9,135   £6,050**

PATRICK NASMYTH – A Wooded Landscape With A Seated Shepherd And His Dog In The Foreground – oil on board – 9¾ x 13½in. *(Geering & Colyer)* **$948   £600**

JEAN-MARC NATTIER, Studio of – Portrait Of A Gentleman Sportsman; and Portrait Of A Lady As Diana – 52 x 39½in. *(Sotheby's)*
$25,916   £17,050 Pair

WILLIAM NEDHAM – A Gentleman On A Grey Hunter With His Hounds – 21¼ x 29½in.
(Sotheby's)   **$3,986   £2,640**

R. NEEDHAM – In The Woods – signed with initials and dated 1875 – heightened with bodycolour – 29 x 21in.
*(Sotheby Beresford
   Adams)*   **$38   £22**

VAN DER NEER – A Moonlit River Scene – bears monogram – on panel – 10¼ x 12½in.
*(Sotheby Beresford
   Adams)*   **$1,108   £660**

VAN DER NEER – River Landscape, Evening – oil – 15 x 19¼in.
*(Laurence & Martin
   Taylor)*   **$830   £480**

AERT VAN DER NEER – A Moonlit River Landscape – signed in monogram – 20¼ x 28in.
(Sotheby's)   **$24,739   £14,300**

NEUMANN

JOHAN NEUMANN – The Danish Ship, Prins Christian Frederik, Engaged Against British Vessels At The Battle of Sjaellands Odde – signed and dated 1901 – 32½ x 53¼in.
(Sotheby's) **$1,420** **£935**

ALFRED ARTHUR BRUNEL DE NEUVILLE – Kittens At The Rabbit Hutch – signed – oil on panel – 12½ x 18in.
(William Doyle Galleries) **$3,600** **£2,130**

E. NEVIL – Whitby; and Robin Hood's Bay, Yorkshire – signed and inscribed – heightened with white – 15 x 11in.
(Sotheby Beresford Adams) **$204** **£121 Two**

GEORGE F. NICHOLLS – A Cheshire Cottage – signed – 12½ x 9in.
(Sotheby Beresford Adams) **$70** **£41**

JOHN E. NICHOLLS – Still Life, Roses, Lillies, Carnations And Other Flowers – signed and dated – oil on board – 24 x 20in.
(Woolley & Wallis) **$283** **£170**

BEN NICHOLSON –A Cornish Land-scape – pencil – 9½ x 13¾in.
(Christie's) **$1,223** **£810**

FRANCIS NICHOLSON – Pont Aberglaslyn, North Wales – signed, inscribed and dated 1806 on the reverse – watercolour – 25 x 35½in.
(Sotheby, King & Chasemore) **$652** **£418**

JOHN MILLAR NICHOLSON – A Busy Harbour Scene At Douglas, Isle Of Man, With Figures And Boats – signed and dated 1883 – watercolour – 13 x 20in.
(Chrystals) **$1,164** **£650**

SIR WILLIAM NICHOLSON – The Hall By The Sea, Margate – signed and dated 1909 – oil on canvas – 21½ x 23½in.
(Christie's) **$2,283** **£1,512**

WINIFRED NICHOLSON – Abstract Composition – gouache – 8¾ x 12in.
(Christie's) **$423** **£280**

E. NICOL – An Irish Quay – heightened with white – 9¼ x 12½in.
(Sotheby Beresford Adams) **$114** **£66**

EDMUND JOHN NIEMANN, SNR. – Fisherfolk And Their Craft On A Beach At Low Tide – signed – 18 x 24in.
(Sotheby's) **$869** **£572**

EDMUND JOHN NIEMANN – 'Bridge Of Dunoon' – signed – oil on canvas – 12 x 18in.
(Sotheby, King & Chasemore) **$558** **£319**

EDMUND JOHN NIEMANN – Shipping In A Harbour – signed – oil on panel – 5.7 x 14.5in.
(Woolley & Wallis) **$885** **£500**

EDMUND JOHN NIEMANN — Sarum, Near Salisbury, Old Sarum In The Distance — signed, inscribed and dated '73 — on panel — 9 x 25in.
(Christie's) $2,176   £1,404

EDMUND JOHN NIEMANN — Carisbrooke, Isle Of Wight — signed — 25 x 45in.
(Lawrence) $3,585   £2,255

HERMANN NIGG — The Sirens — signed and dated 1855 — 64 x 38½in.
(Sotheby's) $2,560   £1,430

GIUSEPPE DE NITTIS — A Landscape With Traveller — signed — oil — 14 x 9.5in.
(Woolley & Wallis) $1,570   £940

JAMES CAMPBELL NOBLE — View Of Venice — signed — 18½ x 22in.
(Christie's & Edmiston's) $640   £400

JAMES CAMPBELL NOBLE — Waiting For Spring, Figure Outside Thatched Cottage — watercolour — 9 x 14in.
(John Hogbin & Son) $20   £12

JOHN SARGENT NOBLE — 'Caught In The Act' — signed and dated 1876 — 28 x 40in.
(Sotheby, King & Chasemore) $2,310   £1,329

GIUSEPPE NOGARI — Portrait Of A Young Girl — 21¼ x 16½in.
(Sotheby's) $2,093   £1,210

NOGARI

MAX NONNENBRUCH – By The Sea – signed – 43 x 31½in.
(Christie's)   **$5,670**   **£3,780**

ADRIANUS CORNELIS VAN NOORT – On The Beach – signed – on panel – 11½ x 15½in.
(Christie's)   **$778**   **£432**

GIUSEPPE NOGARI AND FRANCESCO SIMONINI – Field-Marshal Count Matthias Johannes Von Der Schulenburg On Horseback – 78 x 57in.
(Sotheby's)   **$32,350**   **£18,700**

SIR SIDNEY NOLAN – Leda And The Swan – signed – oil on paper – 11½ x 9½in.
(Sotheby's)   **$1,355**   **£935**

CARL JOHN DAVID NORDELL – Child In Blue Dress – signed – oil on canvas – 24 x 18in.
(William Doyle Galleries)   **$2,800**   **£1,656**

AXEL NORDGREN – A Fjord Landscape With Fisherman In The Foreground – oil on canvas – 38½ x 52¾in.
(Sotheby, King & Chasemore)   **$6,520   £4,180**

ORLANDO NORIE – Fishergirls With The Catch – signed – heightened with body-colour – 9 x 15½in.
(Sotheby's)   **$187   £100**

DAVID DE NOTER – A Lady In An Elegant Interior – signed – 30¾ x 25½in.
(Sotheby's)   **$10,238   £5,720**

PARSONS NORMAN – 'Fritton Lake – Looking South', With Figures In Boat – watercolour – 16½ x 23in.
(Hilhams)   **$144   £90**

WYNAND JAN JOSEPH NUYEN – A Wooded River Landscape With Elegant Figures In A Boat And A Village Beyond – signed and dated '38 – on panel – 12 x 16¼in.
(Christie's)   **$1,166   £648**

329

OCTAVIUS OAKLEY – A Reflective
Moment – signed – watercolour
heightened with bodycolour – 21½ x 15in.
*(Sotheby, King
& Chasemore)* $570   £300

O. OCHUM – Alpine River Landscapes
– one signed – 35 x 51in.
*(Sotheby, King &
Chasemore)* $1,848   £1,056 **Pair**

K. OCKENT – 'Reclining Deer In Woodland' – signed and dated 1858 – 10¼ x
13in.
*(W. H. Lane &
Son)* $101   £58 **Pair**

RODERICK O'CONOR – Reclining Nude
– oil on canvas – 25 x 19in.
(Christie's) $2,446   £1,620

RODERICK O'CONOR – Girl On A Bed
– oil on canvas – 21 x 25in.
(Christie's) $3,098   £2,052

HUGO OEHMICHEN – Sharing The
Apples – signed – 25 x 18¼in.
(Sotheby's) $10,032   £6,600

HELEN OGILVIE – Stone Ruin, Cape
Bridgewater – signed and dated '66 –
tempera on panel – 8½ x 9½in.
(Christie's) $326   £216

C. OGILVY – Study Of The Clipper
'Amy' – signed and dated 1865 – on
canvas – 24 x 36in.
*(Sotheby, King &
Chasemore)* $943   £605

WILLIAM OLIVER – A Distant View Of Samaria – inscribed and dated 1852 – pencil and watercolour – 11 x 14½in. *(Christie's)* **$288 £172**

JOHN OLSEN – 'Sunlight And Avocets On The Lake' – signed and dated '77 – watercolour – 98 x 68cm. *(Geoff K. Gray)* **$515 £295**

WILLIAM OLIVER – A Spanish Beauty – signed and dated 1878 – 19 x 15in. *(Sotheby Beresford Adams)* **$1,848 £1,100**

B. P. OMMEGANCK – A Shepherd Asleep, With Cattle And Sheep In A River Landscape – on panel – 17½ x 22¾in. *(Christie's)* **$2,343 £1,512**

WILLIAM OLIVER, Attributed to – View Of A Windmill, With A Gipsy Encampment – oil on canvas – 18½ x 25½in. *(Sotheby, King & Chasemore)* **$560 £374**

OMMEGANCK

BALTHAZAR PAUL OMMEGANCK –
Crossing The Ford – on panel – 11½ x
14in.
*(Sotheby Beresford
    Adams)*   **$8,130   £4,840**

GEORGE BERNARD O'NEILL –
The Auction – signed – 8¼ x 13in.
(Christie's)   **$11,340   £7,560**

HENRY NELSON O'NEIL – Sleep –
signed and dated 1870 – 24 x 20in.
(Sotheby's)   **$4,950   £3,300**

HENRY NELSON O'NEIL – The Parting Cheer – signed and dated 1861 – 52 x
74in. *(Sotheby's)*   **$59,400   £39,600**

JOHN OPIE – The Gleaner – 29 x 24in.
(Sotheby's)   **$4,919**   **£2,860**

ERNST OPPLER – Liegender Akt – signed – oil on canvas – 19¾ x 25¾in.
(Sotheby's)   **$3,344**   **£2,200**

ORIZZONTE – Classical Landscape With A Traveller Attacked By A Snake – 23½ x 28½in.
*(Sotheby Beresford
      Adams)*   **$2,956**   **£1,760**

EMIL ORLIK – Vase Mit Blumen – signed – oil on canvas on panel – oval 12 x 18in.
(Sotheby's)   **$3,176**   **£2,090**

J. R. ORLON – An Italian Girl With An Urn On Her Head – dated 1847 – oil – 24 x 18in.
(Lawrence)   **$78**   **£49**

VLADIMIR DONATOVICH ORLOVSKY – A Peasant In A Troika – signed – oil on panel – 12 x 16in.
(Sotheby's)   **$1,036**   **£682**

SIR WILLIAM ORPEN – Girl Reading In Bed – brush and grey wash – 5½ x 8¼in.
(Christie's)   **$782**   **£518**

SIR WILLIAM ORPEN – Girl In A Feathered Hat – red chalk and pencil – 13 x 9¼in.
(Christie's)   **$1,386**   **£918**

SIR WILLIAM ORPEN – Death And The Stone Breaker – signed and dated 1900 – pencil heightened with white – on beige paper – 8 x 10¾in.
(Christie's)   **$678**   **£432**

ORPEN

SIR WILLIAM ORPEN – Portrait Of Captain Wood, The Inniskilling Fusiliers – signed – oil on canvas – 30 x 25in.
(Christie's) **$1,695 £1,088**

ORROCK – A Country Churchyard – 12½ x 19½in.
(Sotheby Beresford Adams) **$23 £13**

JAMES ORROCK – Near Milford, Surrey; and Arundel – signed and dated 1897 – 8 x 19in.
(Sotheby's) **$1,050 £682 Pair**

JAMES ORROCK – Harvesters, Storm Approaching – signed and dated 1893 – black pencil, black chalk and watercolour – 7¼ x 18¾in.
(Christie's) **$490 £324**

JAMES ORROCK – A Rest On The Bank – signed and dated 1884 – canvas on board – 20 x 30in.
(Sotheby's) **$535 £352**

JAMES ORROCK – Coastal Scene, Near Criccieth, With Harlech Castle In The Distance – signed – watercolour – 7.5 x 12.5in.
(Woolley & Wallis) **$175 £105**

MARTIN RICO Y ORTEGA – A Venetian Scene – signed – oil on canvas – 18¼ x 29in.
(William Doyle Galleries) **$7,000 £4,142**

JAN VAN OS – A Coastal Scene With A Peasant Farmhouse To The Left And Shipping Beyond – 12¼ x 17in.
(Sotheby Beresford Adams) **$8,316 £4,950**

G. OSBORN – River Landscapes With Fishermen – signed – oil – 10 x 18in.
(Woolley & Wallis) **$500 £300 Pair**

WALTER OSBORNE – An Extensive Landscape – oil on canvas board – 7 x 10¾in.
(Sotheby, King & Chasemore) **$822 £462**

WALTER OSBOURNE – Cattle In A Landscape – signed – oil on canvas – 12½ x 15¾in.
(Sotheby, King & Chasemore) **$4,813** **£2,750**

CARL AUGUST HEINRICH FERDINAND OSTERLEY – A Norwegian Fjord Scene – signed – oil on canvas – 41 x 60in.
(Sotheby, King & Chasemore) **$748** **£440**

EDMUND OSTHAUS – After The Nap – signed, inscribed on the reverse – watercolour on paper – 29¾ x 21¾in.
(Christie's) **$3,300** **£2,200**

OSLO MASTER, The – The Virgin Of Mercy – on panel – 55¼ x 31½in.
(Sotheby's) **$13,376** **£8,800**

A. VAN OSTADE – The Letter – oil – 6 x 5.2in.
(Woolley & Wallis) **$1,503** **£900**

JEAN-BAPTISTE OUDRY, Manner of – Flowers In A Basket – bears signature – 34½ x 27¼in.
(Sotheby's) **$1,203** **£792**

OUTHWAITE

WILLIAM OUTHWAITE – Ann Hatha-way's Cottage; and West Gate, Warwick – signed, inscribed on labels – 10 x 14in.
(Sotheby Beresford Adams)   **$190**   **£110 Pair**

PIERRE JUSTIN OUVRIE – Le Palais De Versailles; and Le Chateau De Neuilly – signed – 31½in. diam.
(Sotheby's)   **$51,150**   **£34,100 Pair**

GEORGE O. OWEN – 'Turnips' – inscribed on reverse and dated 1895 – 9 x 11½in.
(Sotheby, King & Chasemore)   **$594**   **£396**

ROBERT EMMETT OWEN – 'Winter Sunlight' – signed – oil on canvas – 36 x 46in.
(Robert W. Skinner Inc.)   **$3,000**   **£1,875**

ELLEN G. OZANNE – Evening; and Moonlight – signed – 19½ x 24in.
(Sotheby Beresford Adams)   **$75**   **£44 Pair**

K. PACELLI – Two Figures In Front Of A Building – signed – 12½ x 9½in.
(Elliott & Green)   **$760**   **£440**

JOSEPH PAELINCK – Orpheus And Eurydice – 79 x 57in.
(Christie's)   **$15,876**   **£10,584**

JULES PAGE – Crepuscle, Twin Peaks At San Francisco – signed – oil on board – 10¼ x 13½in.
(Butterfield's)   **$1,500**   **£888**

GEORGE PAICE – A Grey And A Companion – signed and dated 1882 – 20 x 27in.
(Sotheby's)   **$702**   **£462**

HAROLD SUTTON PALMER – A Woodland Scene With A Stream – signed – watercolour – 14¼ x 20¾in.
(Geering & Colyer) $758 £480

HAROLD SUTTON PALMER – 'Grasmere' – signed – watercolour – 14 x 21in.
(Woolley & Wallis) $900 £540

HARRY SUTTON PALMER – A Country Cottage At Studland – signed – watercolour – 13¾ x 10in.
(Sotheby, King & Chasemore) $1,793 £1,055

HARRY SUTTON PALMER – A Welsh Valley – signed – watercolour – 14¾ x 20in.
(Sotheby, King & Chasemore) $596 £341

HARRY SUTTON PALMER – 'In The Lledr Valley, N. Wales' – signed and inscribed on a label – watercolour – 14 x 19¾in.
(Sotheby, King & Chasemore) $1,116 £638

HARRY SUTTON PALMER – On The Wye – signed – 18 x 24in.
(Sotheby's) $1,863 £1,210

HARRY SUTTON PALMER – The Wye Evening – signed – 14 x 22in.
(Sotheby's) $1,863 £1,210

PAOLETTI

ANTONIO PAOLETTI – Young Fruit-seller, Venice – signed and inscribed – canvas on board – 21½ x 32in.
(Christie's)   **$7,533   £4,860**

VICENTA DE PAREDES – Cardinal And His Kittens – signed – oil on canvas – 12¾ x 9½in.
(Butterfield's)   **$1,000   £598**

J. S. PARK – Roses In A Vase – bears signature – oil on canvas – 16½ x 13¼in.
(Sotheby, King & Chasemore)   **$182   £104**

JOHN ANTHONY PARK – Farmhouse – signed – oil – 24 x 30in.
(Woolley & Wallis)   **$267   £160**

JOHN ANTHONY PARK – 'Summer In The Harbour, St. Ives' – signed – oil on canvas – 13½ x 18in.
(Sotheby, King &
Chasemore) **$810** **£506**

HENRY H. PARKER – Woolhampton, Berks; and The River Stort, Harlow, Essex – signed, signed and inscribed on the reverse – 12¼ x 18¼in.
(Christie's) **$1,840** **£1,188 Pair**

HENRY H. PARKER – Welsh River Landscape – signed – oil – 24 x 36in.
(Woolley &
Wallis) **$673** **£380**

HENRY H. PARKER – Near Chertsey-on-Thames – signed on the reverse – oil on canvas – 20 x 29½in.
(Dreweatt Watson &
Barton) **$1,800** **£1,200**

HENRY H. PARKER – Silent Waters – signed, inscribed on the reverse – 23 x 25in.
(Sotheby Beresford
Adams) **$2,587** **£1,540**

JOHN PARKER – At Dorchester, Oxfordshire – signed with monogram. and dated – watercolour – 9.7 x 13.7in.
(Woolley &
Wallis) **$267** **£160**

STANLEY PARKER – Caricature Portrait Of Head Of George Bernard Shaw – signed – in pencil – 15 x 10in.
(Lawrence) **$165** **£106**

WILLIAM PARROT – A Fair In The Champs Elysees, Paris – signed and dated 1851 – 45 x 59in.
(Sotheby's) **$40,425** **£26,950**

ALFRED PARSONS – 'Fallen Willows' – signed and inscribed on reverse – oil on board – 9½ x 13½in.
(Sotheby, King &
Chasemore) **$750** **£429**

PARSONS

ARTHUR WILDE PARSONS – An Extensive Coastal Scene With A Beached Fishing Boat Unloading – signed and dated '89 – oil on canvas – 92 x 61.5cm.
(Osmond, Tricks)   **$1,238**   **£728**

ARTHUR WILDE PARSONS – 'Stains Castle, Cruden Bay, Aberdeen', Fishing Smacks In A Rough Sea Before The Castle – signed and dated '81 – watercolour – 52 x 41cm.
(Osmond, Tricks)   **$602**   **£305**

MAX PARSONS – Seascape With Gulls And Sailing Vessels – signed – oil on panel – 10 x 14in.
(John Hogbin & Son)   **$42**   **£25**

RICHARD L. PARTINGTON – Evening, Oakland Estuary – signed and dated '15 – oil on canvas – 18 x 24in.
(Butterfield's)   **$1,100**   **£650**

JULES PASCIN – Jeunes Filles Sur La Plage D'Ostende – signed – 21½ x 18¼in.
(Sotheby's)   **$3,740**   **£2,090**

JULES PASCIN – Portrait De Femme – pencil and pen and indian ink – 7¼ x 5¼in.
(Sotheby's)   **$315**   **£176**

DANIEL PASMORE – The Serenade – signed and dated 1876 – on panel – 13½ x 11¼in.
(Christie's)   **$702**   **£453**

DANIEL PASMORE, JNR. – The Revellers – signed and dated 1871 – 14¼ x 20¼in.
(Christie's) **$1,546** **£864**

T. PATCH – Classical River Scene – oil on canvas – 25 x 38½in.
(Sotheby, King & Chasemore) **$1,272** **£715**

PIERRE PATEL, The Younger – A Southern Landscape – 25½ x 37½in.
(Sotheby's) **$2,508** **£1,650**

FRANK PATON – Beauty And Lictor – signed and dated 1885 – oil on canvas – 23 x 27¼in.
(Geering & Colyer) **$1,530** **£900**

FRANK PATON – Stage Coach At The Chequers Inn, Departure And Arrival – signed and dated 1893 – watercolour over pencil heightened with bodycolour – 6 x 8¼in.
(Sotheby's) **$2,540** **£1,650 Pair**

SIR JOSEPH NOEL PATON – A Midsummer Night's Dream – signed and inscribed – diam. 10in.
(Sotheby's) **$8,663** **£4,950**

EDOUARD L. PATRY – Head And Shoulders Portrait Of Young Woman – signed – oil on canvas – 24 x 24in.
(Edgar Horne) **$362** **£240**

JOHN PAUL – Study Of A Horse In A Stable – signed and dated 1877 – oil on canvas – 20 x 24in.
(Sotheby, King & Chasemore) **$774** **£484**

CHARLES JOHNSON PAYNE, Called Snaffles – The Soldiers – signed and inscribed – pencil and watercolour heightened with white – 20½ x 26in.
(Christie's) **$1,944** **£1,296**

J. PAULMAN – Going To Market; and Flower Gatherers – signed – 16 x 12in.
(Sotheby's) **$1,086** **£715 Two**

EDGAR PAYNE – California Late Afternoon – signed – oil on canvas – 12 x 16in.
(Butterfield's) **$1,300** **£770**

EDGAR PAYNE – Venetian Waters – signed – oil on canvas – 20 x 29in.
(Butterfield's) **$4,500 £2,694**

EDGAR ALWIN PAYNE – Mountain Landscape – signed – oil on board – 9 x 12in.
(Robert W. Skinner Inc.) **$800 £500**

EDGAR ALWIN PAYNE – 'Landscape With Purple Mountains' – signed – oil on board – 9 x 12in.
(Robert W. Skinner Inc.) **$1,050 £656**

WILLIAM PAYNE – View Of Castle And Town Of Okehampton, Devon – inscribed on reverse – oval 7½ x 11in.
(Lawrence) **$542 £341**

REMBRANDT PEALE – George Washington – signed – oil on canvas – 36¼ x 29¼in.
(Christie's) **$60,500 £40,333**

REMBRANDT PEALE – Portrait Of George Washington – signed on the reverse – oil on canvas – 30 x 25in.
(William Doyle Galleries) **$20,000 £11,834**

GEORGE PEARCE – Fishing Boats And Figures By Wooden Quay – signed – oil on canvas – 23½ x 19½in.
(Olivers) **$166 £98**

STEPHEN PEARCE – A Fox-Hound – signed and inscribed on a label – heightened with white – 15 x 18cm.
(Sotheby's) **$58 £35**

CHARLES PEARS – 'Gosport' – signed – on board – 13 x 17¾in.
(Sotheby, King & Chasemore) **$492 £308**

MARGUERITE S. PEARSON – 'The
Artist Before Her Easel' – signed –
oil on canvas – 24 x 18in.
*(Robert W. Skinner
Inc.)*   **$500**   **£312**

PEEL – Welsh River Landscape With Two
Fishermen In The Foreground – oil on
canvas – 26 x 36in.
*(Dreweatt Watson &
Barton)*   **$420**   **£280**

JAMES PEEL – On A Highland Loch –
signed – 13 x 21in.
*(Sotheby Beresford
Adams)*   **$156**   **£93**

JAMES PEEL – View Of Sandhill,
Surrey – signed, and inscribed on a label
on the reverse – 8 x 12in.
(Christie's)   **$676**   **£378**

JOHN PEELE – Child Sleeping On Rocks
– signed and dated 1891– 24 x 30in.
(Du Mouchelles)   **$2,500**   **£1,470**

PEETERS – Shipping In A Swell –
bears signature – on panel – 17¾ x 25in.
(Sotheby's)   **$1,324**   **£770**

THOMAS KENT PELHAM – Cutting Up
The Rhubarb – signed with monogram –
11½ x 9½in.
(Sotheby's)   **$836**   **£550**

THOMAS KENT PELHAM – The Fandango – signed – 25 x 30in.
(Sotheby Beresford Adams) **$1,330** **£792**

GIOVANNI ANTONIO PELLEGRINI – Hercules And Omphale – 39¾ x 33½in.
(Sotheby's) **$24,750** **£16,500**

RICCARDO PELLEGRINI – The Vegetable Seller – signed and dated 1894 – 27¼ x 15½in.
(Sotheby's) **$3,510** **£2,310**

PIERRE-JACQUES PELLETIER – Peniches Sur La Riviere – signed – on panel – 14¾ x 23½in.
(Sotheby's) **$985** **£550**

FRANCESCO PELUSO – A Quarrel – signed – 9½ x 13½in.
(Sotheby Beresford Adams) **$529** **£308**

EDWIN A. PENLEY – Mountain Gorge With Female In Foreground – signed and dated 1887 – watercolour – 20 x 14in.
(Edgar Horne) **$317** **£210**

EDWIN AARON PENLEY – A Rural Scene With Faggot Gatherers By A Cottage – signed and dated 1852 – watercolour heightened with white – 9¾ x 13¾in.
(Sotheby, King & Chasemore) **$299** **£187**

WILLIAM CHARLES PENN – Cyclamen – signed and dated 1947 – 19½ x 15½in.
(Sotheby Beresford Adams) **$19** **£11**

PENNE – A Sportsman And His Dog In A Wooded Landscape – on board – 12¾ x 16in.
(Christie's) **$502** **£324**

HARRY PENNELL – Near Steyning – signed, inscribed on the reverse – 15 x 23½in.
(Sotheby Beresford Adams) **$170** **£99**

JOSEPH PENNELL – The Palace, Venice – pencil and coloured chalks on grey-green paper – 9¼ x 12½in.
(Christie's) **$1,100** **£723**

ALBERT JOSEPH PENOT — Le Bain Du Soir — signed and signed on the reverse — on canvas board — 18 x 21¼in.
(Sotheby's)   **$585**   **£385**

DENIS PEPLOE — Glen Elg, Wester Ross — signed, indistinctly inscribed and dated '51 on the reverse — 20 x 24in.
(Sotheby's)   **$493**   **£264**

PAUL EMILE LEON PERBOYRE — French Cavalry On The March — signed — on panel — 9¼ x 13in.
(Christie's)   **$1,590**   **£1,026**

HERBERT S. PERCY — Milkmaid And Spring Lambs In A Field — signed and dated 1887 — oil on canvas — 12 x 8in.
(Sotheby, King & Chasemore)   **$626**   **£352**

BARTOLOME PEREZ – A Still Life Of Flowers In A Gilt Vase – 35½ x 27¼in. *(Sotheby's)* **$8,527 £5,610**

LEON JEAN BASILE PERRAULT – 'La Jeune Paysanne' – signed – oil on canvas on board – 15¼ x 12in. *(Stalker & Boos)* **$3,000 £1,875**

ENOCH WOOD PERRY – Mother And Child – signed and dated 1881 – oil on canvas – 28½ x 36¾in. *(Christie's)* **$46,200 £30,800**

CHARLES EDWARD PERUGINI – Dressing Up – signed with monogram and dated 1877 – 36 x 28in. *(Sotheby's)* **$10,725 £7,150**

ABRAHAM PETHER – A Moonlit Estuary Scene, Figures And Cattle In The Foreground – oil on panel – 10½ x 16in. *(Hy. Duke & Son)* **$147 £85**

HENRY PETHER – View Of Windsor By Moonlight – signed – 17¼ x 23¼in. *(Sotheby's)* **$1,328 £880**

HENRY PETHER – 'Moonlight Estuary Scene With Sailing Ships And Castle' – signed – oil on canvas – 21¼ x 37in. *(Bracketts)* **$4,000 £2,500**

SEBASTIAN PETHER – A Ruined Church By A Moonlit Lake – signed – 17¼ x 23¼in *(Sotheby's)* **$1,660 £1,100**

SEBASTIAN PETHER – 'A Moonlight River Scene', With A Furnace In The Foreground – signed and dated 1825 – oil on canvas – 17½ x 25in. *(Sotheby, King & Chasemore)* **$1,584 £990**

SEBASTIAN PETHER – Moonlit Lake Scene – signed and dated 1829 – oil on canvas – 25 x 33in.
(Sotheby, King & Chasemore) $979 £550

EDMOND PETITJEAN – Sailing Boats In A Harbour – on panel – 9¾ x 18in.
(Christie's) $1,590 £1,006

EDMOND MARIE PETITJEAN – Town And Cathedral Near A River – signed – oil on canvas – 18 x 26in.
(Butterfield's) $1,600 £958

HIPPOLYTE PETITJEAN – Femme Lisant Une Lettre – oil on canvas – 25¾ x 19½in.
(Sotheby's) $2,174 £1,430

EDWIN ALFRED PETTITT – Courmayeur, Val D'Aosta, Italy – signed and dated 1884, inscribed on the reverse – 13½ x 23½in.
(Sotheby, King & Chasemore) $858 £550

GEORGE PETTITT – Showers And Sunshine, Ullswater From Under Place Fell, Looking Towards Hellvellyn – signed and dated 1858 – 36 x 60in.
(Sotheby's) $1,254 £825

GEORGE PHOENIX – Peasant Farmer And Wife With Geese In An Orchard – signed – oil on canvas – 23½ x 11½in.
(Olivers) $68 £40

PABLO PICASSO – Francoise – signed – lithograph – 64 x 49cm.
(Germann Auktionshaus) $4,198 £2,624

PABLO PICASSO – 'The Nude' – poster
– 68 x 60cm.
(Geoff K. Gray) **$72** **£44**

PABLO PICASSO – 'Sculpture, Modele
Et Sculpture Assise' – signed – pencil –
12¼ x 7¼in.
(Du Mouchelles) **$1,900** **£1,117**

CHRISTIAN PIEPER – A Mother And
Child In An Interior – signed and dated
'96 – 17¾ x 14½in.
(Sotheby's) **$1,420** **£935**

HAROLD H. PIFFARD – The Toast –
signed – 35 x 27in.
*(Sotheby Beresford
Adams)* **$2,217** **£1,320**

HAROLD H. PIFFARD – The Crystal
Ball – signed – 35½ x 27½in.
(Christie's) **$1,933** **£1,080**

WILLIAM HENRY PIKE, Attributed to
– An Italian Market – signed and dated
1889 – on board – 10¼ x 13½in.
*(Sotheby, King &
Chasemore)* **$1,372** **£880**

PILLEMENT – A River Landscape – oil
on panel – 9¼ x 11½in.
*(Sotheby, King &
Chasemore)* **$858** **£505**

PILLEMENT

JEAN-BAPTISTE PILLEMENT – Pastoral Landscapes – signed and dated – 5¼ x 7in.
(Sotheby's)   **$4,620**   **£3,080 Pair**

EMILE AUGUSTE PINCHART – The Armlet – signed and dated 1871 – 22½ x 15¾in.
(Christie's &
   Edmiston's)   **$3,040**   **£1,900**

ADOLPHE PIOT – 'The Young Entertainers Of Two Peasant Clad Children – signed – 46 x 36in.
(Du Mouchelles)   **$11,000**   **£6,110**

PIPER – A Winter Landscape – 16 x 22in.
(Lawrence)   **$87**   **£55**

JOHN PIPER – Romanesque Variations – signed – gouache – 57 x 74cm.
(Sotheby, King &
   Chasemore)   **$884**   **£520**

FAUSTO PIRANDELLO – 'Oggetti' – signed – oil on board – 27½ x 39in.
(Stalker &
   Boos)   **$5,000**   **£2,994**

CAMILLE PISSARRO – Rue St. Lazare – signed and dated '93 – oil on canvas – 29 x 23¾in.
(William Doyle Galleries) **$520,000 £307,692**

CAMILLE PISSARRO – Marche St. Honore – signed and dated 1889 – watercolour on paper – 11¼ x 8¼in.
(William Doyle Galleries) **$45,000 £26,627**

LUCIEN PISSARRO – Trees Near Southminster – stamped with monogram on the reverse – oil on panel – 9¾ x 14in.
(Christie's) **$893 £480**

LUCIEN PISSARRO – Landscape Near Rye – signed with monogram – watercolour, pen and ink – 4½ x 5½in.
(Christie's) **$652 £432**

BONIFAZIO DEI PITATI, Called Bonifazio Veronese – The Adoration Of The Shepherds With Saints Catherine And A Monastic Saint – 45¾ x 66½in.
(Sotheby's) **$38,060 £22,000**

F. PITCHER – Cottage Scenes – signed – 16 x 22in.
(Sotheby's) **$803 £528 Pair**

351

N. SOTHEBY PITCHER – Whaler And Rowing Boats – signed – oil on canvas – 25¼ x 30¼in.
(Sotheby, King &
Chasemore) **$195** **£110**

WILLIAM PITT – Near Iron Bridge, Shropshire – signed, inscribed and dated 1853 – oil on canvas – 15½in. diam.
(Sotheby, King &
Chasemore) **$1,030** **£660**

WILLIAM PITT – The Ferry At Bodinnick Near Fowey With Houses, Figures And A Boat Repair Yard On The Foreshore – signed with initials and dated '68 – watercolour – 33 x 23cm.
(Osmond,
Tricks) **$318** **£185**

PITTO – An Italian Market Scene – signed – on canvas – 19½ x 27½in.
(Sotheby, King &
Chasemore) **$1,115** **£715**

G. PITTO – Market Day – signed – 23¼ x 31¼in.
(Sotheby's) **$2,173** **£1,430**

JOHANN GEORG PLATZER – The Rape Of The Sabine Women; and The Reconciliation Of The Romans And The Sabines – on copper – 15 x 21½in.
(Sotheby's) **$19,800 £13,200 Pair**

ANDRE PLUMOT – A Mother And Child With Animals In A Coastal Landscape – signed and dated 1877 – on panel – 11¾ x 20in.
(Christie's) **$2,916 £1,620**

NICHOLAS POCOCK – Studies Of Roman Architecture – signed – watercolour – 17 x 12in.
(Laurence & Martin Taylor) **$69 £40**

CORNELIS VAN POELENBURGH, Circle of – The Basilica Of Maxentius With A Group Of Dutch Visitors – 25½ x 19¾in.
(Sotheby's) **$6,270 £4,180**

CORNELIS VAN POELENBURGH – Rome And The Tiber – signed in monogram – on copper – 16½ x 21½in. *(Sotheby's)* **$9,075 £6,050**

POITTEVIN

EUGENE LE POITTEVIN – A Beach Scene With Fisherfolk – signed and dated 1835, and signed with monogram – 34½ x 45½in.
(Christie's) **$9,785** **£6,480**

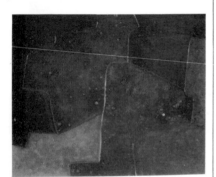

SERGE POLIAKOFF – Composition – signed and dated '65 – 61 x 73cm.
(Germann Auktionshaus) **$2,430** **£1,520**

JAMES POLLARD – Ascot Cup, Glaucus Beating Rockingham and Samarkand – signed and dated 1834, inscribed on a label – 14 x 25in.
(Sotheby's) **$54,868** **£31,900**

ALFRED POLLENTINE – The Grand Canal, Venice – signed, and inscribed on the reverse – 15 x 22in.
(Lawrence) **$1,259** **£792**

ALFRED POLLENTINE – The Grand Canal, Venice – signed and dated '96, inscribed on the reverse – 16 x 24in.
(Sotheby Beresford Adams) **$1,663** **£990**

ALFRED POLLENTINE – Santa Maria Della Salute, Venice – signed, and signed and inscribed on the reverse – 19½ x 29in.
(Christie's) **$1,160** **£648**

ALFRED POLLENTINE – S. Pietro de Castello, Venice; and The Grand Canal From Santa Maria Della Carita, Venice, Looking Towards The Bacino Di San Marco – signed and dated '87 and one signed and inscribed on the reverse – 10¾ x 19½in.
(Christie's) **$2,008** **£1,296** **Pair**

ALBERT POLLITT – Young Anglers – signed and dated 1892 – 13½ x 20in.
(Sotheby Beresford Adams) **$57** **£33**

GEORGE AUGUSTUS POOLE – A Cottage In Summer, Welford On Avon – signed – 19 x 24in.
(Sotheby Beresford Adams) **$19** **£11**

WILLEM DE POORTER – The Idolatory Of Solomon – on panel – 27½ x 21¾in. *(Sotheby's)* **$1,608** **£935**

H. POPE – 'Bell's Farm, Kings Norton' – watercolour – 11 x 7½in. *(G. H. Bayley & Sons)* **$190** **£110**

JAN PORCELLIS – A Damlooper Running Before The Wind – signed – on panel – 14 x 24in. *(Sotheby's)* **$7,920** **£5,280**

SIR ROBERT KERR PORTER – A Smuggler – signed and dated 1799 – watercolour – 14½ x 10in. *(Sotheby, King & Chasemore)* **$187** **£110**

EDWARD ANTOON PORTIELJE – 'Two Women Seated At A Table With Bowls Of Cherries' – signed – oil on canvas – 20 x 25½in. *(Sotheby, King & Chasemore)* **$5,775 £3,850**

PORTIELJE

GERARD PORTIELJE – Men Playing Cards In A Tavern Setting – signed and dated 1883 – oil on canvas – 18 x 24in. *(Du Mouchelles)* **$22,500 £13,235**

FRANS POST – A Plantation In Brazil – signed – on panel – 14 x 16in. *(Sotheby's)* **$198,000 £132,000**

EDWARD HENRY POTTHAST – A Holiday – signed and dated 1923 on a label on the reverse – oil on board – 12 x 16in. *(William Doyle Galleries)* **$42,500 £25,148**

JAMES POULTON – Still Life Of Fruit – signed and dated '51 – 12 x 14in. *(Sotheby Beresford Adams)* **$296 £176**

FRANS POURBUS, The Younger – Portrait Of Guillaume Du Vair – 24 x 21in. *(Sotheby's)* **$29,700 £19,800**

POUSSIN – The Infant Bacchus And Putti Revelling – 39 x 48½in. *(Sotheby Beresford Adams)* **$2,402 £1,430**

NICHOLAS POUSSIN, Follower of – The Family Of Coriolanus Begging Him To Spare Rome – 25½ x 36in. *(Sotheby's)* **$990 £572**

POWELL – 'Manor House By A Stream' – signed – pencil – 14 x 20cm. *(Geoff K. Gray)* **$9 £5**

CHARLES MARTIN POWELL, Follower of – A Frigate And Sailing Vessels At Anchor In A Calm – inscribed – on panel – 12 x 16in. *(Sotheby's)* **$334 £220**

SIR EDWARD JOHN POYNTER – The Princess And The Frog – signed with monogram – 23 x 17in. *(Sotheby's)* **$762 £495**

A. F. DE PRADES – Three-Horse Sleigh Outside A Cabin – bears monogram – on board – 17½ x 23¼in. *(Christie's)* **$1,171 £756**

T. H. PRAGER – 'Two Women And Young Girl Picking Flowers' – signed – oil on canvas – 15½ x 23½in.
(Stalker & Boos) $70   £45

DOUGLAS FIELDEW PRATT – 'Venetian Scene' – signed – watercolour – 19 x 24cm.
(Geoff K. Gray) $135   £90

PRELL – An Elegant Family Outside A Dairy – signed – on panel – 19¼ x 26in.
(Christie's) $2,176   £1,404

JANE R. PRICE – 'Sydney Harbour At Night' – oil on board – 32 x 28cm.
(Geoff K. Gray) $540   £322

W. J. PRINGLE – The Favourite Gun Dog – signed and dated 1833 – 14 x 18in.
(Sotheby's) $902   £594

A. W. PRIOR – Othello And Desdemona Before The Doge – signed and dated 1864 – pencil and watercolour heightened with white – 11½ x 16¾in.
(Christie's) $162   £108

HANS PRENTZEL – Im Schwabenland, Besigheim Am Neckar – signed – 27 x 32in.
(Sotheby's) $2,340 £1,540

PRITCHETT

E. PRITCHETT – The Rialto On The
Grand Canal, Venice – oil – 36 x 65cm.
(Reeds Rains)   **$875   £500**

EDWARD PRITCHETT – The Rialto
Bridge, Venice – signed – 12 x 18in.
(Christie's)   **$1,933   £1,080**

GIULIO CESARE PROCCACINI –
Apollo And Minerva – 45¼ x 79in.
(Sotheby's)   **$8,564   £4,950**

ERNEST PROCTOR – 'Garden Fountain' – signed and dated 1913 – watercolour – 14¼ x 10½in.
*(W. H. Lane &
    Son)*   **$209   £120**

ERNEST PROCTOR – 'The Old Newlyn
Slipway' – oil on canvas – 18 x 14in.
*(W. H. Lane &
    Son)*   **$1,287   £740**

PROUT – A Venetian Canal Scene With
Figures – 17 x 11½in.
(Lawrence)   **$60   £38**

JOHN SKINNER PROUT – A Barge
Passing A Fortified Town Wall – signed
and dated 1858 – watercolour heightened
with white – 17¼ x 13in.
(Christie's)   **$507   £302**

JOHN SKINNER PROUT – Women And
Children In A North European Village
Street – signed and dated 1860 – watercolour heightened with white – 14¾ x
10¾in.
(Christie's)   **$616   £367**

JOHN SKINNER PROUT – 'Stormy Seas
On A Rocky Coast' – watercolour – 11.3
x 16.7cm.
(Geoff K. Gray)   **$360   £205**

S. PROUT – At Rouen – 7½ x 5in.
*(Sotheby Beresford
    Adams)*   **$10   £6**

S. PROUT – Outside The Cathedral –
18 x 13in.
*(Sotheby Beresford
    Adams)*   **$26   £15**

SAMUEL PROUT – Bawbridge, Devon
– signed – pencil and watercolour – 7½
x 10½in.
(Christie's)   **$570   £378**

SAMUEL PROUT – Figures Outside A Building – signed – watercolour – 22 x 17¼in.
(Sotheby, King & Chasemore) **$342** £220

SAMUEL PROUT – A Woman By A Thatched Cottage – signed – pencil and brown wash – 7½ x 10¼in.
(Christie's) **$344** £205

SAMUEL PROUT – Cologne, A Coach Outside A Town House – watercolour – 15 x 10½in.
(Hall, Wateridge & Owen) **$262** £150

SAMUEL PROUT – Caen, Normandy, Figures In The Cathedral Porch – watercolour – 11½ x 16in.
(Hall, Wateridge & Owen) **$455** £260

ALFRED PROVIS – The Young Blacksmiths – signed, inscribed and dated 1862 – oil on canvas – 16½ x 24¼in.
(Sotheby, King & Chasemore) **$5,148** £3,300

ALFRED PROVIS – Kitchen Interior With A Maid And A Day Old Chick – signed – oil on panel – 9 x 13in.
(Graves, Son & Pilcher) **$1,665** £950

ALFRED PROVIS – 'Companions' – signed and dated 1864 – oil – 9½ x 14in.
(Graves, Son & Pilcher) **$1,610** £920

ALFRED PROVIS – Kitchen Interior With A Mother And Daughter – signed and dated 1880 – oil on panel – 11 x 14in.
(Graves, Son & Pilcher) **$2,100** £1,200

JAMES PRYDE – Ruins By A Lake – signed – oil on canvas – 12 x 15in.
(Christie's) **$733** £486

PRYN

HARALD PRYN – A Winter's Day At Kongekilden In Dyrehaven, Klampenborg – signed and inscribed – 27¾ x 37¾in.
(Sotheby's) **$1,839 £1,210**

SCIPIONE PULZONE, Called Gaetano – Portrait Of Saint Pius V – signed or inscribed – 53½ x 40½in.
(Sotheby's) **$2,675 £1,760**

CLIFTON PUGH – 'Eagle Nest' – signed – gouache – 89 x 69cm.
(Australian Art Auctions) **$1,228 £714**

H. PUGH – A Caricature Of A Naval Battle At A Fete – bears signature – 12¾ x 21½in.
(Christie's) **$758 £410**

HOVSEP PUSHMAN – Vanishing Glories – signed – oil on canvas – 28¼ x 21¼in.
(Christie's) **$7,700 £5,133**

JOSEPH KARL PUTTNER, Attributed to — At The Ferry — bears signature and dated — oil on panel — 13 x 18½in.
(Sotheby, King & Chasemore)   **$650   £407**

WILL PYE — Sandsfoot Castle And Portland By Moonlight — oil on canvas — 9 x 13in.
(Hy. Duke & Son)   **$25   £15**

J. B. PYNE — A River Valley — bears signature — 19½ x 29½in.
(Sotheby Beresford Adams)   **$605   £352**

JAMES BAKER PYNE — Gypsies By A Lane In A Highland Village — signed and dated 1838 — pencil and watercolour heightened with white — 9 x 13¼in.
(Christie's)   **$470   £280**

JAMES BAKER PYNE — Nottingham Across The Meadows — signed — 13 x 24in.
(Christie's)   **$1,449   £810**

JAMES BAKER PYNE — A Stream In A Mountainous Landscape — signed and dated 1842 — on board — 12 x 16¼in.
(Sotheby's)   **$1,419   £825**

THOMAS PYNE — Going To The Meet — signed and dated 1879 — 10 x 14¾in.
(Sotheby Beresford Adams)   **$95   £55**

MARTIN FERDINAND QUADAL – Portrait Of A Gentleman – signed – 26 x 20in.
(Sotheby's) **$3,630 £2,420**

ARTHUR QUARTLEY – 'Late Afternoon On The East River' – signed – oil on canvas – 8 x 13in.
(Robert W. Skinner Inc.) **$950 £593**

JOSEPH QUINAUX – Landscape With A Stream, Sheep And Shepherds In The Foreground – signed and dated 1852 – oil – 30 x 39½in.
(Graves, Son & Pilcher) **$2,712 £1,550**

J. QUINTON – Portraits Of Hunters, A Bay And A Grey In Their Stables – signed and dated – oil – 18 x 24in.
(Woolley & Wallis) **$500 £300 Pair**

ARTHUR RACKHAM – The Cat Whom Venus Transformed Into A Woman – signed, inscribed and dated 1912 – pen and black ink and watercolour – 9¾ x 6½in.
(Christie's) **$7,620 £4,536**

RAEBURN – Portrait Of William Douglas, 4th Duke Of Queensbury – oil – 29 x 23.7in.
(Woolley & Wallis) **$460 £260**

WILLIAM H. RAINEY – Tales From The Sea – signed – 37 x 50in.
(Christie's) **$1,546 £864**

ALLAN RAMSAY – Portrait Of Lady Archer, Nee Sarah West, In A Blue Dress – 30¼ x 25½in.
(Christie's) $1,598 £864

WILLIAM RATCLIFFE – Cottages Under Snow, Sweden – signed – oil on canvas – 20 x 24in.
(Christie's) $4,077 £2,700

G. W. RATHBONE – Warkworth Castle, A View From The River – signed and dated 1877 – oil – 17¼ x 23¼in.
(Anderson & Garland) $67 £42

WILLIAM BRUSE ELLIS RANKEN – Woman Looking Out Over The Balcony – initialled and dated 1915 – oil on canvas – 18 x 18in.
(Butterfield's) $600 £359

RAPHAEL, After – Holy Family With St. Anne – on panel – 10 x 8in.
(Sotheby Beresford Adams) $1,016 £605

JOHN RATHBONE – A Wooded River Landscape With Rustics Gathered Around A Fire – 14¼ x 18in.
(Sotheby's) $2,325 £1,540

ROBERT RAUSCHENBERG – Collage – signed and dated '73 – collage on paper – 30¼ x 44¾in.
(Christie's) $2,712 £1,728

SAMUEL RAVEN – Two Pointers – signed with initials on panel – oil – 7 x 9in.
(Woolley & Wallis) $768 £460

RAYNER

LOUIS J. RAYNER – Heriot's Hospital From The Greyfriars Churchyard, Edinburgh – signed – watercolour over pencil heightened with white – 10 x 14¾in.
(Sotheby's) $542   £352

LOUISE RAYNER – Conway – signed – heightened with bodycolour – 11½ x 16½in.
(Sotheby's) $5,420   £3,520

LOUISE RAYNER – A Cathedral Service – gouache – 19 x 14¼in.
(Sotheby Beresford Adams) $444   £264

LOUISE RAYNER – The Market Square, Grantham – signed – heightened with bodycolour – 10½ x 15½in.
(Sotheby's) $5,420   £3,520

HENRY READMAN – A Man And A Small Girl On A Path At The Outskirts Of Whitby Town – signed and dated 1913 – watercolour – 10 x 14¾in.
(Anderson & Garland) $16   £10

MORSTON CONSTANTINE REAM – 'Still Life With Peaches, Grapes And Raspberries' – signed – oil on panel – 10 x 12in.
(Robert W. Skinner Inc.) $1,400   £875

H. RECK – Portrait Of A Meditating Young Girl – signed – oil on canvas – oval 26 x 22in.
(Stalker & Boos) $500   £312

JOHN RECKNAGEL – 'A Breton Woman' – monogrammed and indistinctly dated and inscribed on the reverse – pastel on paper – 39 x 17in.
(Robert W. Skinner Inc.) $800   £500

EDWARD WILLIS REDFIELD – The
Ferry Road At Point Pleasant – signed,
inscribed and dated 1928 – oil on
canvas – 32 x 40in.
(Christie's) $52,800   £35,200

H. REDMORE – Dutch And English
Sailing Vessels Off Chalky Cliffs – oil –
20½ x 27½in.
(Graves, Son &
   Pilcher) $2,362   £1,350

LEONARD REEDY – Indian And Horse
At A Watering Hole – signed and dated;
Cowboys In The Desert – signed – 8 x
11in.
(Du Mouchelles) $800   £470 Pair

LLOYD REES – 'Spanish Landscape' –
signed and dated 1976 – etching – 18
x 13cm.
(Geoff K. Gray) $180   £107

SIR GEORGE REID – Still Life Study
Of Peonies In A Vase – signed with mono-
gram – oil on canvas – 21 x 15in.
(Sotheby, King &
   Chasemore) $792   £528

GEORGE OGILVY REID – A Discussion
– signed and dated 1893 – oil on canvas –
50½ x 33in.
(Sotheby, King &
   Chasemore) $520   £297

REID

JOHN ROBERTSON REID – Saturday Afternoon – signed, signed and inscribed on the reverse – 11½ x 19¾in.
(Christie's &
Edmiston's) **$352 £220**

ROBERT REID – Autumn Landscape – signed and dated 1908 – oil on canvas – 27 x 33½in.
(Butterfield's) **$17,000 £10,180**

STEPHEN REID – 'A Stuart Home' – signed and inscribed on the reverse – oil on canvas – 16 x 12in.
(Sotheby, King &
Chasemore) **$374 £220**

R. R. REINAGLE – 'Borrowdale, Yorkshire' – watercolour – 18½ x 12½in.
(G. H. Bayley
& Sons) **$311 £180**

REMBRANDT, Circle of – A Soldier In A Guardroom – on panel – 25¼ x 18¾in.
(Sotheby's) **$8,360 £5,500**

DEDE RENARD – Landscapes In Brittany – oil on canvas – 12 x 16in.
(Hy. Duke &
Son) **$35 £20 Pair**

PIERRE AUGUSTE RENOIR – Girl In Blue Wearing Veil – signed – pastel on paper – 11½ x 9¼in.
(William Doyle
Galleries) **$42,500 £25,147**

ALAN REYNOLDS – Spring Landscape – signed and dated '52, inscribed on the reverse – on board – 16 x 20in.
(Sotheby's) **$829** **£572**

ALAN REYNOLDS – Bleak Orchard – signed and dated '53 – on board – 16½ x 22½in.
(Sotheby's) **$957** **£660**

FREDERICK GEORGE REYNOLDS – Heidelberg – signed with monogram – 12 x 14in.
(Sotheby Beresford Adams) **$480** **£286**

SIR JOSHUA REYNOLDS – Portrait Of Anthony Ashley Cooper, 4th Earl Of Shaftesbury – inscribed – 48 x 28½in.
(Sotheby's) **$13,288** **£8,800**

SIR JOSHUA REYNOLDS – Portrait Of The Hon. Mary Bouverie, Countess Of Shaftesbury – 48 x 38½in.
(Sotheby's) **$16,610** **£11,000**

HENRICH ENGLEBERT REYNTJENS – Sitting For The Portrait – signed – on panel – 10½ x 14¾in.
(Christie's) **$1,004** **£648**

FELICE A. REZIA – Windsor Castle From The River – signed and dated 1896 – 10 x 14in.
(Laurence & Martin Taylor) **$253** **£150**

LOUIS JOHN RHEAD – Fly Fishing At Beaver Kill Valley, New York – signed – oil on canvas – 18 x 26in.
(William Doyle Galleries) **$1,600** **£946**

RHEAM

HENRY MEYNELL RHEAM – Portrait Of A Girl With A Harbour Behind – signed with initials and dated 1899 – watercolour – 9½ x 14in.
(Hy. Duke & Son)   **$1,816**   **$1,050**

JOSEPH RHODES – A Lake In A Mountainous Landscape – signed and dated – 27½ x 37¾in.
(Sotheby's)   **$2,823**   **£1,870**

OLIVER RHYS – Italian Street Scene – oil – 16 x 12in.
(Morphets)   **$1,539**   **£900**

ARTURO RICCI – Motherly Love – signed and dated '75 – 38½ x 28¾in.
(Christie's)   **$2,916**   **£1,620**

ARTURO RICCI – The Game Of Chess – signed – 16¼ x 11½in.
(Christie's)   **$9,325**   **£5,940**

ARTURO RICCI – The Singing Lesson – signed – 16¼ x 11½in.
(Christie's)   **$8,138**   **£5,184**

P. RICCI – The Courtship – 18 x 12½in.
(Sotheby Beresford
Adams)   **$1,604**   **£968**

FRANK RICHARDS – 'Old Woman
Seated By A Doorway' – signed, inscribed
and dated 1893 – 11 x 8¾in.
(Sotheby, King &
Chasemore)   **$274**   **£154**

FREDERICK DE BOURG RICHARDS –
Valley Of Arkansas – signed – oil on
canvas – 30¼ x 50¼in.
(Christie's)   **$6,050**   **£4,033**

J. I. RICHARDS – A Wooded River Land-
scape With Cattle, Sheep And Country
Folk By A Waterfall – 20¼ x 25½in.
(Christie's)   **$1,098**   **£594**

RICHARD PETER RICHARDS – The
Back Page – signed and dated 1861 –
heightened with bodycolour – 13½ x
9¼in.
(Sotheby Beresford
Adams)   **$287**   **£165**

WILLIAM TROST RICHARDS – 'A Country Church Beneath A Rainbow' – signed
– oil on canvas – 20 x 30in.
(Robert W. Skinner
Inc.)   **$2,000**   **£1,250**

RICHARDSON – On The Tyne, Two
Men Fishing From A Tree-Lined Bank
– 8 x 10in.
(Anderson &
Garland)   **$125**   **£75**

C. RICHARDSON – Vessels Off Whitby –
signed and dated 1875 – 14¾ x 25in.
(Sotheby Beresford
Adams)   **$416**   **£242**

CHARLES JAMES RICHARDSON –
Lord Archer's House, Covent Garden –
signed, inscribed and dated 1817 –
pencil and watercolour – 8½ x 10¼in.
(Christie's)   **$163**   **£108**

RICHARDSON

CHARLES EDWARD RICHARDSON –
'The Connoisseur' – signed and dated
1910 – oil on canvas – 20 x 14in.
(Sotheby, King &
Chasemore) $1,188   £792

J. I. RICHARDSON – Gathering A Posy
– signed with a monogram and dated
1862 – heightened with bodycolour –
14 x 10¼in.
(Sotheby Beresford
Adams) $612   £352

THOMAS MILES RICHARDSON – A
Moorland Landscape With River In The
Foreground – signed with initials and
dated 1850 – watercolour – 8½ x 12in.
(Hy. Duke &
Son) $371   £215

THOMAS MILES RICHARDSON, JNR. –
Peasants In An Alpine Village – signed
and dated 1857 – pencil and watercolour
heightened with white – oval 18½ x
14¾in.
(Christie's) $490   £324

THOMAS MILES RICHARDSON, JNR. –
Newhaven Fishwoman: Study From
Nature – signed, inscribed and dated
1842 – watercolour heightened with
white on pale blue paper – 14 x 10in.
(Christie's) $362   £216

THOMAS MILES RICHARDSON, SNR.
– On The Tyne With Fishermen In The
Foreground – 8 x 10in.
(Sotheby's) $367   £242

WILLIAM RICHARDSON – The Via-
duct, Scarborough; and Scarborough
Castle, Yorkshire – signed with initials
and dated 1852 – heightened with
bodycolour – 9½ x 14½in.
(Sotheby Beresford
Adams) $739   £440 Pair

R. RICHES – 'Coastal Scene' – signed
– watercolour – 10 x 50cm.
(Geoff K. Gray) $54   £32

AGNES M. RICHMOND – 'A Young
Friend' – signed – oil on canvas – 36
x 32in.
(Robert W. Skinner
Inc.) $900   £562

AGNES M. RICHMOND – Lady With A Parasol – oil on canvas – 24 x 20in.
(Butterfield's)   **$1,100   £658**

LEONARD RICHMOND – 'A Panoramic Landscape' – pastel – 18 x 23½in.
(W. H. Lane & Son)   **$70   £40**

HENRY DAVIS RICHTER – Still Life, A Bowl Of Flowers – signed – pastel – 20 x 24in.
(Woolley & Wallis)   **$584   £330**

PHILIP RICKMAN – Three Mallards On A Pond – signed and dated 1979 – watercolour heightened with bodycolour – 41 x 56cm.
(Sotheby, King & Chasemore)   **$884   £520**

HUGH E. RIDGE – At Mousehole, Cornwall – signed – canvas on board – 11 x 14in.
(Sotheby Beresford Adams)   **$45   £27**

F. H. RIDEOUT – Hunting Scenes With Mounted Riders And Hounds – signed and dated 1895 – oil on canvas – 9½ x 13½in.
(Hy. Duke & Son)   **$710   £410 Four**

PHILIP H. RIDEOUT – Coaching Scenes – signed and dated – oil on board – 7.2 x 14.7in.
(Woolley & Wallis)   **$200   £120**

LUIGI DA RIOS – At A Venetian Well – signed and dated 1873 – 29 x 49in.
(Christie's)   **$8,100   £5,400**

AIDEN LASSELL RIPLEY – 'After Lobstering' – signed – watercolour – 16¼ x 20in.
(Robert W. Skinner Inc.)   **$950   £593**

WILLIAM RITSCHEL – Surf On The Rocks – signed – watercolour on paper – 3½ x 5½in.
(Butterfield's)   **$200   £119**

RIVERS – Little Girl Lost, Hampstead Heath – 19 x 31in.
(Sotheby Beresford Adams)   **$498   £297**

RIX

JULIAN RIX – Landscape – signed – oil on canvas – 17 x 23in.
(Butterfield's)   **$350   £207**

WILLIAM GEORGE ROBB – 'Evening By The Lake' – signed – watercolour – 22 x 34cm.
(Geoff K. Gray)   **$108   £65**

HUBERT ROBERT, Manner of – Women Laundering At A Fountain In A Park – 34½ x 48½in.
(Sotheby's)   **$2,006   £1,320**

DAVID ROBERTS – Arabs Of The Tribe Of The Benisaid – signed, inscribed and dated 1839 – pencil and watercolour heightened with white – 13 x 9¾in.
(Christie's)   **$12,717   £8,100**

DAVID ROBERTS – The Interior Of A Norman Cathedral – signed and dated 1825 – pencil and watercolour heightened with white – 13¼ x 7½in.
(Christie's)   **$1,956   £1,296**

HUBERT ROBERT – The Ruins Of A Roman Temple – 15¾ x 11¾in.
(Sotheby's)   **$14,272   £8,250**

DAVID ROBERTS – 'The Island Of Philae, Nubia' – signed and dated 1843 – 30¼ x 60½in.
(Christie's)   **$113,400   £75,600**

DAVID ROBERTS – The River Thames At Waterloo Bridge Looking Towards St. Paul's Cathedral – 10½ x 23¼in. *(Sotheby's)*   **$5,676   £3,300**

DAVID ROBERTS – The New Palace Of Westminster From The Old Horseferry – signed and dated 1861 – 23¾ x 42in.
(Sotheby's) **$23,650 £13,750**

EDWIN ROBERTS – The Secret – signed, inscribed on the reverse – 13½ x 11½in.
(Sotheby Beresford Adams) **$1,339 £770**

WILLIAM ROBERTS – Customers In The Shoe Shop – signed – oil on canvas – 36 x 24in.
(Christie's) **$5,544 £3,672**

WILLIAM ROBERTS – Seated Nude – pencil – 9 x 5in.
(Sotheby's) **$255 £176**

PERCY ROBERTSON – 'Old Chelsea' – signed – etching – 8½ x 7¾in.
(W. H. Lane & Son) **$48 £28**

T. S. ROBINS – 'Stormy Seascape With A Barge' – signed with monogram – on panel – 9½ x 13¼in.
(Bracketts) **$1,280 £800**

FREDERICK CAYLEY ROBINSON – The Foundling – signed and dated 1908 – pencil and coloured wash heightened with bodycolour, on buff paper – 9½ x 11½in.
(Sotheby's) **$10,010 £5,720**

F. ROBSON – York Minster From Stonegate; An Old Alley In York; Pump Court York; and York Minster And Bootham Bar – colour prints – 9 x 6in.
(John Hogbin & Son) **$26 £15 Four**

J. ROBUSTI, Called Tintoretto – King David Receiving The News Of Uriah's Death – 62½ x 87in.
(Sotheby's) **$19,030 £11,000**

ALEXANDER IGNATIUS ROCHE – A July Afternoon – signed – oil on canvas – 15½ x 24in.
(Geering & Colyer) **$646 £380**

RODECK

CARL RODECK – A Forest At Sunset – signed – 22½ x 38in.
(Sotheby Beresford Adams) **$454** **£264**

COLIN GRAEME ROE – A Short Haired Pointer And Two Setters Guard A Grouse And A Game Bag By A Rocky Outcrop – signed and dated (18)99 – oil on canvas – 49.5 x 75cm.
(Henry Spencer & Sons) **$2,685** **£1,500**

ROBERT ERNEST ROE – Shipping In A Choppy Sea – signed and dated 1875 – oil on canvas – 12 x 16in.
(Sotheby, King & Chasemore) **$759** **£506**

ETTORE ROESLER-FRANZ – Prati Di Castelli – signed – watercolour on paper – 14¼ x 21in.
(Butterfield's) **$700** **£414**

C. A. ROGERS – View Of An Industrial Town – signed and dated 1838 – oil on canvas – 25 x 34¾in.
(Sotheby, King & Chasemore) **$783** **£440**

WILLIAM ROGERS – Seascapes – oil – 11 x 15in.
(Capes, Dunn & Co.) **$640** **£400 Pair**

ROLTENHAMER, School Of – Adoration Of The Virgin And Child – oil on copper panel – 6¾ x 5¼in.
(Butler & Hatch Waterman) **$1,260** **£700**

VICTOR ROLYAT – Lake Views – signed – 19 x 29in.
(Sotheby Beresford Adams) **$132** **£77 Two**

ANTON ROMAKO – 'The Young Shepherd' – signed on reverse – oil on board – 20½ x 18in.
(Stalker & Boos) **$450** **£280**

GIOVANNI FRANCESCO ROMANELLI, Circle of – Saint Catherine Of Alexandria – 35½ x 29in.
(Sotheby's) **$1,362** **£792**

SALOMON ROMBOUTS – A Dutch River Landscape With A Farm – on panel – 18 x 21¾in.
(Sotheby's) **$4,567** **£2,640**

GEORGE ROMNEY – Portrait Of A Lady, Probably Lady Betty Compton Seated Wearing A White Dress With A Blue Sash – 29¾ x 24¾in.
(Sotheby's) **$32,164** **£18,700**

THOMAS MATTEWS ROOKE – Fire And Water, or Feeding The Steam Dragon – signed – heightened with bodycolour – 7 x 43in.
(Sotheby's) **$424** **£274**

ROOSENBOOM – Skaters On A Frozen River – indistinctly signed and dated 1842 – oil on canvas – 17 x 21in.
(Sotheby, King & Chasemore) **$2,524** **£1,485**

ROOSENBOOM

NICOLAAS JOHANNES ROOSENBOOM
– Skaters On A Frozen River – signed –
on panel – 9¼ x 13¼in.
(Sotheby's) $770   £430

SALVATOR ROSA, Circle of – Cain And
Abel – 80 x 56¾in.
(Sotheby's)   **$1,755   £1,155**

HARRY ROSELAND – 'With The Fortune Teller' – signed – oil on canvas –
11 x 14in.
*(Robert W. Skinner
   Inc.)*   **$750   £468**

DANTE GABRIEL ROSSETTI – Edith
Williams – signed with monogram and
dated 1879 – coloured chalks – 25 x
17½in.
(Sotheby's)   **$21,450 £14,300**

DANTE GABRIEL ROSSETTI – A Girl
Singing To A Lute – signed and dated
1853 – pen and brown ink – watercolour
and bodycolour – 8¾ x 4in.
(Christie's)   **$11,415   £7,560**

ROTTENHAMMER

G. ROSSI – Festivities Off The Coast Of Naples – signed – oil on canvas – 22½ x 35½in.
(Butterfield's) **$600** **£355**

DANTE GABRIEL ROSSETTI – A Head Of A Girl – signed with monogram and dated 1874 – coloured chalks – 23½ x 19½in.
(Sotheby's) **$44,275 £25,300**

LEOPOLD ROTHANG – 'Woodland Scene' – signed and inscribed on a label – oil on canvas – 18½ x 22in.
(Sotheby, King & Chasemore) **$783** **£440**

JOHANN ROTTENHAMMER – The Resurrection Of Lazarus – on copper – 10½ x 14¼in. *(Sotheby's)* **$4,758 £2,750**

CHARLES ROWBOTHAM – Paddle Steamer On The Orwell At Ipswich – signed and dated 1884 – 5 x 10in. *(Sotheby, King & Chasemore)* **$652** **£418**

CHARLES ROWBOTHAM – Near Scelia Calabria, And On The Island Of Saint Marguerite, Near Cannes – signed and dated – watercolour – 6.2 x 11in. *(Woolley & Wallis)* **$460** **£260 Pair**

THOMAS LEESON ROWBOTHAM – While Father's A-Sailing – signed and dated 1870 – heightened with bodycolour – 8 x 13in. *(Sotheby's)* **$593** **£385**

CECIL M. ROUND – The Path Of The Whirlwind – signed and dated 1885 and inscribed on the reverse – 51½ x 35¼in. *(Sotheby's)* **$769** **£506**

ROUVIERE – Marigolds In Glass Vase – signed – oil on canvas – 37 x 29in. *(Edgar Horne)* **$241** **£160**

THOMAS LEESON ROWBOTHAM – 'Vietri' – signed, inscribed and dated 1874 – watercolour heightened with bodycolour – 7½ x 18in. *(Sotheby, King & Chasemore)* **$387 £242**

THOMAS LEESON ROWBOTHAM –
A View In Southern Italy – signed and
dated 1867 – heightened with bodycolour
– 7 x 17in.
(Sotheby's) $320   £209

THOMAS LEESON ROWBOTHAM –
Sorrento – signed and dated 1861 –
heightened with bodycolour – 9½ x 23in.
(Sotheby's) $575   £374

THOMAS ROWDEN – Cattle At A River's
Edge – signed – watercolour with touches
of white heightening – 14 x 20¼in.
(Christie's) $362   £216

E. ARTHUR ROWE – The Way To The
Bowling Green, Montacute – signed –
watercolour – 9 x 14in.
*(Woolley &
Wallis)* $684   £410

EDMUND ARTHUR ROWE – The Last
Gleam, Melbourne, Derbyshire – 8½ x
16in.
(Sotheby's) $711   £462

G. D. ROWLANDSON – Following The
Hounds – oil – 24 x 36in.
*(Capes, Dunn
& Co.)* $2,240   £1,400

LILIAN ROWNEY – The Fairy Ring –
signed – 14 x 21in.
(Sotheby's) $2,710   £1,760

STANLEY ROYLE – Fishing Port, Nova
Scotia – signed and dated 1933 – 28 x
36in.
(Sotheby's) $877   £605

RUBENS

ARNOLD FRANS RUBENS – Battle
Scenes – signed – 14¾ x 20in.
(Sotheby's) **$6,811 £3,960 Pair**

SCHOOL OF RUBENS – 'Nude With
Grapes' – oil on canvas – 31½ x 25in.
(Stalker &
Boos) **$650 £406**

RUBENS, After – Merrymaking In The
Park Of The Chateau De Steen – oil on
copper – 58.5 x 79.3cm.
(Christie's) **$1,190 £650**

J. VAN RUISDAEL – Landscape With A
Pool Below A Rocky Bank – 33 x 40½in.
(Sotheby's) **$41,866 £24,200**

JACOB RUISDAEL, Manner of –Wooded River Landscapes – 17½ x 16½in.
(Sotheby's) **$1,420 £935 Two**

FRANZ RUMPLER – The Young Peasant
Girl – signed and inscribed – on panel –
10 x 5½in.
(Sotheby's)   **$7,700   £4,400**

G. R. RUSHTON – 'Les Beaux', South
Of France – watercolour – 30 x 25in.
(G. H. Bayley
& Sons)   **$294   £170**

JOHN RUSKIN – Shakespeare's Cliff,
Dover – pencil, pen and brown ink,
brown wash heightened with white on
green paper – 8¼ x 12½in.
(Christie's)   **$507   £302**

GYRTH RUSSELL – Brixham Harbour –
signed – 19½ x 23½in.
(Sotheby's)   **$473   £275**

GYRTH RUSSELL – Harbour Scene – signed – 23½ x 31½in. *(Sotheby's)*
$378 £220

RUST

J. A. A. RUST – A Dutch Canal Scene
With Shipping – 8 x 11in.
(Lawrence) **$332** **£207**

RACHEL RUYSCH – Summer Flowers
And A Turkey Carpet – 29 x 24in.
(Sotheby's) **$41,250** **£27,500**

HENRY RYLAND – Dorothea And The
Roses – signed – on panel – 20 x 14in.
(Sotheby's) **$9,625** **£5,500**

HENRY RYLAND – Golden Autumn –
signed and dated 1907, and signed and
inscribed on the reverse – watercolour –
19½ x 28½in.
(Christie's) **$3,391** **£2,160**

HENRY RYLAND – The Nymph's
Toilette – signed and dated 1906 – water-
colour over pencil – 21 x 14½in.
(Sotheby's) **$762** **£495**

PIETER RYSBRAECK – An Assembly Of
Gods In A Classical Landscape – signed or
inscribed – 39¼ x 51in.
(Sotheby's) **$4,567** **£2,640**

EDWIN ST. JOHN – Townsfolk By The River At Strasbourg – signed and dated '88 – watercolour – 26½ x 46½in.
(Sotheby's)　　**$762**　　**£495**

W. DENBY SADLER – 'Country Gentleman Smoking A Churchwarden' – oil on canvas – 19½ x 15½in.
(Hilhams)　　**$260**　　**£150**

WILLIAM SADLER – A Ship Ablaze Off A Harbour By Night – on panel – 12¾ x 16¼in.
(Sotheby's)　　**$969**　　**£638**

HERMANN SAFTLEVEN – A Rocky River Scene With Shipping – signed in monogram and dated 1680 – on panel – 6¾ x 7¼in.
(Sotheby's)　　**$7,993**　　**£4,620**

ISAAC SAILMAKER, Attributed to – The Landing Of King William III At Torbay, 1688 – 41 x 69¾in.
(Sotheby's)　　**$5,674**　　**£3,740**

GRACE E. SAINSBURY – In The Fields – signed with initials – oil on canvas – 21½ x 14in.
*(Sotheby, King &
　Chasemore)*　　**$549**　　**£352**

J. SALMON – Coastal Scene With Boats – watercolour – 20½ x 14in.
*(G. H. Bayley
　& Sons)*　　**$398**　　**£230**

JOHN CUTHBERT SALMON – Mountain Lakes – signed – 9¼ x 14in.
*(Sotheby Beresford
　Adams)*　　**$75**　　**£44 Pair**

SALMON

JOHN FRANCIS SALMON – A Hay Barge On The Medway – signed and dated 1865 – watercolour – 10 x 20¾in. *(Sotheby's)* $542   £352

JOHN FRANCIS SALMON – Fisherwomen On A Stormy Coast – signed and dated 1853 – watercolour heightened with white and gum arabic – 9½ x 21½in. *(Sotheby's)* $260   £140

JOHN CUTHBERTSON SALMON – Dartmouth Castle; and Inverlochy Castle – signed, one inscribed and dated 1881 – watercolour over pencil, heightened with bodycolour – 21 x 29in. *(Sotheby's)* $677   £440 Two

R. SALMON – Coastal Inlet With A Fishing Boat And Figures In The Foreground – oil on panel – 8¼ x 10¾in. *Dreweatt Watson & Barton)* $2,550   £1,700

ROBERT SALMON – A Night Engagement – signed – 20½ x 30¾in. *(Sotheby's)*
$2,490   £1,640

ANTHONY FREDERICK AUGUSTUS SANDYS – Penelope – coloured chalks on green tinted paper – 30 x 21in.
(Sotheby's)   **$8,663   £4,950**

EDWARD SALOMONS – 'Caudebec' – signed and dated 1901 – watercolour heightened with bodycolour – 21 x 12¼in.
(Sotheby, King &
*   Chasemore)*   **$294   £165**

SALT – Venetian View – 25½ x 36in.
(Sotheby Beresford
*   Adams)*   **$314   £187**

J. SALTER – A View On The Italian Lakes – signed – watercolour – 8 x 11½in.
(Lawrence)   **$147   £93**

A. SANI – Competent Judges – 17 x 20½in.
(Sotheby Beresford
*   Adams)*   **$1,663   £990**

FRANK SALTFLEET – Ploughing – signed – 7 x 10in. *(Sotheby's)* **$1,778 £1,155**

ALESSANDRO SANI – A Musical Interlude – signed – on panel – 19 x 23¾in.
(Christie's)   **$4,860   £2,700**

JAMES SANT – Portrait Study Of A Young Boy – signed with monogram and inscribed – 50 x 40in.
(Sotheby, King &
Chasemore)   **$1,809   £1,034**

SARKIS SARKESIAN – Head Of A Young Woman – signed – oil on board – 13½ x 11½in.
(Stalker &
Boos)   **$350   £210**

FRANCIS SARTORIUS – A Gentleman With A Grey And A Chestnut Hunter In A Landscape – signed and dated 1781 – 13¼ x 18¼in.
(Christie's)   **$1,898   £1,026**

WILLIAM SARTORIUS – Still Life Of Fruit And Flowers On A Ledge Including Tulips, Grapes And Peaches – inscribed – 22¾ x 34¾in.
(Sotheby's)   **$2,270   £1,320**

SASSOFERRATO – The Virgin At
Prayer – 16½ x 13in.
*(Sotheby Beresford
Adams)* **$203** **£121**

ADRIEN JACQUES SAUZAY – A Village Street – signed and dated '77 – on
panel – 13¼ x 24¼in.
(Christie's) **$3,110** **£1,728**

JULES SCALBERT – Spring Blossom –
signed – on panel – 13½ x 9in.
*(Sotheby, King &
Chasemore)* **$584** **£374**

FREDERICK W. SCARBROUGH –
The Upper Pool, London, With St.
Paul's – signed and inscribed – water-
colour heightened with white – 13½ x
20½in.
(Christie's) **$942** **£561**

FRANK W. SCARBOROUGH – 'The Pool
Of London' – watercolour heightened with
bodycolour – 15½ x 21½in.
*(Sotheby, King &
Chasemore)* **$979** **£550**

FRANK WILLIAM SCARBOROUGH –
Limehouse Reach, London; The Thames
At Greenwich – signed – watercolour –
9¾ x 13½in.
*(Sotheby, King &
Chasemore)* **$1,174** **£660 Pair**

FREDERICK W. SCARBROUGH –
Pool Of London, Sunset – signed and
inscribed – watercolour heightened
with white – 9½ x 13½in.
(Christie's) **$847** **£540**

FREDERICK W. SCARBROUGH –
Greenwich Reach, London – signed
and inscribed – watercolour heightened
with white – 9¾ x 13½in.
(Christie's) **$593** **£378**

SCARSELLINO – Christ On The Road
To Calvary – 16½ x 24½in.
*(Sotheby Beresford
Adams)* **$369** **£220**

SCHAFER

FREDERICK F. SCHAFER – Autumn River Landscape – signed – oil on canvas – 20 x 36in.
(Butterfield's) **$700** **£414**

FREDERICK F. SCHAFER – Mount Hood From The Dalles, Oregon – signed – oil on canvas – 40 x 60in.
(Butterfield's) **$3,500** **£2,070**

HENRY SCHAFER – Lisieux, Normandy; and Chartres – signed – heightened with bodycolour – 15½ x 11½in.
(Sotheby Beresford Adams) **$516** **£297 Pair**

HERMAN SCHAFER – The Cathedral Porch, Chartres; and St. Lawrent, Nuremberg – signed and dated 1876, also signed and dated on the reverse – 15½ x 11½in.
(Sotheby's) **$1,505** **£990 Two**

HERMAN SCHAFER – St. Etienne; St. Qintaine – signed with monogram and dated 1882, signed on the reverse – on board – 9 x 7in.
(Sotheby's) **$1,142** **£638 Pair**

SCHEFFER – The Sickbed – 25 x 20½in.
(Sotheby Beresford Adams) **$351** **£209**

ANDREAS SCHELFOUT – Landscape With Foreground Figures And A Distant Town – signed – oil – 6 x 7in.
(Woolley & Wallis) **$434** **£260**

PETRUS VAN SCHENDEL – A Fish Market By Candlelight – signed and dated 1848 – 27¼ x 24in.
(Christie's) **$4,860** **£2,700**

CORNELIS SCHERMER – Ringstekers – signed and dated 1861 – oil on wood – 33.5 x 47cm.
(Germann Auktionshaus) **$3,314 £2,070**

JOHAN SCHERREWITZ – A Peasant And Cows Outside A Barn – signed – 27½ x 39½in.
(Christie's) **$2,176 £1,404**

JOHAN SCHERREWITZ – Low Tide, Scheveningen – signed – on panel – 10¾ x 14in.
(Sotheby's) **$3,010 £1,980**

ANTON SCHIFFER – An Alpine Town By A Lake – signed and dated 1868 – on board – 16 x 21¼in.
(Sotheby's) **$5,871 £3,740**

EMIL JAKOB SCHINDLER – Ragusa, Lovers In An Ornamental Garden – signed – 36½ x 55in.
(Sotheby's) **$28,875 £16,500**

HEINRICH HANS SCHLIMARSKI – An Eastern Dancer – signed – canvas on panel – 58½ x 32¾in.
(Christie's) **$6,361 £4,104**

SCHMITT

ALBERT SCHNYDER – Weide Bei Montfaucon – signed and dated 1954 – oil on wood – 46.5 x 105cm. *(Germann Autktionshaus)* **$11,490   £7,182**

NATHANIEL SCHMITT – Portrait Of A Girl – signed and inscribed – on canvas – 26 x 20in. *(Sotheby, King & Chasemore)*   **$457   £286**

ALBERT SCHNYDER – Nature Morte A La Cruche – signed and dated 1960 on reverse – oil on canvas – 54.5 x 73.5cm. *(Germann Auktionshaus)* **$10,608   £6,630**

JOHN WILLIAM SCHOFIELD – St. Michael's Mount – signed and dated 1904 – 11 x 23in. *(Sotheby Beresford Adams)*   **$230   £132**

CASPAR SCHNEIDER – Rhineland Views – signed and dated 1790 – on panel – 15¾ x 22½in. *(Sotheby's)*   **$15,136   £8,800 Pair**

MAX SCHOLZ – Paying For The Meal – signed and inscribed – on panel – 13¼ x 10¼in. *(Sotheby's)*   **$1,588   £1,045**

PIETER SCHOUBROECK – A Mountainous Landscape – signed and dated – on copper – 6¼ x 9¾in.
(Sotheby's) **$14,273 £8,250**

PIETER SCHOUBROECK – Troy Burning – signed and dated 1605 – on copper – 7 x 10in.
(Sotheby's) **$14,273 £8,250**

PIETER SCHOUBROECK – The Flight From Troy – on copper – 10¼ x 11¾in.
(Sotheby's) **$6,270 £4,180**

ALOIS HANS SCHRAMM – Decorating Buddha's Shrine With Flowers – signed – 33 x 38¾in.
(Sotheby's) **$3,344 £2,200**

ADOLF SCHREYER – Arabs On Horseback – signed – 19¾ x 33½in.
(Sotheby's) **$36,300 £24,200**

FRANZ SCHREYER – Coast Of Naples With Vesuvius In The Background – signed and dated '88 – oil on canvas – 14½ x 22in.
(Butterfield's) **$800 £473**

SCHULTZ – Fishergirls With Their Wares – 11½ x 9½in.
(Sotheby's) **$468 £308**

JOHN SCOTT – Freyja's First Task – inscribed on an old label on the reverse – 60 x 36¼in.
(Christie's) **$4,017 £2,592**

SCOTT

SIR PETER SCOTT – Pintails At Evening
Flight – signed and dated 1933 – 11½ x
16in.
(Sotheby, King &
Chasemore)   **$238   £140**

WILLIAM BELL SCOTT – 'Thou Hast
Left Me Ever Jamie, Thou Hast Left Me
Ever', Robert Burns – signed, titled and
inscribed – watercolour heightened with
bodycolour – 16½ x 26in.
(Sotheby's)   **$4,620   £2,640**

WILLIAM HENRY STOTHARD SCOTT
– Fisherfolk By A River, A Village And
Mountains Beyond – pencil and water-
colour heightened with white – 20¼ x
28¼in.
(Christie's)   **$725   £432**

ALFRED VON SCROTTER – The Huntsman – signed and dated 1886 – on panel
– 11 x 7¼in.
(Sotheby, King &
Chasemore)   **$4,976   £3,190**

EDWARD SEAGO – Summer Afternoon
On The Thurne – signed – oil on board
– 14½ x 20½in.
(Christie's) **$8,969** **£5,940**

EDWARD SEAGO – The Harbour At
Grado, Portugal – signed with initial
and inscribed on the reverse – on board
– 9 x 11in.
(Sotheby's) **$2,073** **£1,430**

EDWARD SEAGO – Pall Mall, June
1953 – signed – watercolour over pen
and black ink – 10½ x 14in.
(Sotheby's) **$2,552** **£1,760**

EDWARD SEAGO – A Windmill – signed
with initial – watercolour – 10¼ x 12½in.
(Sotheby's) **$1,324** **£770**

EDWARD SEAGO – Hotel De Ville, Honfleur – signed – oil on board – 11¾ x
15in. *(Christie's)* **$4,892 £3,240**

SEAGO

EDWARD SEAGO – Drying Sails, Honfleur – signed – pencil and watercolour – 10½ x 14½in.
(Sotheby's)   **$2,838**   **£1,650**

EDWARD SEAGO – Portrait Of A Pilot – signed and dated '42 – on panel – 17½ x 15½in.
(Sotheby's)   **$681**   **£396**

EDWARD BRIAN SEAGO – Slack Water – signed and inscribed – watercolour – 10½ x 14½in.
(Sotheby, King & Chasemore)   **$3,080**   **£1,760**

COLIN SEALY – 'Cornish Farm' – oil on canvas – 14¼ x 18¼in.
(W. H. Lane & Son)   **$87**   **£50**

SEATON – Christchurch Meadow – dated 1891 – 8 x 17in.
(Lawrence)   **$95**   **£60**

ENOCH SEEMAN, Attributed to – Portrait Of Philip Dormer Stanhope, 4th Earl Of Chesterfield – inscribed and inscribed on the reverse – 90½ x 56¼in.
(Sotheby's)   **$3,155**   **£2,090**

ARTHUR SEGAL – Strassenszene – signed and dated 1916 – 27¾ x 35¼in.
(Sotheby's)   **$1,476**   **£825**

ARTHUR SEGAL – Figuren In Einem Zimmer – signed and dated 1918 – on board – 16¼ x 20¾in.
(Sotheby's) **$6,103** **£3,410**

ARTHUR SEGAL – Haus Und Baume – signed – brush and indian ink – 13 x 16½in.
(Sotheby's) **$394** **£220**

GUILLAUME SEIGNAC – 'Diana' – signed – oil on canvas – 12 x 8½in.
(Robert W. Skinner Inc.) **$850** **£530**

PAUL SEIGNAC – Interior Scene Of A Mother With Children, 'Hush, Baby Is Asleep' – signed – oil on board – 16 x 12½in.
(Du Mouchelles) **$6,500** **£3,610**

GEORGE SEITZ – Roses In A Glass Vase With Fruit On A Ledge – signed and dated '68 – 10½ x 8½in.
(Christie's) **$3,850** **£2,484**

G. SELBY – Fishing Views – signed – on panel – 6 x 12in.
(Sotheby Beresford Adams) **$227** **£132 Pair**

SEMENOWSKY

EMILE EISMAN SEMENOWSKY – The Flower Girl – signed and inscribed – on panel – 22 x 15in.
(Sotheby's)   **$1,254**   **£825**

A. SERKERWICZ – A Camp At Nightfall – signed – 15 x 17in.
(Sotheby Beresford Adams)   **$248**   **£143**

D. SERRES – A Masting Hulk And A Man-O'-War Off The Coast – on panel – 15½ x 21in.
(Lawrence)   **$1,923**   **£1,210**

D. SERRES – H.M.S. Centaur and H.M.S. Belleisle At Spithead – 24¾ x 40in.
(Christie's)   **$2,397**   **£1,296**

RAFAEL SENET – A Calm Day, Venice – signed – 19 x 31in. *(Sotheby Beresford Adams)*   **$3,216 £1,870**

MARY SETON – 'Still Life – Vase Of Spring Flowers' – oil on canvas – 11½ x 13½in.
(W. H. Lane & Son)   **$17**   **£10**

FRANZ VAN SEVERDONCK – Sheep In An Extensive Landscape – signed and dated 1873 – on panel – 18¾ x 25½in.
(Sotheby's)   **$3,010**   **£1,980**

FRANZ VAN SEVERDONCK – Sheep In A Landscape – signed and dated 1873 – 18 x 25in.
(Sotheby Beresford Adams)   **$240**   **£143**

JOSEPH SEVERN – Portrait Study Of A Lady Artist – signed and dated 1836 – on canvas – 36 x 28in.
(Sotheby, King & Chasemore)   **$514**   **£330**

JOSEPH ARTHUR PALLISER SEVERN – 'Old Westminster Pier' – signed – watercolour – 13½ x 20½in.
(Sotheby, King & Chasemore)   **$475**   **£297**

MARY SEYMOR – 'Still Life, Hibiscus' – signed – watercolour – 76 x 54cm.
(Geoff K. Gray)   **$198**   **£118**

JAMES SEYMOUR – A Lady And Gentleman On Horseback In A Landscape, A Huntsman With A Horse To Their Right – signed and dated 1738 – 39 x 49in.
(Sotheby's)   **$60,544**   **£35,200**

JAMES SEYMOUR – Groom Holding A Dark Bay Racehorse, On A Racecourse – signed – 34¼ x 38¾in.
(Sotheby's)   **$10,776**   **£7,150**

SEYMOUR

JAMES SEYMOUR – Flying Childers
With Jockey Up – signed and dated
1740 – 35 x 53in.
(Sotheby's)   **$22,704 £13,200**

SHALDERS – The Plough Team Water-
ing – 37½ x 58in.
*(Sotheby Beresford
Adams)*   **$1,404·   £836**

GEORGE SHALDERS – 'A Country
Road' – signed – oil on canvas – 20 x
30in.
*(Sotheby, King &
Chasemore)*   **$880   £550**

GEORGE SHALDERS – A Lane Near
Southend – 6 x 7in.
(Sotheby's)   **$400   £264**

GEORGE SHALDERS – Evening Glow,
Ranmore Common – signed and dated
1865 – bodycolour – 18¼ x 35in.
(Christie's)   **$2,772 £1,836**

T. SHAPLAND – Continental Estuary
Scene With Boats – signed – watercolour
– 11 x 18in.
(Edgar Horne)   **$66   £44**

DOROTHEA SHARP – Paddling –
signed with initials – canvas on board
– 7½ x 9in.
(Sotheby's)   **$606   £419**

JOSEPH HENRY SHARP – Belle Of Portugal Roses – signed – oil on canvas – 24 x 20in.
(Butterfield's) **$10,000 £5,988**

JOSEPH HENRY SHARP – Play Fellows – signed – oil on board – 11 x 8½in.
(Butterfield's) **$1,600 £947**

ELIZA SHARPE – The Village School Room – signed and dated – watercolour – 19 x 24in.
(Woolley & Wallis) **$1,239 £700**

AARON DRAPER SHATTUCK – Mount Washington, Clouds At Summit, Conway – oil on board – 6¼ x 10in.
(Christie's) **$495 £330**

JOHN BYAM LISTON SHAW – When Love Came Into The House Of The Respectable Citizen – signed – watercolour heightened with bodycolour – 18 x 23in.
(Sotheby's) **$3,657 £2,090**

SHAYER – Fisherboys – on board – 10 x 15in.
(Sotheby Beresford Adams) **$406 £242**

SHAYER – Vessels And Figures On A Beach – 18 x 28.5in.
(Woolley & Wallis) **$407 £230**

W. SHAYER – Young Fisherfolk – 24½ x 29in.
(Sotheby Beresford Adams) **$1,848 £1,100**

W. SHAYER – Coastal Scenes With Figures And Boats – signed – 18 x 30in.
(Chrystals) **$1,128 £630**

SHAYER

WILLIAM SHAYER – A Wooded Landscape With A Gipsy Encampment By A
Stream – signed, signed and inscribed
on a label on the reverse – 11¾ x 15¾in.
(Christie's) **$8,120 £4,536**

WILLIAM SHAYER, SNR. – A Shepherdess With Cattle Drinking From A
Well, In A Wooded Landscape – signed
and dated 1867 – 21¼ x 26¾in.
(Christie's) **$2,034 £1,296**

WILLIAM SHAYER, Follower of – Cattle
Watering From A Farm Pond – oil on
canvas – 24 x 20in.
*(Sotheby, King &
Chasemore)* **$660 £440**

**WILLIAM JOSEPH AND CHARLES
SHAYER** – Cottage By A Woodland
Path With Milkmaid And Cattle –
signed – 27½ x 35½in.
(Sotheby's) **$5,298 £3,080**

WILLIAM SHAYER – Refreshment At
The Cottage Door – 13½ x 11½in.
(Sotheby's) **$4,347 £2,860**

**WILLIAM SHAYER AND EDWARD
CHARLES WILLIAMS** – The Approach-
ing Storm – 30 x 50in.
(Christie's) **$2,176 £1,404**

GEORGE SHEFFIELD – Summer Landscapes – signed and dated 1871 – 11½ x 18in.
(Sotheby Beresford Adams) **$191** **£110 Pair**

ERNEST HOWARD SHEPARD – 'The First Shot' – signed – watercolour – 6 x 9in.
(Sotheby, King & Chasemore) **$346** **£198**

H. C. SHEPPARD – Landscapes With Stream, Track And Byre – signed and dated 1914 – watercolour – 13 x 20in.
(Edgar Horne) **$94** **£62 Pair**

WARREN W. SHEPPARD – Contrarini Palace On The Rio Della Macenigo, Venice – signed, inscribed and dated 1901 – oil on canvas – 24¼ x 16in.
(Christie's) **$1,650** **£1,100**

ALBERT J. SHERMAN – 'Blossoms In A Chinese Vase' – signed – oil on board – 35 x 28cm.
(Geoff K. Gray) **$1,265** **£752**

DAN SHERRIN – A Wooded Landscape With Children On A Path – signed – 24 x 42in.
(Christie's) **$690** **£386**

DAVID SHERRIN – 'On The Thames' At Marlow – signed on canvas – 12 x 20in.
(Sotheby, King & Chasemore) **$990** **£660 Pair**

WALTER RICHARD SICKERT – Santa Maria Della Salute – signed – oil on canvas – 23½ x 19in.
(Christie's) **$42,400** **£28,080**

SICKERT

WALTER RICHARD SICKERT – The Laundry Shop, Dieppe – signed – oil on canvas – 20¼ x 16in.
(Christie's) **$5,218 £3,456**

N. SIDEBOTTOM – 'Cottage Interior With Old Man Making Fishing Nets' – watercolour – 13½ x 17¼in.
(Dacre, Son & Hartley) **$86 £50**

PAUL SIEFHERT – Full Length Portrait Of A Lady Seated In An Interior Wearing Chinese Costume – signed and dated 1910 – 61 x 49½in.
(Lawrence) **$559 £352**

GUISEPPE SIGNORINI – Cardinal Pondering A Letter – signed – watercolour – 12¾ x 9½in.
(Du Mouchelles) **$900 £500**

DE SIMONE – British Iron-Clad Man O' War In Naples Harbour – signed and dated 1885 – oil on canvas – 19¾ x 27¼in.
(Sotheby, King & Chasemore) **$1,045 £615**

PAUL SIGNAC – World's Fair, Paris, 1900 – signed and dated 1900 – watercolour and pencil on paper – 9¾ x 11½in.
(William Doyle Galleries) **$10,000 £5,917**

SIMONINI – An Army On The Move, A Plain Beyond – 22 x 37in.
(Sotheby Beresford Adams) **$1,663 £990**

FRANCESCO SIMONINI, Circle of – A Military Encampment – 27½ x 37¾in.
(Sotheby's) **$9,698 £6,380**

FRANCESCO SIMONINI – A Column Of Troops – 22 x 34in. *(Sotheby's)*
$7,612 £4,400

SIMONINI

FRANCESCO SIMONINI – Battles Between Christians And Turks – oval – 58¼ x 42½in. *(Sotheby's)* **$11,798 £6,820** Two

STEFAN SIMONY – 'Alpine Village' – signed and dated – oil on board – 19 x 27cm.
(Geoff K. Gray) **$54 £32**

WILLIAM SIMSON – A Camaldolese Monk Showing The Relics In The Sacristy Of A Roman Convent – signed and dated 1838 – 51 x 41in.
(Christie's & Edmiston's) **$1,040 £650**

H. SINGLETON – Preparing For The Fight – oval 15 x 18¾in.
(Christie's) **$500 £270**

ALFRED SISLEY – La Riviere – signed – pastel on paper – 8¼ x 13¼in.
(William Doyle Galleries) **$7,500 £4,437**

ALFRED SISLEY – L'Abreuvoir De Marly – signed and dated '95 – pastel on paper on canvas – 11¾ x 15½in.
(William Doyle Galleries) **$26,000 £15,384**

KAREL SKRETA – Portrait Of A Man – 17¾ x 13¼in.
(Sotheby's) **$567** **£330**

JOHN FALCONAR SLATER – A Windmill At Sunset – signed – oil – 15½ x 19½in.
(Anderson & Garland) **$51** **£32**

JOHN FALCONAR SLATER – Waves Breaking On The Coast In Summer – signed – oil – 29½ x 49½in.
(Anderson & Garland) **$216** **£135**

JOHN FALCONAR SLATER – The Mouth Of The Tyne, A View West From The Cliffs At Tynemouth Towards The Town Of North Shields – signed – 29½ x 49½in.
(Anderson & Garland) **$600** **£360**

JAMES SMETHAM – The Death Of Earl Siward – 27 x 16in.
(Sotheby's) **$4,235** **£2,420**

JOS DE SMEDT – The Odalisque – signed and dated 1915 – 38½ x 46½in.
(Christie's) **$2,106** **£1,404**

GEORGE HENRY SMILLIE – Path To The Meadow – oil on canvas – 9 x 6¼in.
(Christie's) **$1,100** **£733**

CARLTON A. SMITH – 'Mother's Helper,
Domestic Interior With Women Sewing,
Boy Holding An Apple And Magpie' – oil
– 20¼ x 30½in.
*(Dacre, Son &
Hartley)*   **$3,096**   **£1,800**

CARLTON ALFRED SMITH – Watering
The Pot Plants – signed and dated 1880 –
heightened with white, over pencil – 21
x 14in.
(Sotheby's)   **$1,101**   **£715**

DENZIL SMITH – Dutch Sailing Boats
At Anchor Off A Town – signed with
a monogram – oil on canvas laid on
panel – 15 x 19in.
*(Woolley &
Wallis)*   **$700**   **£420**

FRANCIS HOPKINSON SMITH –
'Venetian Evening' – signed – gouache
– 19¼ x 28¼in.
*(Robert W. Skinner
Inc.)*   **$700**   **£438**

GEORGE SMITH – Fondly Gazing –
signed and dated 1861 – on panel – 16
x 13¼in.
(Sotheby's)   **$3,630**   **£2,420**

GEORGE SMITH of Chichester – An
Extensive River Landscape With Rustics
Resting – 26 x 42in.
(Sotheby's)   **$3,155**   **£2,090**

GRACE COSSINGTON SMITH –
'Street In Kings Cross' – signed – oil on
board – 28 x 25cm.
(Geoff K. Gray)   **$1,535**   **£912**

HELY SMITH – Ships Passing Gibraltar
– signed – 24 x 36in.
(Sotheby's)   **$378**   **£220**

HENRY PEMBER SMITH – 'Moonlit
Coast' – signed and dated '81 – oil on
canvas – 12 x 18in.
*(Robert W. Skinner
Inc.)*   **$300**   **£187**

JAMES BURRELL SMITH – Figures By A Watermill – signed and dated – watercolour – 13.x 8.5in.
(Woolley & Wallis)   **$450**   **£270 Pair**

JAMES BURRELL SMITH – Cattle Watering – signed and dated 1867 – heightened with bodycolour – 14¼ x 22¼in.
(Sotheby's)   **$711**   **£462**

JAMES BURRELL SMITH – The Mill At Warkworth, Northumberland – signed and inscribed on the reverse – 9 x 12½in.
(Sotheby Beresford Adams)   **$425**   **£253**

JAMES BURRELL SMITH – Beach Scene With Boats And A Windmill – signed and dated – watercolour – 8.5 x 19.5in.
(Woolley & Wallis)   **$300**   **£170**

JOHN BRANDON SMITH – Scottish Falls – signed and dated 1876 – 26 x 20in.
(Sotheby's)   **$1,588**   **£1,045**

JOHN WARWICK SMITH – The Ruins Of Habberston Priory – inscribed – watercolour – 5 x 8in.
(Sotheby, King & . Chasemore)   **$561**   **£330**

WALTER GRANVILLE SMITH – Bringing The Boat To Water – signed – oil on canvas – 18¾ x 29½in.
(Christie's)   **$990**   **£660**

WELLS SMITH – Children At Play – oil – 63 x 51cm.
(Reeds Rains)   **$1,312**   **£750**

WILLIAM COLLINGWOOD SMITH – A Beached Ship At Sunset – pencil and watercolour heightened with white on green paper – 10¾ x 13¾in.
(Christie's)   **$235**   **£140**

WILLIAM COLLINGWOOD SMITH –
Constantinople And The Golden Horn
– signed – watercolour – 30 x 51in.
(Sotheby, King &
Chasemore) $8,750   £5,610

WILLIAM COLLINGWOOD SMITH –
The Dreadnought, Seamen's Hospital
Ship, Off Greenwich – pencil and water-
colour heightened with white – 10¾ x
14¼in.
(Christie's) $1,723   £1,026

PALMIRE SMITS – Portrait Of A Boy
– signed – oil – 15.5 x 12in.
(Woolley &
Wallis) $167   £100

E. R. SMYTHE – Home From The Fields –
on board – 10 x 12in.
(Sotheby's) $322   £180

THOMAS SMYTHE – Crossing The
Stream; and A Country Inn – signed –
11½ x 8½in.
(Sotheby's) $2,173   £1,430 **Pair**

JAMES HERBERT SNELL – Eton From Romney Island – signed – watercolour – 14 x 19in.
(Woolley & Wallis) **$267** **£160**

JAMES HERBERT SNELL – A Landscape Scene With Barns – signed and dated '86, and signed and dated on the reverse – oil on canvas – 19¼ x 29¼in.
(Geering & Colyer) **$136** **£80**

PIETER SNYERS – A Still Life, Plums And A Peach On A Ledge – signed – on copper – 16½ x 8in.
(Sotheby's) **$14,045** **£9,240**

REBECCA SOLOMON – A Fashionable Couple – signed and dated – 19 x 21in.
(Christie's) **$2,916** **£1,944**

SIMEON SOLOMON – Shadrach, Meshach And Abednego In The Burning Fiery Furnace – signed with monogram and dated 1863 – watercolour heightened with white – 13 x 9in.
(Christie's) **$14,677** **£9,720**

SIMEON SOLOMON – A Lady At A Window – watercolour – 10¼ x 7¾in.
(Christie's) **$390** **£259**

SIMEON SOLOMON – The Rebuking Conscience – signed with initials and dated 1887 – pencil – 10½ x 13½in.
(Christie's) **$244** **£162**

SIMEON SOLOMON – Atlanta – 18 x 14in.
(Christie's) **$1,506** **£972**

THOMAS SOMERSCALES – The Gathering Storm – signed – oil on canvas – 18 x 12in.
(Sotheby's) **$4,145** **£2,640**

SOMERSET

RICHARD GAY SOMERSET – A
Breezy Day – signed – 17½ x 23½in.
(Sotheby Beresford
Adams) **$132** **£77**

ROBERT GAY SOMERSET – Breaking
Waves – signed – 15½ x 26½in.
(Sotheby Beresford
Adams) **$296** **£176**

JEAN SOUVERBIE – Couple Dans Un
Paysage – signed and dated '36 – oil
on canvas – 25 x 35½in.
(Sotheby's) **$1,755** **£1,155**

JOSEPH EDWARD SOUTHALL – Tor-
cello – signed with monogram and dated
1921 – 10 x 6½in.
(Sotheby's) **$4,620** **£2,640**

EUGENE SPEICHER – Portrait Of
Gloria – signed and inscribed – oil on
canvas – 41 x 34¼in.
(Christie's) **$1,210** **£800**

EUGENE SPEICHER – Portrait Of A
Woman – oil on canvas – 45¼ x 35¼in.
(Christie's) **$1,540** **£1,026**

CHARLES SPENCELAYH – Portrait Of
The Artist, In Black Coat And Waistcoat
– signed and dated 1898 – 24 x 20in.
(Christie's) **$2,008** **£1,296**

CHARLES SPENCELAYH – A Dark Beauty – signed and dated 1922 – 26 x 20in.
(Christie's) **$1,171** **£756**
CHARLES SPENCELAYH – The Pink Dress – signed and dated 1922 – 26 x 20in.
(Sotheby Beresford Adams) **$995** **£572**

CARL SPITZWEG – Madchen Im Gebirge – signed with monogram – oil on canvas – 14 x 10in.
(William Doyle Galleries) **$47,500 £28,106**

SIR STANLEY SPENCER – Me And Hilda, Dresses And Children – signed and dated – pencil on brown paper – 15¾ x 10½in.
(Christie's) **$1,140** **£756**

CARL SPITZWEG – Selbstbildnis – monogrammed and dated 1836 – oil on wood – 18.5 x 16cm.
(Germann Auktionshaus) **$18,564 £11,602**

SPOHLER

JACOB JAN COENRAAD SPOHLER – Figures In A Frozen River Landscape – signed – 25 x 36in.
(Sotheby's) $3,938   £2,200

G. SPONDINI – 'The Bouquet' – signed – oil on panel – 12½ x 8½in.
(Sotheby, King & Chasemore) $1,694   £968

CORNELIS SPRINGER – A Winter Town Scene With Figures By A Canal – signed with initials and dated 1837 – on panel – 10½ x 12¾in.
(Christie's) $3,098   £2,052

LEONARD RUSSELL SQUIRREL – The Market-Place, Stratford-on-Avon – signed and dated 1963 – pencil and watercolour – 8½ x 17in.
(Christie's) $541   £345

LOUIS VAN STAATEN – On The Amstel, Near Amsterdam – signed – watercolour – 11 x 15.2in.
(Woolley & Wallis) $385   £230

LOUIS VAN STAATEN – 'Near Flushing', A Canal Scene With Windmill, Houses And Shipping – signed – watercolour – 16 x 24in.
(Lawrence) $384   £242

LOUIS VAN STAATEN – Dutch Canal Views – signed – heightened with body-colour – 10½ x 15in.
(Sotheby Beresford Adams) $210   £121 Pair

LOUIS VAN STAATEN – Amsterdam – signed – watercolour – 11 x 15.2in.
(Woolley & Wallis) $317   £190

LOUIS VAN STAATEN – Overschie – signed – watercolour – 15 x 24in.
(Edgar Horne) $309   £205

W. S. STACEY – Wooded Landscape With Cattle – watercolour – 20 x 14in.
(G. H. Bayley & Sons) $380   £220

W. S. STACEY – Group With A Horse, Cart And Figures On A Rocky Moorland Road – watercolour – 21 x 13½in.
(G. H. Bayley & Sons) $380   £220

WALTER S. STACEY – Wooded River Landscape With Children Fishing – signed – watercolour – 14.5 x 21in.
(Woolley & Wallis) $267   £160

FREDERICK STAFFORD – The Night Express – signed – watercolour – 14½ x 21in.
(Sotheby, King & Chasemore) **$127** **£75**

FREDERICK STAFFORD – Southern Railway, South Western Section – signed – watercolour – 21¼ x 14½in.
(Sotheby, King & Chasemore) **$110** **£65**

CLARKSON STANFIELD – Driving The Piles – sketch – paper on board – 9½ x 7in.
(Sotheby Beresford Adams) **$332** **£198**

STANFIELD

CLARKSON STANFIELD – A Bell Tower At Sorrento, Italy – black chalk and watercolour heightened with white on blue paper – 7¼ x 11in.
(Christie's) **$362** **£215**

CLARKSON STANFIELD – The Gulf Of Salerno – signed – 28 x 43½in.
(Sotheby's) **$29,700** **£19,800**

CLARKSON STANFIELD – Three-Masted Sailing Vessels In A Harbour, With A Group Of Men And Women In The Foreground Waiting To Embark – signed and dated 1831 – oil on canvas – 29½ x 41¼in.
(Geering & Colyer) **$15,405** **£9,750**

CLARKSON STANFIELD – A Mountainous River Landscape With Figures On A Path – signed and dated 1850 – 10 x 13¾in.
(Christie's) **$773** **£432**

W. CLARKSON STANFIELD – A Man Of War And Other Shipping In Coastal Waters, A Dinghy In The Foreground – signed – oil on panel – 11 x 15½in.
(Hy. Duke & Son) **$1,038** **£600**

WILLIAM CLARKSON STANFIELD – 'The Entrance To Portsmouth Harbour' – signed and dated 1829 – watercolour with scratching out, heightened with white – 11¼ x 17¼in.
(Sotheby, King & Chasemore) **$5,808** **£3,630**

B. STANLEY – A River In Spring – signed – 15 x 23in.
(Sotheby Beresford Adams) **$58** **£33**

ELOISE HARRIET STANNARD – Still Life With Melon, Grapes And Assorted Fruits On A Ledge – signed and dated 1903 – 22½ x 29in.
(Christie's S. Kensington) **$13,360** **£8,000**

HENRY JOHN SYLVESTER STANNARD – Trees On A River Bank – signed – watercolour heightened with white – 13½ x 23½in.
(Christie's) **$474** **£302**

HENRY JOHN SYLVESTER STANNARD – A Little Ray Of Sunlight – signed – heightened with bodycolour – 13½ x 22½in.
(Sotheby's) **$847** **£550**

HENRY JOHN SYLVESTER STANNARD
– 'Feeding The Ducks' – signed – water-
colour – 9½ x 13½in.
(Sotheby, King &
Chasemore) **$1,056** **£704**

HENRY JOHN SYLVESTER STANNARD
– Driving Sheep – signed and dated '08
– heightened with scratching out – 22½ x
31in.
(Sotheby's) **$932** **£605**

**HENRY JOHN SYLVESTER
STANNARD** – Hambledon – signed –
10 x 14in.
(Sotheby Beresford
Adams) **$628** **£374**

HENRY SYLVESTER STANNARD –
An Autumn Landscape With Three Chil-
dren At A Stile – signed – watercolour –
9.5 x 13.5in.
(Woolley &
Wallis) **$635** **£380**

THERESA SYLVESTER STANNARD –
The Garden Path – signed – watercolour
– 9½ x 6½in.
(Sotheby's) **$813** **£528**

G. STANTON – River Views – signed –
19 x 29in.
(Sotheby Beresford
Adams) **$38** **£22 Pair**

SIR ROBERT PONSONBY STAPLES –
At The Seaside – signed – on canvas –
20 x 16in.
(Sotheby, King &
Chasemore) **$4,290** **£2,750**

STARK – A View Of Norwich, With
Figures And Cattle In The Foreground –
oil on board – 17¾ x 23¾in.
(Geering &
Colyer) **$1,304** **£825**

STARK

STARK – A Wooded Landscape With A Waggoner, A Shepherd And His Sheep – bears indistinct signature – 21½ x 26½in.
(Christie's) **$718** **£388**

ARTHUR JAMES STARK – Landscape With A Figure On A Track – watercolour over pencil heightened with white – 6 x 16¼.
(Sotheby's) **$243** **£130**

JAMES STARK – In The Forest, St. Leonard's, near Windsor, With A Fallen Oak – dated 1875 – canvas on panel – 15¾ x 23in.
(Christie's) **$1,506** **£972**

FRED STAUFFER – Landschaft – signed and dated '27 – oil on canvas – 65.3 x 90.5cm.
(Germann Auktionshaus) **$4,860** **£3,038**

STAVEREN – A Hermit – 10 x 8in.
(Sotheby Beresford Adams) **$240** **£143**

EDWIN STEELE – Still Life With Fruit – signed – 23 x 16in.
(Sotheby Beresford Adams) **$10** **£6**

JAN STEEN – A Seated Woman Reading A Letter – signed; and A Beer Drinker Asleep – bears signature – on panel – 9¼ x 6½in.
(Sotheby's) **$7,920** **£5,280 Pair**

PHILIP WILSON STEER – View Over The Solent – signed and dated 1919 – watercolour – 9½ x 13½in.
(Christie's) **$652** **£432**

PHILIP WILSON STEER – The South
Downs – signed and dated 1926 –
watercolour – 12½ x 18½in.
(Christie's)   **$847**   **£561**

PHILIP WILSON STEER – Calm
Estuary – signed and dated 1933 – water-
colour – 7¼ x 11¾in.
(Christie's)   **$390**   **£259**

PHILIP WILSON STEER – 'Shirehamp-
ton, Near Bristol' – inscribed on a label
– watercolour – 9 x 13½in.
(Sotheby, King &
Chasemore)   **$299**   **£187**

THEOPHILE-ALEXANDRE STEINLEN
– Femme Nue – signed with initials –
charcoal – 14½ x 10¼in.
(Sotheby's)   **$787**   **£440**

THEOPHILE ALEXANDRE STEINLEN – Au Marche – signed – black crayon
on paper – 21½ x 18¼in. *(Christie's)*   **$1,441 £918**

STEINLEN

THEOPHILE ALEXANDRE STEINLEN
– La Vendeuse De Fleurs – signed –
black crayon on paper – 23¾ x 18½in.
(Christie's)   **$1,610   £1,026**

FRANCIS PHILIP STEPHANOFF – 'The
Advance' – signed – on canvas – 25 x
30in.
(Sotheby, King &
Chasemore)   **$2,310   £1,540**

CECIL STEPHENSON – Untitled 1938 –
signed and dated – tempera – 36 x 28in.
(Sotheby's)   **$925   £638**

IGNAZ STERN, Attributed to, Called Stella – Charity – signed or inscribed –
31 x 39in. *(Sotheby's)*   **$2,508 £1,650**

GEORGE STEVENS – Still Life – signed and dated 1845 – oil on canvas – 30¾ x 25¾in.
(Sotheby, King & Chasemore) **$1,828** **£1,045**

CHARLES STEWART – Beached Fishing Vessels – signed and dated 1891 – oil – 10 x 14in.
(Sotheby, King & Chasemore) **$369** **£231 Pair**

JULIUS STEWART – Reclining Nude By An Oriental Screen – oil on canvas on board – 28¼ x 47¼in.
(Christie's) **$1,760** **£1,173**

GEORGE BLACKIE STICKS – A Misty Evening, An Angler Sitting On The Bank Of The Tyne By Haughton Castle – signed and dated 1896 and inscribed on the reverse – 17¾ x 13¾in.
(Anderson & Garland) **$418** **£250**

HARRY STICKS – Old Lime Kilns On The South Tyne – signed and inscribed on the reverse – oil on canvas – 12 x 18in.
(Edgar Horne) **$378** **£250**

VINCENT G. STIEPEVICH – 'After The Ball' – signed – oil on canvas – 21 x 16in.
(Stalker & Boos) **$800** **£500**

MORITZ STIFTER – Mediaeval Beauties – signed – on panel – 7¼ x 5in.
(Sotheby's) **$1,575** **£880 Pair**

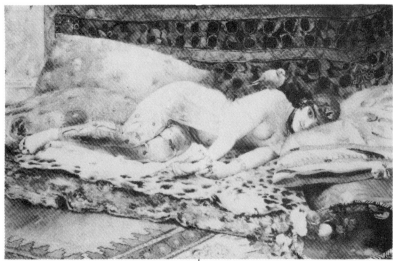

CHARLES STOECKLIN – A Reclining Odalisque – signed – 30½ x 42¾in.
(Sotheby's)   **$4,134   £2,310**

MARIANNE STOKES – Angels Entertaining The Holy Child – signed – 59 x 69in.
(Sotheby's)   **$7,700   £4,400**

CONSTANTIN STOILOFF – Wolves Attacking A Sleigh – signed – oil on canvas – 7½ x 11½in.
(Sotheby, King & Chasemore)   **$1,072   £715 Pair**

ADRIAN STOKES – Studies Of A Nude Male And Female Figures – signed – in crayon – 29 x 19in.
(Lawrence)   **$55   £35**

MARCUS STONE – The Rose Garden – 10 x 12in.
(Sotheby Beresford Adams)   **$830   £495**

MARCUS STONE – A Stolen Kiss –
signed – 60 x 28in.
(Sotheby's) **$41,250 £27,500**

MARCUS STONE, Follower of – Holding
Court – on canvas – 25 x 30in.
(Sotheby, King &
Chasemore) **$514 £330**

R. STONE – The Kill; The Chase – signed
– oil on panel – 5½ x 12in.
(Sotheby, King &
Chasemore) **$866 £495 Pair**

WILLIAM STONE – Old Farm Near
Llangollen, North Wales – signed,
inscribed on the reverse – 19 x 26½in.
(Sotheby Beresford
Adams) **$248 £143**

WILLIAM STONE – Old Park House,
Near Leominster, Herefordshire – signed,
inscribed on the reverse – 19 x 26½in.
(Sotheby Beresford
Adams) **$574 £330**

ABRAHAM STORCK, In The Manner Of
– Warships Off Greenwich – oil on can-
vas – 24 x 35½in.
(Butterfield's) **$2,750 £1,646**

STORCK

STORCK – A Southern Port – 29 x 43½in.
(Sotheby's)   **$2,459   £1,430**

ARTHUR CLAUDE STRACHAN – Young Girls By Thatched Cottage Doorways – signed – watercolour heightened with white – 12 x 18in.
(Christie's S. Kensington)   **$2,005   £1,200 Pair**

CLAUDE STRACHAN – A Saucer Of Milk – signed – watercolour heightened with white – 10¾ x 14½in.
(Christie's)   **$1,863   £1,242**

CLAUDE STRACHAN – The New Bone – signed – watercolour heightened with white – 7¼ x 10½in.
(Christie's)   **$1,944   £1,296**

WILLIAM STRANG – Portrait Of A
Lady, Seated, Holding A Fan – signed
and dated 1914 – 36 x 30in.
(Christie's &
Edmiston's) **$5,440** **£3,400**

JAN STRIENING – Washing Day; and
Tea Time – signed – 18 x 23in.
(Sotheby Beresford
Adams) **$3,880** **£2,310 Two**

TOBIAS STRANOVER – Still Life Of
Fruit With A Parrot – 26 x 23½in.
(Sotheby's) **$3,678** **£2,420**

SIR ARTHUR ERNEST STREETON –
'Venetian Scene' – signed – watercolour
– 32 x 40cm.
(Geoff K. Gray) **$1,354** **£906**

ALFRED WILLIAM STRUTT – Taming
The Shrew – signed – 35 x 60in.
(Sotheby Beresford
Adams) **$20,697** **£12,320**

**FRANCES STRICKLAND, Attributed
to** – Winter Hunt – oil on board –
oval 12½ x 16½in.
(Butterfield's) **$600** **£355**

G. MURRIE STUART – Spring In The
Weald Of Surrey – 19 x 29in.
(Sotheby Beresford
Adams) **$170** **£99**

STUART

CHARLES STUART – Still Life Study Of Fruit On A Marble Ledge – signed and indistinctly dated – 24½ x 30in.
(Sotheby, King & Chasemore) **$908** **£605**

DEDRICK BRANDES STUBER – View Of The City – signed – oil on board – 16 x 20in.
(Butterfield's) **$650** **£385**

R. STURROCK – Corfe Castle Village At Dusk – signed – oil – 20 x 24in.
(Woolley & Wallis) **$200** **£120**

SUTZE – 'Setting Off On A Picnic' – signed – oil on canvas – 12 x 18in.
(Sotheby, King & Chasemore) **$885** **£506**

SVEND SVENDSEN – Entrance To The Garden – signed – oil on canvas – 16 x 24in.
(Butterfield's) **$350** **£210**

WALTER STUEMPFIG – Summer Idle – oil on canvas – 22 x 27in. *(Christie's)*
$2,640 £1,748

FRANCIS SWAINE – Capture Of The Chausey Islands, 1756, A British Squadron In The Gulf Of St. Malo – signed – 25¼ x 35¾in.
(Sotheby's) **$3,784 £2,200**

JOSEPH HAROLD SWANWICK – A Street In Tunis – signed with initials – pencil and watercolour – 6½ x 9¼in.
(Christie's) **$339 £216**

JOSEPH HAROLD SWANWICK – A Farm Near Algiers – signed and dated '95 – watercolour heightened with white – 9¾ x 6½in.
(Christie's) **$177 £302**

ALBERT GERRITS SWART – Landscape With A Cottage By A Pond – signed – oil on canvas – 19½ x 27¼in.
(Du Mouchelles) **$1,000 £588**

JOHN SYER – 'A Mountain Torrent', A Gushing Rocky Waterfall With A Lake And Mountains In The Distance – signed and dated '73 – watercolour – 74 x 52cm.
(Osmond, Tricks) **$310 £180**

JOHN SYER – An Alpine Lake Scene With Figures In Three Punts In The Foreground And Snow Capped Mountains In The Distance – signed and dated '71 – watercolour – 35 x 22cm.
(Osmond, Tricks) **$206 £120**

JOHN GUTTRIDGE SYKES – 'Homeward Bound', Horses Beside A Stream With Farm Buildings Beyond – signed – watercolour – 9½ x 13½in.
(W. H. Lane & Son) **$104 £60**

JOHN GUTTRIDGE SYKES – 'Seascape In Grey' – watercolour – 5 x 7in.
(W. H. Lane & Son) **$69 £40**

JOHN SYER – Off Clovelly; and The Return Of The Fishing Boats – signed and dated '62 – 12 x 20¼in.
(Christie's) **$2,845 £1,836 Pair**

GEORGE GARDNER SYMONS – Early Spring Landscape – oil on canvas – 50 x 60¼in.
(Christie's) **$12,100 £8,066**

JEAN TASSEL – The Virgin And Child With A Jesuit Saint – on panel – 7½ x 5¾in.
(Sotheby's) **$1,427** **£825**

RAFFAELE TAFURI – Gondolas On A Sunlit Venetian Canal – signed and inscribed – 30½ x 20¾in.
(Sotheby's) **$4,330** **£2,420**

DINGWELL B. TATE – The Sunderland Fishing Fleet Becalmed Below A Full Moon – signed and dated 1925 – watercolour – 7¼ x 11in.
(Anderson & Garland) **$18** **£11**

J. TALMAGE-WHITE – 'In The Olive Woods Of Anacapri' – signed – watercolour – 13 x 9in.
(Hy. Duke & Son) **$484** **£280**

WILLIAM TATTON – Winter – signed and dated 1896 – watercolour – 12¾ x 18½in.
(Sotheby, King & Chasemore) **$594** **£396**

JOHN TAVARE – Windsor Castle – signed and dated 1836 – 13 x 17½in.
(Sotheby Beresford Adams) **$96** **£55**

RUFINO TAMAYO – 'Poling Boats' – signed and dated '49 – watercolour – 16 x 13½in.
(Stalker & Boos) **$3,750** **£2,245**

JOHN FREDERICK TAYLER – 'The Day's Bag' – signed with initials and dated 1872 – watercolour – 15 x 21in.
(Sotheby, King & Chasemore) **$1,238** **£825**

JOHN FREDERICK TAYLER – 'Hunting Party On A Woodland Path' – signed with initials – watercolour heightened with bodycolour – 10¼ x 14½in.
(Sotheby, King & Chasemore) **$580** **£363**

FREDERICK TAYLER – Study Of A Girl Holding A Horse's Head – signed with monogram and dated 1875 – 10¼ x 8¼in.
(Sotheby, King & Chasemore) **$363** **£242**

HENRY KING TAYLOR – Shipping Near Honfleur – oil – 24 x 36in.
(Woolley & Wallis) **$1,380** **£780**

LEONARD CAMPBELL TAYLOR – A Game Of Cribbage – signed – 20½ x 15¼in.
(Christie's) **$1,840** **£1,188**

WALTER TAYLOR – Summer Flowers In A Vase – signed, also signed on the reverse – on board – 12¾ x 13in.
(Sotheby's) **$56** **£33**

HENRI TEBBIT – 'Landscape With Stream' – signed – watercolour – 20 x 30cm.
(Geoff K. Gray) **$180** **£107**

TENIERS – The Wedding Feast – on panel – 18 x 25½in.
(Sotheby's) **$7,230** **£4,180**

TENIERS – Peasants In An Interior – on panel – 10¾ x 14½in.
(Sotheby's) **$4,186** **£2,420**

DAVID TENIERS, Follower of – A Kitchen Interior With Figures – bears signature – oil on canvas – 15½ x 22in.
(Sotheby, King & Chasemore) **$1,567** **£1,045**

TENIERS

DAVID TENIERS, The Younger – The Interior Of An Inn – signed and dated – on panel – 13½ x 9¾in.
(Sotheby's) **$24,750 £16,400**

FRITS THAULOW – Factory Buildings By A Bridge In Winter – signed – 25 x 31¼in.
(Sotheby's) **$34,650 £23,100**

DAVID TENIERS, Manner of – The Interior Of A Barn With Figures – 20½ x 25½in.
(Sotheby's) **$4,681 £3,080**

HENRY M. TERRY – The Country Fiddler – signed – watercolour – 21¼ x 15½in.
(Sotheby's) **$390 £253**

HARRY GEORGE THEAKER – 'Vebezia' – signed and inscribed on the reverse – 18 x 10in.
(Sotheby, King & Chasemore) **$1,039 £693**

HARRY GEORGE THEAKER –
Drink To Me Only With Thine Eyes –
signed – heightened with bodycolour –
19½ x 26in.
(Sotheby's)   **$880**   **£572**

HARRY GEORGE THEAKER – 'The
Bridge Of Life' – signed, inscribed on the
reverse – watercolour – 17½ x 13in.
(Sotheby, King &
Chasemore)   **$429**   **£286**

HARRY GEORGE THEAKER – 'The
Queen's Council' – signed – watercolour
– 17¾ x 26in.
(Sotheby, King &
Chasemore)   **$759**   **£506**

JOHANN ALEXANDER THIELE – River
Landscapes – one signed – 11¾ x 15½in.
(Sotheby's)   **$5,328**   **£3,080 Pair**

ANTHONY THIEME – At Dockside –
signed – oil on board – 11¾ x 15¾in.
(Christie's)   **$1,650**   **£1,100**

ANTHONY THIEME – 'On The Shore'
– signed – oil on canvas on board – 8
x 10in.
(Robert W. Skinner
Inc.)   **$600**   **£375**

ANTHONY THIEME – 'Winter Landscape In New Hampshire' – signed – oil on canvas – 25¼ x 30in.
(Robert W. Skinner Inc.) **$1,800** **£1,125**

ANTHONY THIEME – 'Bright Light' – signed – oil on canvas on board – 8 x 10in.
(Robert W. Skinner Inc.) **$600** **£375**

JOSEPH THOMA – A Garden In Constantinople – signed – on panel – 14½ x 22¾in.
(Sotheby's) **$1,420** **£935**

G. THOMAS – The Alchemist – 21½ x 18½in.
(Sotheby's) **$2,284** **£1,320**

J. THOMAS – A Farmyard Scene – oil in canvas – 20 x 30in.
(Sotheby, King & Chasemore) **$1,156** **£680**

THOMAS THOMAS – A Keeper's Cottage, Nr. Dolgelly, North Wales – signed – oil on canvas – 29½ x 50½in.
(Sotheby, King & Chasemore) **$462** **£308**

A. WORDSWORTH THOMPSON – 'Farm Boys Loading A Horse-Drawn Wagon' – signed – oil on canvas – 20 x 16in.
(Robert W. Skinner Inc.) **$1,900** **£1,187**

ALFRED THOMPSON – 'A Japanese Girl' – signed – oil on canvas – 36 x 24in. *(Sotheby, King & Chasemore)* **$1,214** **£682**

G. THOMPSON – Rural Scenes – signed – 16 x 24in. *(Sotheby Beresford Adams)* **$264** **£154 Two**

J. THOMPSON – Portrait Of John Thomas Smith – signed, inscribed and dated 1851 – oil on canvas – 36 x 28in. *(Sotheby, King & Chasemore)* **$316** **£198**

GEORGE THOMSON – A Woman Sitting By An Open Window – 24 x 18in. *(Sotheby's)* **$1,515** **£1,045**

ARCHIBALD THORBURN – Two Cock Pheasants And Two Hen Pheasants In Woodland At The Edge Of A Field – signed and dated 1931 – 27 x 37cm. *(Henry Spencer & Sons)* **$11,200** **£7,000**

ARCHIBALD THORBURN – Mute Swan
– signed – watercolour and bodycolour
– 7 x 9½in.
(Sotheby's)   **$4,743   £3,080**

ARCHIBALD THORBURN – Buntings
– signed and dated 1924 – watercolour
and bodycolour on grey-green paper –
10¾ x 7¼in.
(Christie's)   **$5,443   £3,240**

ARCHIBALD THORBURN – A Wood-
cock Nestling Among Bracken In A
Woodland Landscape – signed and dated
1906 – 28 x 34cm.
*(Henry Spencer &
Sons)*   **$3,680   £2,300**

ARCHIBALD THORBURN – A Cock
Grouse In Flight – signed and dated
1903 – pencil and watercolour heightened with white on grey paper – 7¼ x
11½in.
(Christie's)   **$5,080   £3,024**

ARCHIBALD THORBURN – Grouse At
A Drinking Pool – signed and dated
1905 – watercolour heightened with
white on green paper – 10½ x 7¼in.
(Christie's)   **$4,536   £2,700**

WILLIAM THORNLEY – On The Shore
– signed – 10 x 18in.
(Sotheby's)   **$1,672   £1,100 Two**

WILLIAM THORNLEY – Incoming Sailing Ships – signed – oil on canvas – 10 x 16in.
(Butterfield's) **$1,000 £598**

WILLIAM THORNLEY – Masted Vessels Off The Pier – signed – oil on canvas – 10 x 16½in.
(Butterfield's) **$1,100 £658**

WILLIAM THORNLEY – Hay Barges Off The Coast – signed – 12 x 20in.
(Sotheby Beresford Adams) **$998 £594**

WILLIAM THORNLEY – A Misty Day, Scarborough; and St. Michael's Mount, Cornwall – signed and inscribed – 10 x 16in.
(Sotheby's) **$1,839 £1,210 Two**

WILLIAM THORNLEY – Hulks Off Portsmouth – signed – oil on canvas – 34 x 29cm.
(Henry Spencer & Sons) **$805 £450**

JOSEPH THORS – A Woodland Landscape – signed – oil on canvas – 9 x 12in.
(Sotheby, King & Chasemore) **$629 £370**

JOSEPH THORS – Rural Scenes – signed – oil on canvas – 9½ x 13in.
(Sotheby, King & Chasemore) **$1,309 £770 Pair**

GASTON THYS – The Bather – signed and dated 1891 – 89¼ x 34½in.
(Christie's) **$5,670 £3,780**

GEOFFREY TIBBLE – Studio Breakfast –
signed, inscribed and dated '51 on the
reverse – 27 x 22in.
(Sotheby's)   **$558   £385**

GIOVANNI DOMENICO TIEPOLO – An
Elderly Bearded Soldier – 22½ x 17¾in.
(Sotheby's)   **$12,375   £8,250**

LOUIS COMFORT TIFFANY – 'Resting'
– signed – oil on board – 13 x 17¼in.
*(Robert W. Skinner
    Inc.)*   **$2,300   £1,438**

WALTER F. TIFFIN – The Via Mala
1868 – inscribed on the verso; and
Mountain Landscape With Deer Grazing
And A River – oil on board – 13.2 x
11.2in.
*(Woolley &
    Wallis)*   **$434   £260 Two**

LOUIS TIMMERMANS – A River Scene
With A Steamer And Sailing Boats Off A
Town – signed – on panel – 16¼ x 12¾in.
(Christie's)   **$585   £378**

LOUIS TIMMERMANS – Sailing Ships
Moored Off Touen, Normandy – signed
– on panel – 10½ x 8¾in.
(Sotheby's)   **$826   £462**

CHARLES E. S. TINDALL – 'At Bombala' – watercolour – 30 x 33cm.
(Geoff K. Gray)   **$225   £134**

TINTORETTO, After – The Miracle Of
St. Mark – 27½ x 35½in.
*(Sotheby Beresford
    Adams)*   **$1,330   £792**

W. V. TIPPETT – Cattle Grazing Before
A Stone Bridge And A Church On The
Frome – signed and dated '93 – oil on
canvas – 76 x 50cm.
*(Osmond,
    Tricks)*   **$240   £140**

TIRONI – The Rialto San Giorgio
Maggiore – 23¾ x 38in.
(Sotheby's)   **$5,676   £3,300 Pair**

JOHANN HEINRICH TISCHBEIN –
Portrait Of A Poet, Possibly Torquato
Tasso – 20½ x 16in.
(Sotheby's) **$662** **£385**

JACQUES JOSEPH TISSOT – A Covered
Courtyard – signed – watercolour height-
ened with bodycolour – 15 x 21in.
(Sotheby's) **$5,775** **£3,300**

JACQUES JOSEPH TISSOT – The Fan –
signed – 14½ x 19in.
(Sotheby's) **$80,850** **£46,200**

JACQUES JOSEPH TISSOT – By The
Window – on board – 20 x 14in.
(Sotheby's) **$26,950** **£15,400**

JAMES JOSEPH TISSOT – Reading The
News – signed – 34 x 20½in.
(Christie's) **$275,400** **£183,600**

TITO

SANTO DI TITO – The Holy Family With Saint Elizabeth And The Infant Baptist – 58¼ x 44in.
(Sotheby's)   **$24,739 £14,300**

RALPH TODD – A Fisher Girl On A Quay – signed and dated – watercolour – 15.5 x 12in.
(Woolley & Wallis)   **$768   £460**

CLIFTON TOMSON, Follower of – Study Of A Horse And A Dog, With A Country House In The Background – oil on canvas – 22½ x 29½in.
(Sotheby, King & Chasemore)   **$4,125   £2,750**

RALPH TODD – A Cornish Fishergirl – signed – watercolour – 15 x 10½in.
(Sotheby, King & Chasemore)   **$660   £440**

HENRY TONKS – Head Of A Girl In Profile – signed – watercolour and pencil – 13¼ x 9½in.
(Christie's)   **$1,223   £810**

ADAM WOLFGANG TOPFFER – The Bridal Procession – signed and dated 1816 – 25¾ x 34¾in.
(Sotheby's) **$62,700 £41,800**

FRANCIS WILLIAM TOPHAM – At A Spanish Fountain – signed and dated 1859 – watercolour heightened with white – 27¼ x 34¼in.
(Christie's) **$1,451 £864**

FRANK WILLIAM WARWICK TOPHAM – 'Waving The Flag' – signed – oil on canvas – 20 x 24in.
(Sotheby, King & Chasemore) **$1,020 £638**

GIULIO DEL TORRE – The First Smoke – signed and dated 1900 – on panel – 9½ x 7¼in.
(Sotheby's) **$3,010 £1,980**

LODEWIJK JAN PETRUS TOUTENEL – Burgermeister Six Inspecting Rembrandt's Studio – signed – 28¾ x 23in.
(Sotheby's) **$2,675 £1,760**

JAMES TOWERS – A Wood In Spring – signed and dated 1886 – 29 x 19in.
(Sotheby Beresford Adams) **$124 £71**

CHARLES TOWNE – Drovers With Cattle Watering On The River Bank Below Barnard Castle – signed and dated 1833, also indistinctly inscribed on a label – 12¾ x 17in.
(Sotheby's) **$6,811 £3,960**

HENRY SPERNON TOZER – 'Threading The Needle' – signed and dated 1907 – watercolour – 8¼ x 12in.
(Sotheby, King &
Chasemore) **$535** **£315**

HENRY SPERNON TOZER – 'Brewing Up' – signed and dated 1907 – watercolour – 9 x 12in.
(Sotheby, King &
Chasemore) **$596** **£341**

HENRY SPERNON TOZER – A Quiet Evening – signed and dated 1921 – 13½ x 19¾in.
(Sotheby Beresford
Adams) **$435** **£253**

HENRY SPERNON TOZER – 'By The Fireside' – signed and dated 1906 – watercolour – 9 x 12in.
(Sotheby, King &
Chasemore) **$577** **£330**

W. TRAIES – Figures Fetching Water By A Fountain In An Extensive Landscape – oil on tin – 23¾ x 30in.
(Dreweatt Watson &
Barton) **$780** **£520**

FRANCESCO TREVISANI, Attributed to – The Penitent Magdalen – 22 x 18¼in.
(Sotheby's) **$3,960** **£2,640**

PAUL TROGER – The Lamentation – on metal – 16 x 9¾in.
(Sotheby's) **$4,950** **£3,300**

CORNELIS TROOST, Circle of – A Park With Many Birds And An Aviary; and An Avenue, With A Lady And Gentleman Feeding Deer – on panel – 16 x 19¼in.
(Sotheby's)   **$7,612   £4,400 Pair**

WILHELM TRUBNER – Ludgate Hill, London – signed – 25¾ x 19¼in.
(Sotheby's)   **$19,250   £11,000**

EDWARD TUCKER – The Castle Of Chillon – signed – 11 x 15½in.
*(Sotheby Beresford
    Adams)*   **$174   £104**

EDWARD TUCKER – On Coniston Water – signed – heightened with bodycolour – 10½ x 18½in.
*(Sotheby Beresford
    Adams)*   **$382   £220**

HENRY SCOTT TUKE – Schooners At The Harbour Mouth – signed – watercolour – 14 x 20in.
(Sotheby's)   **$1,196   £825**

HENRY SCOTT TUKE – The Waterfall – signed – watercolour – 11¾ x 8¼in.
(Christie's)   **$423   £280**

HENRY SCOTT TUKE – Study Of A Barque At Falmouth – canvas mounted on board – 15½ x 18½in.
(Sotheby's)   **$756   £440**

HENRY SCOTT TUKE – Near Perival – signed and indistinctly dated – watercolour – 5 x 8in.
(Christie's)   **$260   £172**

TUNNARD

JOHN TUNNARD — Abstract — signed and dated '48 — gouache and watercolour — 14½ x 21½in.
(Sotheby's)   **$925**   **£638**

CHARLES FREDERICK TUNNICLIFFE — A Pointer — signed — black chalks — 14 x 19in.
(Sotheby Beresford Adams)   **$662**   **£385**

S. TURK — 'Rural Landscape With Cattle And Stream' — signed and dated 1882 — oil on board — 10½ x 14¾in.
(Bracketts)   **$224**   **£140**

TURNER — Merton College Garden, Oxford — pencil and watercolour — 11¾ x 10½in.
(Christie's)   **$398**   **£237**

TURNER — An Italian Lake Scene — oil — 10 x 12in.
(Lawrence)   **$85**   **£53**

TURNER — Bolton Abbey — watercolour — 6.7 x 9.7in.
(Woolley & Wallis)   **$250**   **£150**

TURNER — The Grand Canal, Venice — 15 x 18in.
(Lawrence)   **$49**   **£31**

AGNES TURNER — London Bridge — signed — 14½ x 22in.
(Lawrence)   **$369**   **£231**

AGNES TURNER — St. Pauls — signed — 14½ x 22in.
(Lawrence)   **$370**   **£231**

CHARLES YARDLEY TURNER — 'Woodland Girl With Basket' — signed and dated 1906 — oil on canvas — 24 x 36in.
(Robert W. Skinner Inc.)   **$1,600**   **£1,000**

DANIEL TURNER — A View Of Lambeth Palace From The River — signed — 17¼ x 27½in.
(Sotheby's)   **$2,460**   **£1,430**

DANIEL TURNER — A View Of The Royal Hospital From The Windmill At Battersea — signed — 14¾ x 19½in.
(Sotheby's)   **$1,324**   **£770**

GEORGE TURNER — The Gypsies Encampment — signed, inscribed and dated 1868 on reverse — oil on board — 24 x 34cm.
(Henry Spencer & Sons)   **$860**   **£480**

GEORGE TURNER – 'Autumn Gold, A Scene Near Haslemere, Surrey' – signed, inscribed on the reverse and dated 1884 – oil on canvas – 20 x 30in.
(Sotheby, King & Chasemore) **$2,062** **£1,375**

GEORGE TURNER – 'A Lane Near Dovedale' – signed and inscribed on reverse, dated 1904 – oil on canvas – 24 x 36in.
(Sotheby, King & Chasemore) **$1,386** **£792**

GEORGE TURNER – 'Spring, Knowle Hills, Derbyshire' – signed, inscribed on the reverse and dated 1885 – oil on canvas – 20 x 30in.
(Sotheby, King & Chasemore) **$1,023** **£682**

J. M. W. TURNER, Attributed to – 'Sailing Ships' – watercolour – 4½ x 6in.
(Stalker & Boos) **$400** **£259**

W. H. M. TURNER – A Horse Fair At Barnet, Essex – signed and dated 1863, inscribed on a label – 13½ x 19½in. *(Sotheby's)* **$1,328 £880**

TYLER

JAMES GALE TYLER – Sailing Vessel
Under The Moonlight – signed – oil
on canvas – 19 x 16in.
(Butterfield's)   **$700**   **£414**

THOMAS NICHOLSON TYNDALE –
North Mundham, Sussex – signed – 7 x
10in.
(Sotheby's)   **£440**   **£286**

**WALTER FREDERICK ROOFE
TYNDALE** – A Mother And Child In A
Courtyard – signed – watercolour – 10 x
6¾in.
*(Sotheby, King &
Chasemore)*   **$1,605**   **£902**

WALTER FREDERICK ROOFE TYNDALE – Mother And Child Grinding Corn
On A Parapet – signed and dated 1897 – watercolour – 6¼ x 9½in. *(Sotheby,
King & Chasemore)*   **$297 £175**

WALTER UFER – Study Of Iris –
signed and dated '96 – watercolour on
paper – 9½ x 13in.
(Butterfield's)   **$450**   **£269**

FRITZ K. VON UHDE – 'A Sewing Bee
In Holland' – signed – oil on canvas – 40
x 53in.
(Du Mouchelles) **$28,000** **£15,555**

FRANZ RICHARD UNTERBERGER –
A Lake Scene – signed – 7¾ x 14in.
(Christie's)   **$1,255**   **£810**

LESSER URY – Sonntagmorgen im
Tiergarten, Berlin – signed – pastel on
paper – 19¾ x 13¼in.
(Christie's)   **$22,042 £14,040**

JUAN PEYRO URRIA – Blind Man's
Bluff – signed and inscribed – on panel
– 11 x 17¾in.
(Christie's)   **$5,832**   **£3,240**

MAURICE UTRILLO – La Bievre A
Bourg-La-Reine, Um 1921 – signed – oil
on canvas – 31 x 37.5cm.
*(Germann
      Auktionshaus)* **$35,358 £22,099**

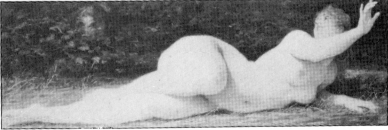

ADO URON – Surprised – signed and dated 1889 – 20 x 62½in. *(Sotheby's)*
$2,763 £1,760

UTRILLO

MAURICE UTRILLO – La Chapelle Des Pyrenees – signed – oil on board on panel – 12½ x 15¾in.
(Christie's) **$45,781 £29,160**

MAURICE UTRILLO – Sacre-Coeur De Montmartre, um 1931 – signed – oil on card – 61 x 50cm.
(Germann Auktionshaus) **$61,878 £38,674**

MAURICE UTRILLO – Rue Chappe a Montmartre – signed – oil on canvas – 20 x 24½in.
(Christie's) **$93,258 £59,400**

MAURICE UTRILLO – La Rue Saint-Vincent et le Campanile du Sacre-Coeur – signed – oil on canvas – 18¼ x 15in.
(Christie's) **$67,824 £43,200**

THOMAS UWINS – Hop-Picking On The Farnham Plantations: A Study – pencil and watercolour – 7¾ x 4¾in.
(Christie's) **$678 £432**

VALENTYN UYTVANCH – Portrait Of Felix Timmermans – signed with monogram – oil on canvas – 12¼ x 10¼in.
(Christie's) **$508 £324**

PIERRE HENRI DE VALENCIENNES –
Figures In A Classical Landscape – signed
and dated 1788 – 32 x 47in.
(Sotheby's) **$56,100 £37,400**

J. PIO VALERO – Flirtations – signed
– oil on canvas – 30 x 21½in.
(Butterfield's) n **$3,750 £2,245**

**MAERTEN VALKENBORCH, Follower
of** – A Vegetable Market – on panel –
12½ x 18¼in.
(Sotheby's) **$3,678 £2,420**

FELIX VALLOTTON – Nu Debout –
signed with initials – pen and ink on
paper – 12½ x 6in. *(Ch*
(Christie's) **$1,187 £756**

FELIX VALLOTTON – Femme Au Collier De Perles – signed and dated '12 –
oil on canvas – 61.5 x 50.5cm.
(Germann
Auktionshaus) **$14,144 £8,840**

VALTAT

LOUIS VALTAT — Nature Morte Aux Raisins — signed — oil on canvas — 15 x 22in.
(Butterfield's) **$8,500** **£5,089**

FLORENCE E. VALTER — Springtime — signed — watercolour — 14 x 20¾in.
(Sotheby, King & Chasemore) **$500** **£295**

JOHANN VANDERBANCK, In The Manner Of — Portrait Of A Lady — oil on canvas — 50 x 40in.
(Butterfield's) **$1,000** **£590**

B. VANDERBERG — Figures In A Frozen River Landscape — signed and dated 1843 — 10 x 12in.
(Sotheby's) **$826** **£462**

VANDERMIER — Marshland Landscape With Geese And A Girl Before A Farm — signed and dated 1875 — 15 x 39in.
(Christie's & Edmiston's) **$3,520** **£2,200**

VARLEY — A Landscape Sketch — 3½ x 5½in.
(Lawrence) **$38** **£24**

J. VARLEY — St. Michael's Mount, Cornwall — watercolour — 9.5 x 14in.
(Woolley & Wallis) **$334** **£200**

JOHN VARLEY, Follower of — Landscape With Villagers Near A Castle — 12 x 10in.
(Sotheby's) **$267** **£176**

JOHN VARLEY — Cottages And A Church By A Lane — dated 1807 — pencil — 9½ x 12½in.
(Christie's) **$163** **£97**

JOHN VARLEY — Llannberris, Lake At The Foot Of Snowdon With Dolbadern Tower, N. Wales — signed and dated 1812, and signed, inscribed and dated on the reverse — watercolour — 10¼ x 20¼in.
(Christie's) **$907** **£540**

JOHN VARLEY, JNR. — On The Mawddach, Wales — signed — 10 x 14½in.
(Sotheby Beresford Adams) **$27** **£16**

VARLIN – Birmingham – signed – oil on canvas – 67 x 138cm.
(Germann Auktionshaus) **$24,310 £15,190**

CARLOS VAZQUEZ – A Terrace In The South Of France, and A View Of Cap Ferrat – signed – oil – 23 x 27.5in.
(Woolley & Wallis) **$370 £210 Pair**

ELIHU VEDDER – 'Study Of An Ideal Head' – inscribed and signed – oil on canvas – 13½ x 10in.
(Robert W. Skinner Inc.) **$850 £530**

WILLIAM CHARLES MEREDITH VAN DE VELDE – Mountain Views Near The Mediterranean Coast – signed, one dated 1886 – pencil and watercolour – 10½ x 14½in.
(Christie's) **$470 £280 Pair**

EUGENE VERBOECKHOVEN – The Return Of The Hunt – signed and dated 1851 – oil on canvas – 45 x 70in.
(William Doyle Galleries) **$67,500 £39,940**

LOUIS VERBOECKHOVEN – Sailing Boats And A Steamer Off A Jetty – signed – on panel – 14¾ x 21¼in.
(Sotheby's) **$2,340 £1,540**

A. H. VERBOOM – Travellers On A Road Beside A River – inscribed – on panel – 21½ x 29¼in.
(Sotheby's) **$4,730 £2,750**

VERBRUGGEN – A Still Life Of Flowers – inscribed – 18¾ x 15¼in.
(Sotheby's) **$4,540 £2,640**

JAN PIETER VERDUSSEN – Brigands Attacking A Baggage Train – 13½ x 16¾in.
(Sotheby Beresford Adams) **$6,468 £3,850**

VERELST

HARMAN VERELST – Portraits Of Samuel Graves Of Mickleton; and His Wife Susanna – inscribed – 28¾ x 24½in. *(Sotheby's)* **$6,312 £4,180 Pair**

SIMON VERELST – A Still Life Of Flowers In A Vase – 28¾ x 24in. *(Sotheby's)* **$11,550 £7,700**

ALBERTUS VERHOESEN – Poultry In A Wooded River Landscape – signed and dated 1876 – on panel – 10¼ x 12½in.
(Christie's) **$2,678 £1,728**

ALBERTUS VERHOESEN – Poultry By A Ruin – signed and dated 1862 – 13¾ x 18¼in.
(Christie's) **$2,333 £1,296**

L. J. VERMEULEN – A Winter Landscape With Figures On The Ice, With A Castle Beyond – signed – on panel – 16 x 20in.
(Christie's) **$1,458 £810**

ARTHUR LANGLEY VERNON – The Ferry – signed – 11¾ x 18¾in.
(Christie's) **$1,933 £1,080**

EMILE VERNON – Amongst The Roses – signed and dated 1919 – 25¾ x 21½in.
(Sotheby's) **$18,287 £10,450**

EMILE VERNON – 'Study Of A Jug Of Carnations' – signed – oil on canvas – 24 x 20in.
(Sotheby, King &
Chasemore) **$1,174** **£660**

PAUL VERNON – Gypsies – signed – oil on panel – 16 x 12¾in.
(Butterfield's) **$700** **£414**

ANTONIO VERRIO – Portrait Of Charles II – signed – 29¼ x 24½in.
(Sotheby's) **$9,125** **£6,050**

WOUTER VERSCHUUR – The Interior Of A Stable With Sportsmen And Animals – signed – 30¼ x 38½in.
(Christie's) **$42,400** **£28,080**

P. G. VERTIN – A Street Scene In Winter – bears signature – on panel – 7½ x 5¾in.
(Sotheby's) **$1,102** **£616**

SALOMON LEONARDUS VERVEER – Figures In A Street In A Canalside Town – signed – 21¾ x 27¼in.
(Sotheby's) **$4,330** **£2,420**

A. VESCOVI — Amstrande Bei Freport; and Strande Bei Stavanger — signed — 15 x 26in.
(Sotheby Beresford Adams) **$803** **£462 Pair**

JULES JACQUES VEYRASSAT — Charrette De Recolte — signed — oil on wood — 21.5 x 41cm.
(Germann Auktionshaus) **$6,629** **£4,145**

ALFRED H. VICKERS — A View Of Aberdeen Harbour With A Steam Boat — signed, signed, inscribed and dated 1883 — 8 x 16in.
(Christie's) **$810** **£453**

ALFRED VICKERS, SNR. — The Entrance To Portsmouth Harbour — 9¾ x 13½in.
(Sotheby's) **$1,419** **£825**

ALFRED VICKERS, SNR. — 'Cromford Derbyshire' — inscribed on reverse — oil on canvas — 14 x 21in. *(Sotheby, King & Chasemore)* **$847 £484**

VICENTINO, NICCOLÒ. See BOLDRINI.

VICENZA, PASQUALINO DE. See ROSSI.

VICKERS, ALFRED, an English landscape painter, was born at Newington, Surrey, in 1786. He was self-taught, and studied from nature, and from the works of the Dutch masters. His pictures were pleasant, but without much individuality or real insight into nature. He exhibited at the Royal Academy, the British Institution, and at Suffolk Street from 1814 to 1868, and died in the latter year.

VICKERS, ALFRED GOMERSAL, an English marine, landscape, and subject painter, was born in Lambeth in 1810. He was the son of Alfred Vickers, by whom he was taught. From the age of seventeen, he began to exhibit at the Royal Academy, in Suffolk Street, and at the British Institution. He was commissioned by Charles Heath to make drawings in Russia for publication in the 'Annuals.' For this work he received £500. He was just beginning to be known, when he died in Pentonville, January 12th, 1837. His sketches were sold at Christie's. Four of his water-colour drawings are in the South Kensington Museum.

VICO, ENEA, (VICUS, or VIGHI,) engraver and archæologist, was born at Parma in the year 1523. He went at an early age to Rome, where he was first instructed by Tommaso Barlacchi, an engraver and print-seller, for whom, in 1541-2, he engraved a series of twenty-four grotesques. He soon reached excellence, studying successively the manners of Giulio Bonasone, Agostino Veneziano, Caraglio, and especially Marc Antonio. Passavant dates from about 1550 the development of a manner of his own, remarkable for delicacy of execution and the skilful use of fine, closely-set lines. Cosmo I. invited him to Florence, where he engraved some of the best works of Michelangelo, with portraits of Charles V. and Henry II. (that of the former monarch has been erroneously stated to have been engraved by him on wood, in which it does not appear that he ever worked at all). He also worked for a time in Venice. In 1554 he brought out engravings of twelve imperial medals with descriptions; in the following year a 'Treatise on Medals,' and in 1557 a series of Empresses, with their biographies. He also engraved a variety of medals, and a set of thirty-six antique gems. He died at Parma in 1567. Bartsch assigns 494 plates to him, and Passavant 503. When he did not sign his plates with his name at length, he marked them with the initials Æ. V., sometimes on a tablet, and sometimes without it. He also occasionally signed A E N. V. F The following his most noteworthy prints:

Charles V., surrounded by emblematical figures, inscribed, Inventum sculptumque ab Aenea Vico Parmense, MDL.

Bust of Giovanni de' Medici, in a border. 1550.

Bust of Cosmo de' Medici, when young.

Bust of Alfonso II., Duke of Ferrara.

The Army of Charles V. passing the Elbe; from his own design.

The Battle of the Amazons; inscribed, Bellum Amatorum. 1543.

Female Figure, with her arms extended, over which appears an Owl; after Parmigiano. 1548.

Vulcan and Venus (a free subject); after the same. 1543.

Jupiter and Leda; after Michelangelo.

Bacchanalian subject; after the same.

Vulcan and the Cyclops; after Primaticcio.

Muses upon Parnassus.

Apollo and Cupid; after Baccio Bandinelli.

Academy of Baccio Bandinelli; after the same.

The Conversion of S. Paul; after F. Salviati.

The Battle of the Lapithæ and Centaurs; after the same. 1542.

Judith with the Head of Holofernes; after Michelangelo.

The Entombment of Christ; after Raphael. 1548.

The Death of Lucretia. 1541.

The Annunciation; after Titian.

A set of twelve Vases; from designs by Polidoro da Caravaggio.

A set of fifty plates of National Costumes; from his own designs.

VICO, FRANCESCO DE, a painter whose name is only known from two entries in the archives of the hospital at Milan. On September 4, 1472, Vico, "who had painted the Duke and Duchess on a canvas placed in the chapel " [of the hospital], was ordered to "re-fashion" these heads "after the manner of those over an altar in the Cathedral," and in the same year he received a certain sum on account for two paintings representing "the Pope and the rulers of Milan." Vico's canvases were kept in the small chapel which in the 15th and 16th centuries stood in the centre of the great courtyard of the hospital, and every year, on the occasion of the Festa del Perdono, they were publicly exhibited for a few days, and were hung on either side of the principal entrance; hence later writers confused them with Vincenzo Foppa's paintings in the colonnade, though these were frescoes and represented totally different subjects, namely, the ceremonies attending the laying of the foundation stone of the hospital. The chapel in the courtyard was destroyed in the 17th century, and Vico's canvases probably perished at the same time and were replaced by copies. These copies are still preserved in the council chamber of the hospital, and in spite of their obviously late character are spoken of by some writers as Vico's original works. They represent Francesco Sforza and Bianca Maria kneeling before Pope Pius II., who grants them permission to build the hospital, and the Duke and Duchess, attended by their followers, making their offerings at the altar of the Annunciation.   C. J. Ff.

VICTOORS, JAN, (FICTOORS, FICTOOR,) a Dutch painter, was born at Amsterdam in 1620. He was educated in the school of Rembrandt, and worked in his atelier in 1635-40. He must not be confused with Johannes Victor, whose proper surname was Wolfvoet (q. v.). His works are better known than those of some other pupils of Rembrandt, but scarcely anything is recorded of his life. Some of his pictures show much affinity with those of his master, but his hand was apt to get heavy. Very many of his subjects are taken from the Old Testament, but he also painted genre, landscapes, peasant assemblies, markets, charlatans, &c. The date of his death is uncertain, but it took place at Amsterdam after 1672. Works:

Amsterdam. R. Museum.	Joseph interpreting the Dreams. 1648.	
"	"	The Dentist. 1654.
"	"	The Pork Butcher.
Antwerp.	Museum.	Village Wedding.
Brunswick.	Gallery.	Esther and Haman. 1632.
"	"	David and Samuel.
"	"	Capture of Samson.
Copenhagen.	"	Ruth and Boaz.
		(And three others.)
Dresden.		The Finding of Moses. 1653.
Louvain.	Museum.	The Prophetess Anna. 1643.
London.	Bridgewater Gallery.	Tobias blessing his Son.

ALFRED H. VICKERS, Attributed to –
Figures Walking Along A Country Road –
oil on canvas – 11½ x 23¼in.
(Sotheby, King &
Chasemore) **$858** **£550**

HENRY HAROLD VICKERS – 'Landscape With Sheep And Shepherd' –
signed and dated 1903 – gouache on
panel – 5¾ x 8in.
(Stalker &
Boos) **$425** **£275**

E. E. VIDAL – Men-of-War In Action In
Coastal Waters – signed and dated 1812
– watercolour – 11 x 16in.
(Hy. Duke &
Son) **$294** **£170**

VICTOR VIGNON – La Remouleuse
– signed – oil on panel – 12½ x 9¼in.
(Sotheby's) **$518** **£330**

DAVID VINCKBOONS – The Hurdy-
Gurdy Player – on panel – 9½ x 16in.
(Sotheby's) **$39,600** **£26,400**

FRANCESCO VINEA – A Fine Vintage
– signed and dated 1872 – on panel –
8 x 5in.
(Sotheby's) **$3,150** **£1,760**

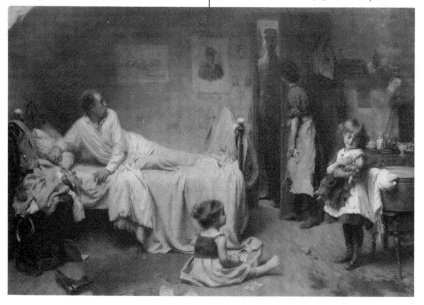

CHARLES VIGOR – The Arrest – signed – 50 x 70¾in. *(Christie's)*
$8,910 £5,940

JANOS VISKI – A Horse Round Up –
signed – 23 x 31in.
(Christie's)   **$874**   **£486**

FRANCOIS XAVIER VISPRE – Portrait Of The Marchioness of Hertford As A Child, In A White Dress And Cap, With A Dog, By A Table – signed – 30 x 26in.
(Christie's)   **$4,748**   **£3,024**

J. VIVIAN – The Grand Canal, Venice – signed – 32 x 50in.
(Lawrence)   **$1,504**   **£946**
J. VIVIAN – Venice, A View Of Scuola di S. Marco And Stalls On The Compo S.S. Giovanni e Paolo From Ria Dei Mendicente – signed – oil – 24 x 42in.
(Woolley & Wallis)   **$1,536**   **£920**

F. VOET – Portrait Of A Lady – 28 x 23in.
(Sotheby's)   **$1,712**   **£990**

ARY DE VOIS – A Gentleman – on panel – 8 x 6¼in.
(Sotheby's)   **$4,350**   **£2,530**

J. C. VOLLERDT – A River Landscape – on metal – 9 x 12in.
(Sotheby's)   **$950**   **£550**

ANTOINE VOLLON – A River Landscape
– signed – 12 x 17¼in.
(Sotheby's) **$802** **£528**

ANTOINE VOLLON – Nature Morte
Aux Patisserie, Pichet Et Verve – signed
– on panel – 15 x 16½in.
(Christie's) **$2,138** **£1,188**

JOHANNES VORSTERMANN – Huntsman And Hounds In An Extensive Landscape – on metal – 12 x 16¼in.
(Sotheby's) **$8,026** **£5,280**

J. VOS – Tulips, Roses, Morning Glory
And Other Flowers In A Vase On A
Ledge – on panel – 20¼ x 15¼in.
(Christie's) **$3,682** **£2,376**

S. VRANCX – Turkish Prisoners Of War
Obtaining Sulphur – on panel – 23¼ x
31¼in.
(Sotheby's) **$8,564** **£4,950**

HANS VREDEMAN DE VRIES – The
Interior Of A Gothic Cathedral With Figures
– indistinctly signed and dated – on panel
– 24½ x 37½in.
(Sotheby's) **$2,845** **£1,650**

ADALBERT WAAGEN – A Wooded Landscape With A Figure By A Chalet – signed and dated 1862 – 13½ x 11in.
(Christie's)   **$1,088   £702**

FRITZ WAGNER – Good Bouquets – signed – 10 x 8¼in.
(Christie's)   **$2,176   £1,404 Pair**

THOMAS FRANCIS WAINEWRIGHT – Herne Bay – signed, inscribed and dated 1861 – watercolour heightened with white – 13¼ x 26¼in.
(Christie's)   **$544   £324**

THOMAS FRANCIS WAINEWRIGHT – 'Haywards Heath', Ayrshire Cattle And Sheep In A Pastoral Landscape – signed and dated 1868 – watercolour – 49 x 34cm.
(Osmond, Tricks)   **$739   £430**

JAMES CLARK WAITE – 'Milking Time' – signed and inscribed on reverse – oil on canvas – 33 x 26in.
(Sotheby, King & Chasemore)   **$2,431   £1,430**

JAMES CLARKE WAITE – A Fisherman's Tale – signed and dated 1875 – oil on canvas – 23 x 30in.
(Sotheby, King & Chasemore)   **$4,890   £3,135**

CHATTY WAKE – Portrait Of Miss Sybil Graham, Half Length, Seated – coloured chalk on buff paper – 32 x 22½in.
(Sotheby's)   **$567   £330**

ROLAND SHAKESPEARE WAKELIN – 'Church At North Ryde' – signed with initials and dated '52 also inscribed – pen and wash – 18 x 25cm.
(Geoff K. Gray)   **$405   £241**

ROLAND SHAKESPEARE WAKELIN –
'Still Life, Green Vases And Roses' – oil
on board – 49 x 36cm.
(Geoff K. Gray)   **$722**   **£430**

ERNEST WALBOURN – 'Expectation',
A Coastal Scene With A Young Lady
Leaning On A Wall And Gazing Out To
Sea – signed – oil on canvas – 19 x 29in.
(Hall, Wateridge &
Owen)   **$2,538**   **£1,450**

WILLIAM WALCOT – The Great Court,
Trinity College, Cambridge – signed and
dated 1917 – watercolour, gouache and
coloured inks – 19½ x 23¾in.
(Christie's)   **$896**   **£594**

SIR WILLIAM WALCOT – A View Of St.
Peters, Rome – signed – heightened with
bodycolour – 19 x 17in.
(Sotheby's)   **$677**   **£440**

DAME ETHEL WALKER – Nude Study
– canvas mounted on board – 9½ x 13in.
(Sotheby's)   **$170**   **£99**

JAMES WILLIAM WALKER – 'Collecting
Driftwood', With Cliffs In Background –
inscribed – watercolour – 10 x 16½in.
(Hilhams)   **$344**   **£215**

JOHN EATON WALKER – A Spanish
Beauty – signed – on board – 17¾ x
13¾in.
(Sotheby Beresford
Adams)   **$435**   **£253**

**GOTTFRIED WALS, Called Goffredo
Tedesco** – A Farm Amid Trees Beside A
River – on copper – diam. 25cm.
(Sotheby's)   **$9,134**   **£5,280**

JACOB VAN WALSCAPELLE – Summer
Flowers In A Stone Vase – 24½ x 18in.
(Sotheby's)   **$22,836**   **£13,200**

MARTHA WALTER – The Breakfast Table – oil on canvas – 23¾ x 20in.
(Christie's)   **$5,500**   **£3,666**

F. WALTERS – Country Scenes, A Mother And Her Small Girl Feeding Ducks At The Edge Of A Pond; and A Small Girl Carrying A Basket On A Path By A Bridge – signed – 9½ x 13¼in.
(Anderson & Garland)   **$309**   **£185 Pair**

ELIJAH WALTON – Study Of An Arab With A Mosque In The Background – signed, inscribed and dated 1877 – watercolour – 28 x 20in.
(Sotheby, King & Chasemore)   **$545**   **£341**

GEORGE STANFIELD WALTERS – Paddle Steamer On A Lake – signed and dated 1869 – watercolour – 9 x 12¾in.
(Sotheby, King & Chasemore)   **$514**   **£330**

GEORGE STANFIELD WALTERS – A Fishing Boat And Other Shipping – signed – watercolour – 12 x 9in.
(Woolley & Wallis)   **$234**   **£140**

S. WALTERS – Dutch Sailing Boats In A Squall – bears signature and dated 1832 – on panel – 13¼ x 18in.
(Christie's)   **$558**   **£302**

ELIJAH WALTON – A Friend In View – signed and inscribed – watercolour – 28 x 20in.
(Sotheby, King & Chasemore)   **$721**   **£451**

WILHELM WANDERER – A Courting Couple – signed and dated 1843 – 23 x 18½in.
(Christie's)   **$4,860**   **£2,700**

EDWARD WARD – Lady Jane Grey At The Traitors' Gate – signed and dated 1871 – 19 x 22½in.
(Christie's)   **$1,170**   **£756**

HARRY WARD – Life Guards Leaving Windsor – signed – 12 x 16in.
(Sotheby Beresford Adams)   **$612**   **£352**

JOHN WARD of Hull – A Riverside Capriccio With A Dutch Galliot And Two Sailors In The Foreground – 9 x 7in.
(Sotheby's)   **$1,661**   **£1,100**

JAMES CHARLES WARD – Rest By The Wayside – signed and dated 1872 – oil on canvas – 24 x 20in.
(Sotheby, King & Chasemore)   **$990**   **£660**

WILLIAM H. WARD – A Still Life Study Of Grapes And A Bird's Nest – oil on canvas – 12 x 10in.
(Sotheby, King & Chasemore)   **$969**   **£570**

ARTHUR WARDLE – Bloodhounds Stopped By Water – signed – watercolour heightened with white – 20¼ x 16in.
(Christie's)   **$308**   **£205**

WARDLE

ARTHUR WARDLE – At The Rabbit
Warren: Two Children Ferreting –
signed – watercolour – 19 x 24¼in.
(Christie's) $1,050   £626

ARTHUR WARDLE – Two Borzois –
signed – oil – 33 x 29in.
(Graves, Son &
Pilcher) $4,550   £2,600

R. E. WARMINGTON – Rydal Lake –
watercolour – 13 x 26in.
(Edgar Horne) $234   £155

FRANK WASLEY – Entrance To The
Grand Canal With Shipping And Gondolas
– signed and dated – oil – 24 x 42in.
(Woolley &
Wallis) $442   £250

JOHN WILLIAM WATERHOUSE –
Narcissus – signed and dated 1912 –
37 x 24½in.
(Christie's) $48,600   £32,400

JOHN WILLIAM WATERHOUSE –
Gather Ye Rosebuds While Ye May –
signed – canvas on board – 27 x 20in.
(Sotheby's) $9.075   £6,050

SIR ERNEST ALFRED WATERLOW –
'Down To The Water' – signed – oil on
canvas – 22 x 32in.
(Sotheby, King &
Chasemore) $2,406 $1,375

MARCUS WATERMAN – 'Picking Apples'
– initialled and dated '85 – oil on canvas
– 12 x 16in.
(Robert W. Skinner
Inc.) $600   £375

REG WATKISS – 'Cottages Before A
Mountain' – oil on board – 13 x 11in.
(W. H. Lane &
Son) $14   £8

JOHN DAWSON WATSON – The Rom-
ance – signed – watercolour heightened
with white – 7¾ x 5¾in.
(Christie's) $520   £345

JOHN DAWSON WATSON – 'The Call Of
The Hunt' – signed and dated 1875 –
watercolour – 9¾ x 14in.
(Sotheby, King &
Chasemore) $264   £176

JOHN DAWSON WATSON – 'Will He
Never Come Back' – signed with initials
and dated 1871 – oil on canvas – 24 x
16in.
(Sotheby, King &
Chasemore) $457   £286

R. WATSON – The Bass Rock – indistin-
ctly signed – 12 x 18in.
(Christie's &
Edmiston's) $288   £180

A. WATTS – A Country Path – signed
and dated 1906 – 9½ x 20in.
(Sotheby Beresford
Adams) $56   £33

F. W. WATTS – Henley-On-Thames –
21 x 33in.
(Christie's) $837   £540

FREDERICK WATERS WATTS – A
Woodland Cottage – signed – 30 x 40in.
(Sotheby's)   **$18,271 £12,100**

FREDERICK WATERS WATTS –
Cottages By A Still River – 35 x 46in.
(Sotheby's)   **$29,700   £19,800**

GEORGE FREDERICK WATTS – A
Bacchante – 35½ x 27¼in.
(Sotheby's)   **$8,663   £4,950**

FREDERICK JUDD WAUGH – Tumbl-
ing Seas – signed – oil on canvas – 25¼
x 30in.
(William Doyle
    Galleries)   **$2,000   £1,183**

GEORGE FREDERICK WATTS – The
Creation Of Eve – 34 x 34in.
(Sotheby's)   **$5,390   £3,080**

CONSTANT WAUTERS – The Odalisque
– signed and indistinctly dated – 27¼ x
21½in.
(Sotheby's)   **$2,175   £1,430**

EMILE CHARLES WAUTERS –
Cavaliers – signed – 29 x 17½in.
(Christie's)   **$3,260   £2,160 Pair**

R. C. WEATHERBY – 'Portrait Of A
Cleric' – signed – oil on canvas – 30¼ x
25in.
*(W. H. Lane &
Son)*   **$348   £200**

MARY WEATHERILL – View On Lake
Maggiore – 19 x 17in.
(Lawrence)   **$140   £88**

ALFRED C. WEATHERSTONE – Small
Talk – signed – 11 x 15½in.
(Sotheby's)   **$406   £264**

EDWARD WEBB – Bridge Over A River
– watercolour – 6.5 x 9.7in.
*(Woolley &
Wallis)*   **$650   £390**

JAMES WEBB – 'Rotterdam' – signed,
inscribed on reverse amd dated 1877 –
30 x 50in.
*(Sotheby, King &
Chasemore)*   **$7,920   £5,280**

JAMES WEBB – An Estuary Scene –
signed – on panel – 11½ x 28in.
*(Sotheby, King &
Chasemore)*   **$4,976   £3,190**

JAMES WEBB, Circle of – A Coastline
With Sailing Vessels In A Calm – on panel
– 15¾ x 27in.
(Sotheby's)   **$434   £286**

WILLIAM EDWARD WEBB – Peel Harbour And Castle With Boats And Figures –
signed and dated 1893 – 22 x 37in.
(Chrystals)   **$6,086   £3,400**

WILLIAM EDWARD WEBB – 'Harbour
Scene With Shipping' – signed and
dated 1892 – oil on canvas – 22 x 38in.
*(Sotheby, King &
Chasemore)*   **$3,080   £1,925**

WILLIAM EDWARD WEBB – Manx
Coastal Scene With Figures And Boats –
signed and indistinctly dated – 7½ x 11½in.
(Chrystals)   **$1,146   £640**

WEBSTER

THOMAS WEBSTER – 'Take Your
Medicine' – signed with monogram and
dated 1866 – on panel – 13¼ x 19¾in.
(Christie's)   **$1,004**   **£648**

HENRY WEEKES – 'Humble Friends' –
bears inscription and dated 1866 – oil
on canvas – 16 x 24in.
*(Sotheby, King &
    Chasemore)*   **$1,815**   **£1,210**

EDWIN LORD WEEKS – 'A Desert
Town' – oil on canvas – 11 x 18½in.
*(Robert W. Skinner
    Inc.)*   **$300**   **£188**

EDWIN LORD WEEKS – Desert Harvest
– signed and dated – oil on canvas –
35½ x 59½in.
(Butterfield's)   **$8,000**   **£4,790**

J. WEENIX – A Still Life Of Game –
33 x 26½in.
(Sotheby's)   **$2,648**   **£1,540**

ARTHUR HOWES WEIGALL – Firewood Sellers In Marien Platz, Munich –
signed and dated 1864 – on panel – 12½
x 9½in.
(Christie's)   **$3,682**   **£2,376**

JULIAN ALDEN WEIR – 'On The Farm'
– signed – oil on canvas – 15 x 19½in.
*(Stalker &
    Boos)*   **$4,000**   **£2,597**

JULIAN ALDEN WEIR – Mill On The
Itchen – signed and inscribed – watercolour and gouache on paper on board
– 9 x 11¾in.
(Christie's)   **$2,200**   **£1,466**

BENJAMIN WEST – Rinaldo And Armida – grisaille – on paper on board – 15½ x 19in.
(Sotheby's) **$3,654** **£2,420**

GEORGE WEISS – Musing Over A Letter – signed and dated '93 – oil on board – 7¾ x 5½in.
(Butterfield's) **$400** **£235**

L. K. WELCH – A Study Of A Cart Horse – 10 x 7in.
(Lawrence) **$87** **£55**

MABEL R. WELCH – 'Spanish Musicians' – inscribed on reverse – oil on canvas – 41 x 40in.
(Robert W. Skinner Inc.) **$750** **£468**

BENJAMIN WEST – Portrait Of George III – on metal – 10¼ x 8in.
(Sotheby's) **$4,983** **£3,300**

FRIEDRICH WENDLER – An Afternoon's Fishing – signed – 12 x 10in.
(Sotheby's) **$3,544** **£1,980**

JOSEPH WALTER WEST – 'A Pageant In The Piazza, Fifteenth Century Venice' – signed with monogram, dated 1930, and inscribed on the reverse – tempera on gesso on wood – 18 x 16in.
(Sotheby, King & Chasemore) **$809** **£506**

WEST

RICHARD WESTALL – Helen Of The Scaean Gate, Come To View The Combat Between Paris And Menelaus – signed – 60¼ x 75½in.
(Sotheby's)   **$4,318   £2,860**

JOSEPH WALTER WEST – 'The Pet Rabbit' – signed with monogram and dated 1869 – watercolour on card – 15½ x 12½in.
(Sotheby, King & Chasemore)   **$563   £352**

WALTER J. WEST – Currie, Near Edinburgh – signed, inscribed on a label – 10¼ x 14¾in.
(Sotheby Beresford Adams)   **$51   £30**

RICHARD WESTALL – Three Angels Writing A Book – 50¼ x 40in.
(Christie's)   **$1,399   £756**

FRITZ WESTENDORP – 'Village Harbor Scene With Figures' – signed – oil on panel – 10 x 16in.
(Stalker & Boos)   **$450   £280**

RICHARD WESTALL – A Mother And Child With A Dead Bird – 50¼ x 40in.
(Christie's)   **$600   £324**

J. WEYL – River Bank Scenes – oil – 14 x 29cm.
(Reeds Rains)   **$770   £440 Pair**

HENRY CLARENCE WHAITE – View Of The River Conway – signed – watercolour – 20 x 29in.
(Woolley & Wallis) $785 £470

JAMES WHAITE – Cockle-Pickers At Penmaenmawr, North Wales – signed – watercolour – 12 x 17.5in.
(Woolley & Wallis) $418 £250

WHEATLEY – A Tea Party – on panel – 15 x 19in.
(Sotheby Beresford Adams) $905 £539

FRANCIS WHEATLEY – A Farmyard Scene – 23½ x 29½in.
(Sotheby's) $3,594 £2,090

JAMES ABBOTT McNEILL WHISTLER – The Beach Near Marseilles – signed – oil on panel – 8½ x 12½in.
(Christie's) $73,386 £48,600

JAMES ABBOTT McNEILL WHISTLER – Surf Breaking On The Beach – signed with monogram – watercolour on paper – 6¼ x 10in.
(William Doyle Galleries) $16,500 £9,763

T. WHITCOMBE – Troops Boarding 'La Hermione' – oil on panel – 9½ x 11½in.
(Hy. Duke & Son) $726 £420

THOMAS WHITCOMBE – Shore Scene With Fishermen Rigging Their Boats; and Shipping Off The South Coast – signed with initials – oil on panel – 10½ x 13½in.
(Woolley & Wallis) $6,930 £4,500 Pair

THOMAS WHITCOMBE – British Men Of War Off The Coast With A Longboat In The Foreground – signed – 17¾ x 15½in.
(Sotheby's) $9,080 £5,280

WHITE

H. G. WHITE – 'The Cliffs At Tintagel'
– watercolour – 8½ x 13½in.
*(W. H. Lane &
    Son)*   **$12**   **£7**

WHITEHEAD – In The College Grounds,
Ely – 11 x 14in.
(Lawrence)   **$53**   **£33**

FREDERICK WILLIAM WHITEHEAD –
The Ford At 'Beggarly Broom' – signed
and inscribed on the reverse – oil on
canvas – 12 x 18in.
*(Sotheby, King &
    Chasemore)*   **$627**   **£418**

THOMAS WORTHINGTON WHITTREDGE
– Kentucky River Near Dic River – signed
and inscribed on the reverse – oil on board
– 9½ x 11in.
(Christie's)   **$14,300**   **£9,533**

**THOMAS WORTHINGTON
WHITTREDGE** – The Rainbow –
Autumn Catskills – signed – oil on
canvas – 11½ x 16¾in.
*(William Doyle
    Galleries)*   **$7,250**   **£4,289**

**THOMAS WORTHINGTON
WHITTREDGE** – The Brook – signed –
oil on canvas – 14½ x 11¾in.
*(William Doyle
    Galleries)*   **$3,000**   **£1,775**

JOHN WHORF – 'Fishing Boats' – signed
– oil on canvas – 28 x 36in.
*(Robert W. Skinner
    Inc.)*   **$1,300**   **£812**

JOHN WHORF – 'Fishing' – signed –
watercolour – 15 x 22in.
*(Robert W. Skinner
    Inc.)*   **$2,200**   **£1,375**

DUNCAN MacGREGOR WHYTE −
Hebridean Shore − signed and dated 1902
− 51 x 39¾in.
(Sotheby's)   **$720**   **£418**

FREDERICK JOHN WIDGERY − 'The
Dart Near Sharpham' − signed − water-
colour − 11 x 17½in.
(W. H. Lane &
Son)   **$90**   **£52**

T. WIDGERY − Rocky Coastal Scene
Off Bude − signed − watercolour −
10¾ x 18in.
(W. H. Lane &
Son)   **$54**   **£32**

W. WIDGERY − The End Of A Day's
Shoot − oil on canvas − 52 x 74in.
(Sotheby, King &
Chasemore)   **$1,870**   **£1,100**

AUGUSTUS WIJNANTZ − Figures On
A Country Lane − signed − 7¼ x 9in.
(Sotheby's)   **$1,208**   **£770**

JAN WIJNANTS − Landscape With A
Decayed Oak − signed and dated 1675 −
40½ x 34½in.
(Sotheby's)   **$24,750**   **£16,500**

JAN WILDENS, Circle of − Diana And
Her Handmaidens In A River Landscape
− on panel − 25¾ x 41½in.
(Sotheby's)   **$2,173**   **£1,430**

JAN WILDENS, Attributed to − A Manor
House On A River With Travellers Among
Trees − 31¾ x 39½in.
(Sotheby's)   **$9,900**   **£6,600**

WILDING

R. T. WILDING – 'Setting Out For The Catch' – signed – watercolour – 37 x 52cm.
(Geoff K. Gray) **$180** **£105**

R. T. WILDING – Fishing Boats Off The Coast – 5½ x 8¼in.
(Laurence & Martin Taylor) **$253** **£150 Pair**

ALF WILDSMITH – 'Rural Landscape With Cart Horses' – watercolour – 15½ x 19½in.
(Dacre, Son & Hartley) **$104** **£60**

LEMUEL MAYNARD WILES – Forest Creek – signed and dated 1882 – oil on canvas – 20 x 16in.
(Butterfield's) **$500** **£295**

SIR DAVID WILKIE, After – 'The Parish Beadle' – oil – 28 x 36in.
(Woolley & Wallis) **$250** **£150**

N. WILKINSON – A River Scene With Anglers – watercolour – 9 x 14in.
(G. H. Bayley & Sons) **$484** **£280**

W. H. WILKINSON – A Manx Stream – signed, inscribed on a label – 13 x 18in.
(Sotheby Beresford Adams) **$134** **£77**

MAURICE WILKS – Fishermen's Cottage, Northwest Coast, Co. Donegal – signed – 24½ x 29½in.
(Sotheby's) **$1,135** **£660**

EDWARD WILLIAMS, Circle of – Rustics In A Wooded Landscape – 17 x 21in.
(Sotheby's) **$601** **£396**

EDWARD CHARLES WILLIAMS – View On The River Yare – 22 x 28¼in.
(Christie's) **$4,253** **£2,376**

EDWARD CHARLES WILLIAMS – Llyn-y-Dywarchen, Snowdonia – signed, and inscribed on a label on the reverse – 10 x 14in.
(Christie's) **$676** **£378**

HARRY WILLIAMS – A Fishing Village – signed and dated 1893 – 16 x 12½in.
(Sotheby Beresford Adams) **$41** **£24**

TERRICK WILLIAMS – Lagoons, Venice – signed and inscribed – pastel – 9 x 11.2in.
(Woolley & Wallis) **$601** **£360**

W. WILLIAMS – Landscape In Surrey – oil on canvas – 9 x 5½in.
(G. H. Bayley & Sons) **$588** **£340**

WALTER WILLIAMS – A Highland River – signed and dated 1864 – 24 x 36in.
(Sotheby's) **$770** **£506**

WALTER WILLIAMS – 'Near Plymouth' – signed, inscribed and dated 1857 – oil on canvas – 16½ x 24½in.
(Sotheby, King & Chasemore) **$1,020** **£600**

WARREN WILLIAMS – Old Conway, North Wales – signed – watercolour – 10.5 x 19.5in.
(Woolley & Wallis) **$250** **£150**

WARREN WILLIAMS – An Old Anglesey Mill, Cemaes Bay – signed – heightened with bodycolour – 18 x 11½in.
(Sotheby Beresford Adams) **$480** **£286**

FREDERICK WILLIAMSON – Sheep Grazing, Near Ewhurst, Surrey – signed and dated 1894 – 17 x 27in.
(Sotheby's) **$780** **£506**

FREDERICK WILLIAMSON – Cattle And A Drover On The South Downs – signed and inscribed – 13¼ x 20½in.
(Sotheby, King & Chasemore) **$1,003** **£590**

P. WILLIOT – Winter Scene – signed – oil on canvas – 9½ x 12in.
(Butterfield's) **$1,300** **£778**

HENRY BRITTAN WILLIS – Summer Landscape With Cattle And A Yacht On An Estuary – signed – watercolour – 17.5 x 29.5in.
(Wooley & Wallis) **$735** **£440**

JOHN RILEY WILMER – The Physician's Daughter, Giletta de Narbonne, from Boccaccio's Decameron – signed and dated 1920 – 12 x 10in.
(Sotheby's) **$2,202** **£1,430**

CHARLES EDWARD WILSON – Young Shepherd Blowing Dandelions – signed – watercolour – 10¼ x 15¼in.
(Sotheby, King & Chasemore) **$940** **£528**

J. T. WILSON – River Landscape With Cattle, 'Near Taunton' – signed – 13 x 21in.
(Laurence & Martin Taylor) **$169** **£100**

JOHN WILSON – Fisherfolk Unloading Their Catch On The Seashore – signed – on panel – 15½ x 20in.
(Sotheby's) **$2,325** **£1,540**

JOHN 'JOCK' WILSON – A Fresh Breeze – inscribed on the reverse – 17 x 17in.
(Sotheby's) **$1,588** **£1,045**

RICHARD WILSON, Circle of – Villa
Of Maecenas – 17¼ x 13¼in.
(Sotheby's)   **$1,672   £1,100**

EDMUND MORISON WIMPERIS, Manner
of – A View Of A Valley With Sheep In
The Foreground – bears monogram – oil
on canvas – 14 x 22¾in.
(Sotheby, King &
Chasemore)   **$380   £253**

EDMUND MORISON WIMPERIS – The
Norfolk Broads – signed with initials –
12 x 20in.
(Sotheby's)   **$585   £385**

EDMUND MORISON WIMPERIS – 'Aut-
umnal Winds' – signed – oil on panel –
17½ x 23½in.
(Sotheby, King &
Chasemore)   **$352   £198**

EDMUND MORISON WIMPERIS –
Hemingford Grey, Huntingdonshire
– signed and dated '91 – 15½ x 23in.
(Christie's)   **$702   £453**

EDMUND MORISON WIMPERIS –
'The Coming Storm' – signed with
initials and dated – oil – 24 x 36in.
(Woolley &
Wallis)   **$2,171   £1,300**

WINKLER – Supper Time; and Father's
Knee – signed – 25 x 20½in.
(Sotheby Beresford
Adams)   **$756   £440 Two**

PETER DE WINT – Cattle Before A
Wood – watercolour – 13¼ x 10¼in.
(Christie's)   **$1,875   £1,242**

PETER DE WINT – Cattle And Deer In
A Park By Ruins, Traditionally Identi-
fied As Torre Abbey – watercolour –
11¾ x 18¼in.
(Christie's)   **$1,088   £648**

WILLIAM TATTON WINTER – Summer Landscape With Two Figures And A Punt – signed – watercolour – 19 x 29in. *(Woolley & Wallis)* **$862** **£560**

PETER DE WINT – A Man Standing By Two Carts, A Cottage Among Trees Beyond – pencil and watercolour on buff paper – 9¼ x 9in. *(Christie's)* **$1,995** **£1,188**

WILLIAM TATTON WINTER – Herding – signed – heightened with bodycolour and scratching out – 13½ x 18in. *(Sotheby's)* **$542** **£352**

WILLIAM TATTON WINTER – Bathampton Mill – signed and inscribed – 11½ x 9½in. *(Sotheby, King & Chasemore)* **$214** **£143**

WILLIAM TATTON WINTER – 'The Avenue – Longpre', A Dutch Landscape With A Tree Lined Road, Two Figures And A Punt – signed and dated 1912 – watercolour – 54 x 37cm. *(Osmond, Tricks)* **$1,204** **£700**

WISINGER-FLORIAN

OLGA WISINGER-FLORIAN – A Woodland Path – on board – 17¼ x 14in.
(Sotheby's) **$3,511 £2,310**

GASPARD VAN WITTEL, Called Vanvitelli – Isola Bella, Lago Maggiore – signed – 17 x 29in.
(Sotheby's) **$46,200 £30,800**

MARTHA WITTWER-GELPKE – Kathedrale – watercolour – 37 x 27.5cm.
(Germann Auktionshaus) **$1,856 £1,160**

JOSEPH WOLF, Attributed to – A Pair Of Hawks – circular 23in.
(Sotheby's) **$836 £550**

GEORGE WOLFE – St. Ives From Hayle Sands – signed – watercolour – 14 x 31in.
(Lawrence) **$805 £506**

WILLIAM BARNES WOLLEN – The Aide De Camp – signed and dated 1907 – heightened with white – 17 x 13in.
(Sotheby's) **$814 £528**

ALFRED WOLMARK – The Haystack – signed with monogram – 19¾ x 15¾in.
(Sotheby's) **$567 £330**

GARNET RUSKIN WOLSELEY – Children Gathering Flowers – signed – 14½ x 19in.
(Lawrence) **$130 £82**

E. WOLSKY – Fighting Off The Wolves – signed – 11¾ x 20in.
(Sotheby's) **$1,588 £1,045 Pair**

WOLSTENHOLME – Fox Hunting – oil – 15 x 21in.
(Lawrence) **$242** **£121**

CHARLES HAIGH WOOD – The Time Of Roses Or Gather Ye Rosebuds While Ye May – signed – 37 x 48in.
(Sotheby's) **$19,250** **£11,000**

FRANK WOOD – Battleships In Harbour – signed and dated 1914 – 36 x 53½in.
(Sotheby's) **$719** **£418**

LEWIS JOHN WOOD – A Street In Rouen – signed and dated 1886 – 24 x 18in.
(Chrystals) **$960** **£600**

LEWIS JOHN WOOD – Chartres Cathedral – signed and dated 1853 on the reverse – on board – 16 x 12in.
*(Sotheby Beresford
  Adams)* **$718** **£418**

DAVID WOODLOCK – 'A Spring Brood', A Country Lass Feeding Young Chicks – signed – watercolour – 9½ x 6½in.
*(Locke &
  England)* **$868** **£560**

DAVID WOODLOCK – The Hall Farmyard, Bidston – signed – 9¼ x 6½in.
*(Sotheby Beresford
  Adams)* **$267** **£154**

RICHARD CATON WOODVILLE – Into Battle – signed – heightened with bodycolour – 10½ x 7½in.
*(Sotheby Beresford
  Adams)* **$142** **£82**

MABEL MAY WOODWARD – 'Woman Knocking At A Door' – signed – oil on board – 10 x 13¼in.
*(Robert W. Skinner
  Inc.)* **$650** **£406**

WOODWARD

MARY WOODWARD – Holland Park Walk – signed and dated 1895 – 13 x 10½in.
(Lawrence)   **$70**   **£44**

HENRY CHARLES WOOLLETT – Patience – signed – 9 x 12in.
(Sotheby's)   **$150**   **£99**

ALFRED JOSEPH WOOLMER – Cockles And Mussels – signed and inscribed on the reverse – oval 16 x 14in.
(Sotheby's)   **$334**   **£220**

J. WOOTTON – A Classical Wooded Landscape With Pastoral Figures By A Pool – 19½ x 25¾in.
(Christie's)   **$2,198**   **£1,188**

ARCHIBALD JAMES STUART WORTLEY – A Portrait Of Miss Tombs, Later Lady Newton-Butler – signed with monogram and dated 1889 – 41 x 27½in.
(Sotheby's)   **$12,513**   **£7,150**

WOUVERMANS – A Military Encampment – bears monogram – 8 x 10¾in.
(Sotheby Beresford Adams)   **$850**   **£506**

WOUVERMANS – The Horse Fair – 23 x 27in.
(Sotheby Beresford Adams)   **$5,359**   **£3,190**

PHILIPS WOUWERMANS – A Rocky Landscape With Travellers By A River – signed or inscribed in monogram and dated 16(49?) – 25¾ x 31¼in.
(Sotheby's)   **$14,272 •**   **£8,250**

GEORGE WRIGHT – White Horse And Three Hounds In A Stable – oil – 16 x 22in.
(Dacre, Son & Hartley)   **$770**   **£500**

GEORGE WRIGHT – A Shooting Party – signed – 14 x 21in.
(Christie's)   **$4,352**   **£2,808**

WRIGHT of Liverpool – British Men Of War Engaging French Men Of War Off Ramsay, Isle Of Man – 36 x 49¾in.
(Sotheby's) **$4,162 £2,420**

GEORGE WYATT – A Village Street Scene – signed – watercolour – 7 x 10½in.
(Sotheby, King & Chasemore) **$148 £83**

WILLIAM WYLD – Rear Of The Market In Venice – 20 x 34in.
(Chrystals) **$2,720 £1,700**

WILLIAM LIONEL WYLLIE – London From The Monument – signed and dated 1870, inscribed on the reverse – 28½ x 48in.
(Sotheby's) **$38,500 £22,000**

WILLIAM LIONEL WYLLIE – 'Making Ready For The Start'·– signed and inscribed – watercolour heightened with white – 9¾ x 16in.
(Sotheby, King & Chasemore) **$915 £572**

JAN WYNANTS – A Fallen Tree And Plants In A Landscape – signed – 19½ x 25in.
(Sotheby's) **$2,512 £1,650**

K. DE WYSS – Interior Scene – inscribed – oil on canvas – 26½ x 24in.
(Sotheby, King & Chasemore) **$783 £440**

EDGAR YAEGER – Interior Still Life Scene – signed and dated 1935 – watercolour – 11¼ x 8¼in.
(Stalker & Boos) $160   £95

SYDNEY JANIS YARD – Cattle In A Sunny Meadow – signed – watercolour on paper – 9½ x 13½in.
(Butterfield's) $350   £207

JACK BUTLER YEATS – View From The Train, Lough Owel – signed – oil on panel – 9 x 14in.
(Christie's) $4,240   £2,808

JACK BUTLER YEATS – 'The Dry Season After The Heavy Wet' – signed – pen and ink – 4½ x 5½in.
(Sotheby, King & Chasemore) $500   £295 Three

ALEXANDER YOUNG – A Dutch Harbour Scene – signed and dated '89 – 15½ x 26½in.
(Christie's) $1,674   £1,080

J. YOUNG – A Scene From The 'Tempest', King Lear And Caliban At The Height Of The Storm – indistinctly signed and dated – oil – 15½ x 9½in.
(Anderson & Garland) $54   £34

T. YOUNG – A Distant View Of Blakeney-on-Sea – 11 x 15in.
(Christie's) $558   £302

WILLIAM JAMES YULE – Girl In Crimson – signed – oil on canvas – 30½ x 30½in.
(Geering & Colyer) $9,350   £5,500

WILLIAM JAMES YULE – Three Young Girls In A Field – oil on canvas – 24½ x 29½in.
(Geering & Colyer) $3,570   £2,100

WILLIAM JAMES YULE – A Group Of Spanish Gypsy Girls Dancing In A Meadow – oil on canvas – 50¼ x 47¼in.
(Geering & Colyer) $2,805   £1,650

WILLIAM JAMES YULE – A Head And Shoulders Portrait Of A Lady In A High-Necked White Blouse With A Black Ribbon, And A Black Hat – oil on canvas – 29 x 24½in.
(Geering & Colyer) $1,020   £600

EUGENIO ZAMPIGHI – The Anniversary
– signed – 17 x 22½in.
(Christie's) **$5,184** **£3,456**

JAKOB ZIEGLER-SULZBERGER –
Der Rheinfall – signed and dated 1863
– oil on canvas – 36 x 49cm.
*(Germann
Auktionshaus)* **$1,105** **£690**

ANTONIO MARIA ZANETTI, The Elder
– River Landscape With Boats At A
Jetty – gouache on leather – 46.5 x 62.2
62.2cm.
(Sotheby's) **$3,108** **£1,980**

JAKOB ZIEGLER-SULZBERGER –
Schaffhausen – signed and dated 1863
– oil on canvas – 36 x 49cm.
*(Germann
Auktionshaus)* **$3,535** **£2,210**

MIHALY VON ZICHY – The Bear Hunt – signed and dated 1869 – brush and
brown ink and watercolour, heightened with bodycolour – 6¾ x 11in. *(Sotheby's)*
$535 £352

ZIMMERMANN

MAX ZIMMERMANN – A Wooded River Landscape With A Rider – signed and dated 1846 – 32¾ x 42¼in.
(Christie's)   **$1,004**   **£648**

GEORGE FREDERICK ZINK – Pensive Thoughts – signed and dated 1888 – heightened with bodycolour – oval 9 x 7½in.
(Sotheby's)   **$237**   **£154**

J. ZOFFANY – Portrait Of John Paulin, Esq., Of Chelsea, Wearing A Brown Coat, Standing In A Landscape – 50 x 40in.
(Lawrence)   **$734**   **£462**

J. ZOBEL – Peasants Loading Boats – signed – on panel – 5½ x 8in. *(Sotheby's)*
$1,420 £935

ANDERS ZORN – 'Nude Bathing' –
signed – pencil – 22 x 17cm.
(Geoff K. Gray) **$45** **£26**

ZUCCARELLI – Imaginary River Land-
scape With Shepherd And Sheep And
Other Figures – oil – 20.2 x 39.5in.
(Woolley &
Wallis) **$1,503** **£900**

F. ZUCCARELLI – A Southern River
Landscape With Girls Fishing – 15¼ x
18in.
(Sotheby's) **$2,459** **£1,430**

F. ZUCCARELLI – A River Landscape
With Figures On A Path – 40¼ x 49¾in.
(Sotheby's) **$7,190** **£4,180**

FRANCESCO ZUCCARELLI – The
Ascension Of Christ – a sketch – 15½ x
20¾in.
(Sotheby's) **$18,150** **£12,100**

JACOPO ZUCCHI, Follower of – The
Olympian Gods – on panel – 13 x 9¼in.
(Sotheby's) **$3,344** **£2,200**

IGNACIO ZULOAGA y Zabaleta –
Portrait Of A Gentleman, Half Length,
Seated At A Table – signed – 47 x 57½in.
(Christie's) **$5,086** **£3,240**

ADRIANUS JOHANNES ZWART – A
Canal Landscape With Figures By Farm
Buildings – signed – 15 x 25in.
(Christie's) **$680** **£378**

MARIE AUGUSTIN ZWILLER – A
Female Nude – signed – 21¼ x 14¼in.
(Christie's) **$544** **£302**